Reluctant
Accomplice

Military portrait of Konrad Jarausch, 1939

Reluctant Accomplice

**A Wehrmacht Soldier's
Letters from the Eastern Front**

~

EDITED BY
Konrad H. Jarausch

With contributions by
Klaus J. Arnold and Eve M. Duffy
Foreword by Richard Kohn

PRINCETON UNIVERSITY PRESS
PRINCETON AND OXFORD

Library of Congress Cataloging-in-Publication Data

Jarausch, Konrad, 1900–1942.
[Stille Sterben. English]
Reluctant accomplice : a Wehrmacht soldier's letters from the
Eastern Front / edited by Konrad H. Jarausch ; with contributions by
Klaus J. Arnold and Eve M. Duffy ; foreword by Richard Kohn.
p. cm.
Includes bibliographical references and index.
ISBN 978-0-691-14042-1 (hardcover : alk. paper) 1. Jarausch, Konrad,
1900–1942—Correspondence. 2. Soldiers—Germany—Correspondence.
3. World War, 1939–1945—Personal narratives, German. 4. World War,
1939–1945—Atrocities. 5. World War, 1939–1945—Campaigns—
Eastern Front. 6. World War, 1939–1945—Moral and ethical aspects
7. Intellectuals—Germany—Correspondence. I. Jarausch, Konrad Hugo.
II. Arnold, Klaus Jochen, 1968– III. Duffy, Eve M. IV. Title.
D811.J364 2010
940.54'1343092—dc22
[B]
2010021714

British Library Cataloging-in-Publication Data is available

⌣ CONTENTS ⌣

⟳ PREFACE ⟳

The exact role of the military in the Nazi genocide during World War II remains difficult to assess because of the wide variety of combat experiences and occupation actions on the eastern front. During the postwar years the "myth of the clean Wehrmacht" helped to exonerate former generals and facilitate the Federal Republic's rearmament as well as NATO membership. However, the shocking photographs of soldiers committing atrocities, presented by a controversial exhibition of the Hamburg Institut für Sozialforschung, discredited this apologetic legend, suggesting instead that the entire army might have been involved in war crimes. This charge triggered angry rebuttals by veterans like ex-chancellor Helmut Schmidt that their units were without blame, until Holocaust historians like Omer Bartov assembled evidence that proved the Wehrmacht's general complicity in the "war of annihilation" beyond doubt. But what is still heatedly debated is the exact degree of involvement of different units at the front and in the hinterland in antipartisan reprisals, political executions, and shooting of Jewish civilians.

Inspired by this controversy, I decided to reexamine my father's letters from the field, since they offer a nuanced picture of what German soldiers thought and did during the war. This resolve turned into a curious voyage of discovery that tested my loyalties as a son and professionalism as a historian. Growing up in a dead father's shadow in post-war Germany was not easy, because a contentious teenager could not argue with a ghost. When generational rebellion brought me to the United States, we were separated not only by my distaste for his conservative-nationalist politics but also by a vast physical and cultural distance. No doubt, a desire to explain the collaboration of educated Germans with the Nazis was one of the motives behind my becoming a historian who explored topics like the academic illiberalism of students or the perversion of ethics among professionals. But I remained reluctant to carry such investigations into my own family, since it meant painful disclosures of things some members would rather forget. It took until my retirement from the directorship of the Zentrum für Zeithistorische Forschung in Potsdam to muster the courage to confront this legacy.

This unusual source consists of some 350 letters sent by Konrad Jarausch, a high school teacher and journal editor, from occupied Poland, training grounds in Germany, and POW camps in Russia between September 1939 and his death in January 1942. Although as a member of the reserves he could only report from the perspective of the rear, he was close enough to witness the devastating impact of the "breath of war." A first set of letters focuses on the Polish campaign, describing the chaos in the wake of the German advance, the treatment of POWs, and the interactions of the population with the occupation regime. A second section of the correspondence deals with the details of the training of recruits in Poland as well as in Germany, illustrating the process of militarization of civilians in the Wehrmacht. The final and most original group of letters presents a chilling account of the mass death of Russian POWs in the German receiving camps for want of adequate food supply. In between there are close descriptions of army life and ten unpublished essays on the suffering of the conquered East that provide an inside view, close to the perspective of an ordinary soldier.

It seemed important to share these documents with the public, since they are more detailed and analytical than comparable messages from the field. Most collections available in English, like the last letters from Stalingrad, only contain selections from widely different individuals. Other editions like Karl Fuchs's show the naive enthusiasm of Nazified youths, while Willy Reese's confession describes the horror of the actual fighting. In contrast, Jarausch's letters document the experience of a single, mature academic over two and one half years and contain more critical reflections on the war. Although they are personal in tone, since most were addressed to his wife, brother, and friends, they are written in a clinical language and present meticulous descriptions. When the military historian Klaus Jochen Arnold attested to their unusual character, we decided to collaborate and prepare an accurate transcription. Along with a personal introduction and an explanation of their significance for military history, we published a selection from this correspondence and some fifty pictures as *"Das stille Sterben . . ." Feldpostbriefe von Konrad Jarausch aus Polen und Russland, 1939–1942.*

For the German edition we ultimately settled on a form of presentation that would constitute a "letter diary" of Konrad Jarausch's experiences in Poland, the Reich, and Russia. On the one hand, the frequency of correspondence presented the opportunity of having almost daily progress reports, but on the other it also posed the challenge of considerable repetition and overlap. Instead of aiming for a full-length scholarly edition or a narrative interspersed with only a few snippets of quotations, we chose a selective and annotated presentation that would preserve the integrity of the author's voice and convey the vividness of the descriptions as well as the depth of his reflections. For this reason we reproduced several complete letters at the beginning so as to give a sense of their style, but subsequently eliminated many redundancies and trivial references of interest only to the family. Since we aimed for easy readability, we kept our commentary to a minimum, only explaining the rationale of the edition and providing separate introductions into his personal life as well as military career. German reviewers seem to have found this editorial compromise workable.

Due to the cultural distance to German topics, this English-language edition is both somewhat shorter and more elaborate. While the letters have been carefully translated by Eve Duffy, the introductions were recast considerably. Since interest in the minutiae of the German war machine is limited in the United States, only about half of the correspondence has been kept. Additional notes have been added so as to make the text more intelligible for readers with little background knowledge. In response to the preoccupation with memory, the personal introduction has been expanded by the addition of a new postwar section. In order to locate information where it is most needed, the military history essay has been broken up into specific introductions for each section of the letters, dealing with the onslaught on Poland, military training there and in the Reich, and the Soviet campaign. Since letters tend to touch upon many different subjects, each chosen text received a brief title, highlighting an aspect of particular importance. Finally, Richard Kohn, a leading American military historian, has added a foreword on the differing experiences of German and American soldiers in World War II.

As a lost voice from the past, the letters must themselves stand in the center of this volume, with the various introductions playing merely a subsidiary role. But since sources rarely "speak for themselves," they need to be edited in such a manner as to make them audible to a later audience. The selected letters are therefore given a brief header and then identified by date, place, and correspondent, whenever possible. But the texts have been stripped of merely formulaic greetings as well as good-byes in the interest of saving space. In the letters chosen, the coherence of the text has been respected, even if their contents wander from one subject to another, because that is the charm of personal correspondence. The translation has striven for a crisp and accessible English style that avoids any pretence of historicity. In order to preserve readability, we have resisted the Teutonic temptation to display our learning in elaborate footnotes; instead, a minimalist commentary merely identifies persons and places, explains forgotten military events, and deciphers intellectual allusions. Only in some especially important cases have suggestions for further reading been added.

The significance of this wartime correspondence lies in the ambivalent role of its author as reluctant accomplice in and clear-eyed witness to important aspects of the war in the East. Although too old to engage in actual fighting, Konrad Jarausch was close enough to the front to provide detailed descriptions of German occupation policy in Poland, graphic comments on the training of new recruits, and shocking accounts of the mass death of Russian POWs, somewhat neglected by the burgeoning Holocaust literature. At the same time, he had the leisure to record sustained reflections on the historical meaning of the war, the prospects of the fighting and the (im-)morality of the German cause that go beyond the usual concerns of soldiers, voiced in letters home. Especially his conflicted attitude, hoping for and wanting to participate in a German victory while increasingly noticing and being repelled by Nazi brutality, sheds fresh light on the contradictory feelings of decent professionals who supported the war. Finally, his discovery of solidarity with Russian POWs also offers an inspiring example of the possibility of recovering a shared humanity amid catastrophe.

Konrad H. Jarausch
Berlin and Chapel Hill, spring 2010

⌒ FOREWORD ⌒

Richard H. Kohn

War "is not an occasional interruption of a normality called peace," wrote the distinguished literary scholar, Princeton professor of English Samuel Hynes. Instead, "it is a climate in which we live." Thus "we are curious" about war—indeed "more than curious, we are engaged and compelled by it." But because war is so sprawling a human phenomenon, we are intimidated by its sheer size and ubiquity in history. So, observed Hynes, we "seek the reality in the personal witness of the men who were there."

Most all of the published individual testaments, whether in the form of memoirs, diaries, autobiographies, oral interviews, or collections of letters like this volume, have concerned high command or combat, "the actual killing"—but neglecting, as Hynes has written, the "important but noncombatant business of war-making that takes place away from battlefields: the planning, the code breaking, the quartermastering, the acts of diplomacy and government, which command the labors of so many people . . . all necessary, honorable tasks." In studying war narratives, Hynes concentrated on combat, seeking documents that spoke "with a voice that is stubbornly distinctive, telling us what it was like for *this* man, in *his* war, the particular . . . the *human* tale of war."

This collection of letters by Konrad Jarausch, covering the first years of World War II in Poland, Germany, and Russia, possesses this distinctive human and personal quality. This correspondence covers the important experience behind the lines away from combat, providing insight into modern war from the perspective of a highly educated, thoughtful, noncommissioned officer keenly observing his surroundings and candidly expressing, mostly to his wife, his moods and feelings, his worries, and his larger thoughts about the war. We learn not only how German soldiers lived in the years from 1939 to 1942 but also what so many tens of thousands were doing, thinking, feeling, and experiencing.

Konrad Jarausch was far from a typical soldier, yet so much of what he saw and felt, and the way he reported it, was typical of the soldier experience in modern times. He details his movements and changes of location and the modes of transportation. He recounts the comings and goings of the people around him almost as though keeping a record for future reference. He succumbs to the slavery of military routine, like soldiers all the way back to ancient times: the barrage of orders, the daily tasks, and for the twentieth century, the bureaucracy and mind-numbing paperwork. The monotony of schedule was especially difficult for Jarausch because of his education and restless, reflective mind. But that intellect gave him the ability to recreate most vividly what soldiers have always faced: the tediousness of their lives and their constant fatigue.

Like for so many soldiers, for him writing could be a release from the frustrations of long hours of waiting, followed by frenetic activity. Jarausch could lose himself in communicating with friends and loved ones, describing realistically his environment and conversing through prose about what he was seeing and experiencing, how it affected his outlook on his previous life or his plans for the future. The landscape of Poland and the character of the farms, buildings, and towns caught his eye at the beginning of the war. Like most soldiers he was outdoors far more than in civilian life, so he commented on the weather and the terrain. A beautiful day could raise his spirits and momentarily relieve the discomfort of extreme heat or cold, or rain or snow. But always there were the obstacles weather threw up in the way of armies, even away from the combat, particularly mud or frozen ground. Weather always made soldiers obsess about shelter. Being behind the lines, that was rarely a problem, but the conditions were nevertheless primitive, sometimes sleeping several to a room in commandeered public buildings. Lack of privacy often wore down this bookish noncom who liked to spend his spare time reading and thinking, and who did not connect to other soldiers who spent their off duty time in idle chatter (often on subjects that a person of his background found almost always superficial and all too often distasteful), or card playing.

Like other soldiers, however, Jarausch was subject to swings in mood and a nagging gloom that he mostly kept out of his correspondence with his wife but that still crept into the tone or the subject of his writing. The prospect of leave, or promotion (especially becoming an officer), and at times the possibility of being released from service because of his age or physical condition, often led to false hopes. Rumors and worries captured his attention: promotion or transfer, leave to return home, news that might mean the war would end and he could be demobilized led to endless speculation. Sometimes he would be enervated by the stress or by his duties. He would become lackadaisical as bureaucracy robbed him of energy and motivation. The physical strains wore him down, particularly the long marches when he served in a training regiment back in Germany. He would have to fight off the loneliness, and always, always the separation from his family ached in his heart. The birth of his son, while a joy, intensified the longing for his wife and home. "Being apart in this manner does eat away at one's spirit and energy." The limited, focused, routinized world of the soldier dominated by repetitive duties even without the stress of danger could deaden even as intellectual and self-contained a man as he.

If the contents of these letters are similar to those of other soldiers in other wars, the quality of their descriptions and the cumulative picture that emerges of one individual's military experience is not. Konrad Jarausch was a most singular reporter and observer, a shy, sensitive man who read constantly (Karl Marx and Aeschylus in the original Greek) and expressed great joy at finding books. He strove to learn Russian when in charge of a kitchen feeding Soviet prisoners, using precious spare time, ignoring his fatigue, to study with the help of Russian tutors. He differed in age, education, interests, and temperament from his comrades. He had an unusual eye not only for the people and lands he encountered but also for their psychology and culture. He contextualized what he saw in larger political and cultural terms, worrying, for example, about what might become of the great cities of Warsaw and Paris given the destructiveness of modern armies. His richly drawn pictures and personal empathy put us inside his mind and let us see with his eyes, and experience with his feelings, the war behind the lines and in the training establishment of the German army during its first and most victorious years of World War II. One senses in these letters an earnest, mature, responsible man caught up in a grand historical event that he understands but increasingly laments, as the reality of what is happening to him and to others, and to his own decency and humanity, weakens his beliefs in National Socialism and German superiority.

While the brutality and depravity common to combat are absent from Jarausch's experience, an increasing sense of fatalism creeps into his letters—the same kind that infected so many battlefield soldiers. Aware that at his age he could not keep up with his younger comrades, recognizing that he would not become an officer or have the luck to be demobilized, he nevertheless worked diligently to do his duty and to see to the people under his care. This is not the typical picture of German soldiers American readers have come to expect, either from the classic narratives of combat published in the 1960s—the famous *Last Letters from Stalingrad*, or the memoir of the Alsatian youth who served in an SS division, *The Forgotten Soldier*—or some more recent memoirs and films that have tended to spread blame for the many atrocities of the eastern front across most all the German forces.

What makes these letters different from other testimonies is their growing realization of being caught up in a transformation of warfare that turned the fighting in the East into an ideological "war of annihilation." While still rejoicing in the initial German victory, he began to worry about the political consequences of the reprisals, shootings, and ethnic cleansing during the Polish campaign. Jarausch also noted with disgust the progressive Nazification of the troops, reinforced by the tough combat training of young recruits that obliterated the humanistic scruples of the older officers. While not describing the "Holocaust by bullets," he recorded not without sympathy instances of appalling ghettoization, physical exploitation, and killing of the Jews that he encountered during the course of his duties. And finally the letters reveal an underlying conflict of conscience due to their writer's becoming aware of his own responsibility for the horror of guarding Soviet prisoners. Controlling them with too few guards, providing food when there was too little to keep so many from starving to death, pointed to a personal complicity that called the justification of the entire war in question. Although by 1941 Jarausch was already inured to much of the difficulty of soldiering, his personal role in as well as the general immorality of the warfare against Russia troubled him so much that he was ready to call it "more murder than war."

In the end, these letters transmit a deep sense of tragedy, for in the reading one notices Jarausch's growing mental as well as physical fatigue, his understanding that the war would go on for a very long time, and that he like so many thoughtful people were being forced into a callousness that he neither foresaw nor ever accepted. His essential decency never left him. His disillusionment with National Socialism grew along with his sympathy for the defeated prisoners whom he was charged to feed but could not adequately help. In the end, Jarausch succumbed to disease but never to that sense of dread or the loss of compassion that affects so many soldiers, or to the degradation that affected so many caught up in the mass killing that characterized the war he fought. Judging by his letters, he remained to the end a caring man, and in doing so gives us hope that even in a desperate war, it is possible for people to resist the forces and the circumstance that rob us of our humanity.

Reluctant
Accomplice

IN SEARCH OF A FATHER

Dealing with the Legacy of Nazi Complicity

∿

The missing father who had died in Russia in January 1942 hovered like a phantom over my entire childhood. Since he was ordered back to the front three days before my birth in Magdeburg on August 14, 1941, and passed away in a field hospital in Roslawl five months later, I was never able to see him in person, though he remained a constant presence in my life. Try as I might, I could not resolve the contradiction between the photograph of a slender, bespectacled academic in uniform and my mother's praise for his intellectual brilliance, pedagogical charisma, and personal modesty. For my mother, a bereaved widow just over forty years of age, cultivating the memory of her deceased husband through contacts with his former pupils, colleagues, and friends was a psychological necessity, since she was unable to find a new partner. But for a small, malnourished boy the premature death proved to be quite a burden, because his absence created material impoverishment and emotional confusion: Who could ever live up to the standard of such a virtual superfather?

Only as a result of my subsequent training as a historian did I gradually realize that I shared this fate with millions of other "children of the war." Most of them were so busy trying to survive without fathers that the long-term effects

1

of a fatherless childhood during or after the war have only recently become a subject of scholarly reflection.[1] Many German "half-orphans" repressed their resentment and sought to compensate for their disadvantage by dedicated study and hard work, only finding the time to reflect on the psychological costs of their success after their retirement. Especially the sons of famous perpetrators like Hans Frank, former governor general of Poland, or Will Vesper, a leading Nazi writer, reacted with visceral hatred and made their sires responsible for all their personal misfortunes.[2] Whether children never knew or subsequently lost their father, their retrospective encounters with their missing progenitors create a double challenge: On the one hand, it requires finding out about the unsavory actions of a parent in the Third Reich, and on the other it involves dealing with one's own subsequent reactions to those actions.

The search for an absent father poses the general question of complicity with the Third Reich on a more personal level, undercutting both individual excuses and collective evasions. Efforts to uncover secrets from the family past are likely to reveal a spectrum of attitudes, ranging from enthusiastic support for Hitler to active resistance against Nazi atrocities, with most cases showing collaboration rather than opposition. Finding damning evidence that one's own parents were involved makes their silences and euphemisms regarding their role in the Third Reich or the Holocaust suddenly appear in a more sinister light. Moreover, if decent people like one's own relatives were implicated, one can no longer blame only a small number of prominent National Socialist Party (NSDAP) or Schutzstaffel (SS) members for the war or hold impersonal structures responsible for the genocide. Not surprisingly, Harald Welzer has found that many Germans are willing to condemn the Third Reich in general, while claiming that their "grandpa was no Nazi" in particular.[3] For the half-orphaned *Kriegskinder*, this quest turns out to be more complicated yet, because a missing father cannot be interrogated and confronted.

A frank analysis of their family's role in the Third Reich therefore confronts the war's children with their own ambivalent feelings toward a past that will not go away. Instead of being proud of their relatives and emotionally close to them, the discovery of their troubling NS involvement creates a sense of personal betrayal and deep embarrassment. When a father is absent, there is also a feeling of abandonment that arouses resentment instead of filial love. Because of his tarnished record, the missing parent cannot serve as a positive role model, but rather becomes an example of what not to do. This leads to a generational rejection, vividly described by the journalist Wibke Bruhns in her reconstruction of the development of her father from an accomplice to a member of the resistance. Negative feelings tend to govern subsequent life decisions to a surprising degree, influencing choices through the resolve to be different.[4] The effort by German children of the war to find their absent fathers therefore faces cognitive difficulties in understanding their parents' actions and triggers strong emotions about their postwar consequences.

As a case in point, in search of my own father I have tried to resolve these dilemmas by close examination of an incomplete but still considerable source base. While virtually all contemporaries who might have been able to talk about their life together have passed away in the meantime, my father's older brother wrote a detailed family memoir in the 1960s, based on his own records, which was intended as a posthumous memorial. Moreover, Konrad Jarausch coedited two volumes of essays and published numerous articles in the pedagogical journal *Schule und Evangelium*, which he coedited, reflecting his political and philosophical views before and during the Third Reich. Finally, his wife, Elisabeth Charlotte Jarausch, preserved some family documents like his military passport, many photographs and some letters from before the war, as well as his correspondence from the field, which form the basis of this edition.[5] Together with a few other archival fragments, a reading of these documents suggests some tentative answers to the question of why a decent and educated Protestant would follow Hitler and support the war until he himself, his family, and the country were swallowed up by it.

National Upbringing

Konrad Jarausch hailed from a Silesian family that had settled in Berlin around the turn of the twentieth century. Since his own father, Wilhelm Hugo, was the third son, he could not inherit the family farm in Misselwitz near Brieg. Instead he was apprenticed to a storekeeper and moved to the growing German capital in 1891 like many other young Silesians in search of opportunity. Five years later he married Anna Grenz, a petite beauty, and bought a store, dealing in colonial wares and delicatessen items, in the Nollendorfstrasse at the western edge of Schöneberg, one of the more affluent neighborhoods of Berlin. Because the couple's parents were unable to contribute much to its considerable purchase price of 2,200 Marks, they lived in modest circumstances, always worried about being able to pay the next installment of their loan. Especially during holidays, the family often returned to Silesia until the farm was sold in 1908, but only thrift and doing without could sustain a bourgeois living standard after they hired a household maid.[6]

August Wilhelm Hugo *Konrad* was born at 6:30 a.m. on December 12, 1900, in Berlin-Schöneberg as the second son; he was named after several of his ancestors. His brother, Bruno, the elder by three years, recalled: "We brothers got along well and only rarely quarreled with each other." The younger sibling was initially fairly lively and shared the few toys of his brother. However, the parental store did not do well and had to be sold at a loss of 400 Marks in 1902. After a lengthy search their father found a new, somewhat busier shop in the Oldenburgstrasse in the less fashionable Moabit, which he rented at first. Because of the costly move, Konrad's third birthday was "quite meager; he only got a little bag of sweets." After Easter 1907, he enrolled in the preparatory school of the Friedrich-Werdersche Gymnasium, one of the best classical secondary institutions in Berlin. Since to the amazement of his teachers he had already learned to read with his older brother, he was able to skip a grade, helped by special tutoring in writing during the summer. At this early age he was already an outstanding pupil: "Konrad was always valedictorian or salutatorian" of his class.[7]

When the new store became more profitable, the childhood of both brothers slowly improved in material terms. An old acquaintance quipped that both were "as well-behaved as any Berlin boys," because they had to help out in the shop and were not supposed to make trouble. Bruno also recalled that "we boys were proud of our genuine navy suits from Kiel," because they were like many others caught up in the Kaiser's naval enthusiasm. For Christmas the younger got "a castle" with guardhouse and lead figures of the imperial couple, and later on an Anker stone construction set. From 1910 on, summer vacations were spent at the Baltic Sea, and later on also on the Island of Rügen, where the boys built big sand castles. Konrad improved his small allowance through

Konrad and Bruno Jarausch in 1904

private lessons in the homes of Jewish families as well as in the house of the painter Lovis Corinth. On March 11, 1915, he was confirmed in the Heilandskirche in Moabit, where he participated in a Bible study group. Recalling their intense conversations about religious questions, a school friend later wrote that both acquired "a world-view, which was deeply rooted in Christianity."[8]

The First World War was "a difficult time" for the now prosperous Jarausch family. Due to strict rationing of food the turnover in the store dropped considerably, forcing father Wilhelm to work in the city office for bread supply. At the same time Bruno was drafted as a wireless operator. On October 20, 1917, Konrad passed an emergency *Abitur* examination, in which he got an "excellent" in deportment and mathematics, a "good" in religion, German, Latin, Greek, History, Physics, and Handwriting, but only a "satisfactory" in French, English, and Sport. "In his homework he displayed great industry." His circle of friends, composed of Hans Hempel, Johannes Dietrich, Günter Roß, and Theodor Dorn, who subscribed to the *Großdeutsche Blätter* of Admiral von Throta, was patriotically inclined. Subsequent duty in the "National Auxiliary Service" delayed the beginning of Konrad's university studies until June 1918, when the seventeen-and-a-half-year-old was drafted into the field artillery, serving in the Pomeranian city of Thorn. Since he disliked riding, taking care of horses, and the "rudeness" of his comrades, these must "have been hard weeks for him." Only the Armistice and the November Revolution saved him from being sent to the front.[9]

When peace returned, Konrad Jarausch studied in Berlin from 1919 to 1924 except for a brief sojourn in Freiburg during the summer of 1920. Inspired by the historical novels of Felix Dahn, he majored in German literature and history,

Soldier in World War I, fall 1918

attending lectures by luminaries such as Dietrich Schäfer, Georg von Below, Gustav Kosinna, and Eduard Spranger. He also minored in Protestant theology, intent on exploring religious issues like "the spiritual world of the ancient Germans."[10] On February 21, 1925, he defended his doctoral dissertation on "Popular Beliefs in the Icelandic Sagas," which his advisors, Gustav Neckel and Gustav Roethe, judged magna cum laude. His research focused on "the ensemble of ideas" that guided the actions of heathen Germanic tribes, the "last great creation of a vanishing time" before the arrival of Christianity. Since an academic career was unlikely, he passed the examination for Gymnasium teaching with an "excellent" in November 1925 and obtained an additional certificate for the teaching of religion in January 1927. His brother considered him an "exceedingly scrupulous researcher, who only drew conclusions when he had no doubt about their correctness."[11]

These challenging studies left little time for social contacts and occasional diversion. Since his parents financed him, "Konrad was quite modest during his time at the university; our father's purse was to be spared as much as possible." Therefore he was unable to travel to Iceland in order to explore the location of his dissertation, and his mother had to darn his suit. During his Freiburg semester he did hike with his brother through the Black Forest, with both subsisting on oatmeal and hot chocolate. In order to have some social life, he joined the German Christian Student Association (DCSV), led by ex-chancellor Georg Michaelis, which devoted itself to the study of the Bible and discussed national and social questions in the journal *Die Furche*. Former classmates and new acquaintances formed a friendship circle called "lethe," after the mythological Greek river bordering on the Elysian fields. One of the newcomers to this group was

Student in Berlin, early 1920s

the historian Franz Petri, with whom he collaborated in the Hungarian institute in Vienna during the winter semester of 1925/26. The leftist, modernist strains of Weimar culture therefore hardly made any impact on his social circle or his outlook.[12]

As with many of his peers, this education reinforced in Konrad Jarausch a Protestant-national mindset, but widened its perspective from the state to the people. His petit bourgeois childhood during the Empire fostered an unquestioning acclamation of the monarchy as well a boundless enthusiasm for the navy and for colonies. He became politically conscious at the very zenith of nationalist propaganda, which glorified the heroism of German arms with speeches, parades, and flags on the map. The ensuing defeat hit him all the harder because his images of the war were not de-mythologized through the shock of battle. "We experienced the terrible collapse of the world of our childhood and youth in 1918/19 by clinging with passionate resolve to the belief that everything must rise again more beautifully and purely." After the breakdown of the Wilhelmian order much of his age cohort turned to the *Volk*, a myth of cultural and social community, which was supposed to reunite the fragmented country and lead Germany to new greatness. Only Konrad Jarausch's reading of the classics and his Christianity tempered this nationalism by suggesting an alternate understanding of humanity.[13]

Protestant Pedagogy

Although the deteriorating economy slowed public hiring during the late 1920s, Konrad Jarausch eventually succeeded in gaining a position in a Prussian secondary school. He completed his practical training at the classical high school in Berlin-Friedenau between 1926 and 1927 as well as at the Arndt-Gymnasium in Dahlem during the following year. In the subsequent examination on March 14, 1928, he only received a grade of "good," but this mark was still high enough to enable him to be appointed as *Studienassessor* on April 1. After a successful probationary term, he obtained the "strongly desired" job at a modern secondary school in Schwedt, a garrison town of about 10,000 inhabitants on the banks of the Oder River in eastern Brandenburg. His established colleagues welcomed him with open arms and he befriended the art teacher Fritz Merwart, whose post-impressionist landscapes displayed considerable talent. His relief about gaining a professional foothold during the onset

11

of the Great Depression was only overshadowed by the sudden death of his supportive father in January 1929, which made it necessary to sell the family store two years later.[14]

Combining his scholarly interests with teaching practice, he involved himself in Protestant pedagogy so as to improve the teaching of religion in public schools. In 1929 he published his examination essay on "Teaching the Gospel of St. Mark in Eighth Grade" in the journal of the Protestant Teachers' Association, *Schule und Evangelium*. In contrast to the existential theology of Karl Barth and the biblical criticism of Rudolf Bultmann, he sought, following the neo-Lutheran Friedrich Gogarten, "to unfold the purity of faith even in the work of the school."[15] In spite of his academic training, he joined "the criticism of the liberal image of Jesus" and understood the gospels not as "historical documents, but as testimony of faith," that is, as "the voice of God." For a teacher such an existential concept of faith posed the challenge "of making the words of the text speak in such a way that pupils can hear in them the message of God's kingdom and of Christ who proclaims it." Between the extremes of a cultural Protestantism and an emotional Pietism, he searched for a popular "pedagogy on a Reformation basis."[16] Since Magdalene von Tiling, a German National Peoples' Party Landtag deputy, also promoted this neo-Lutheranism, he began to collaborate with her and moved back to Berlin as "research fellow" of the Protestant School Association in the fall of 1930.[17]

During the decline of the Weimar Republic, Konrad Jarausch kept searching for a firm ideological basis for constructing a new social order, inspired "by faith in creation." Since he considered neither Pietist inwardness nor Lutheran social action sufficient, he wrestled with the question of "how the immense chaos of modern life can once

Hiking with pupils in 1930

more be conquered and transformed into a sensible order."
In pedagogical practice he worried about "the dissolution
of discipline" due to the cult of personality, arguing "that
the relationship between teacher and pupil is governed by
an eternal law, which has to be recognized and fulfilled ob-
jectively."[18] Moreover, he feared the proliferation of "isolated
individuals" who "hardly have any other future today than
their submersion in an enslaved fascist or communist mass."
As a Prussian to boot he rejected "unrestrained individualism" as well as Marxist collectivism in principle, but his ideas
about a hierarchical, estatelike reconstruction of the state
on the basis of the *Volk* remained curiously vague. Therefore
he formulated his rejection of "rational democracy" more
clearly than his neoconservative alternative of an organic
"life-order of the people."[19]

Toward the end of the 1920s he met Elisabeth Charlotte,
the older sister of his friend Franz Petri, and fell in love. The
temperamental Lotte was born in Wolfenbüttel in 1901, but

13

her father, a librarian at the famous Georg August Biblio-
thek, had died early, while her mother, a parish nurse, passed
away in 1919. Her unusual intellectual ambition contrasted
with the bitter poverty of her circumstances. In 1922 she finally graduated from an academic high school—an unusual
accomplishment for a young woman without means. Although she had to support herself, she studied French, religion, and history in Munich, Berlin (1925–26), and Marburg.
Under the direction of the Luther specialist, Karl Holl, she
wrote a master's thesis "On the Influence of Pietism on German Social Life," which was judged to be "excellent." After
a stay in Geneva to improve her French, she completed her
practical training in Beuthen and Gleiwitz in Upper Silesia
and started teaching in a charity Girls' High School in Leob-
schütz. Shared interests inspired a frequent correspondence
between Lotte and Konrad, in which he sympathized with
her beginner's difficulties with words like "chin up!"[20]

After much deliberation Konrad Jarausch decided on
March 19, 1931, to pose the crucial question per letter: "Have
you already considered, whether we could go through life together?" Instead of passionately pleading for a joint future, he
listed his scruples: "You will not have an easy time with me,"
since work tended to absorb him completely. "At my side you
have to count on the possibility of spending your life as the
wife of a high school teacher in a small East German town."
But in spite of hinting at health concerns, he concluded on
an upbeat note: "A positive answer would make me very,
very glad." Overcome with emotion, Lotte Petri immediately answered in an almost illegible scrawl: "Your letter has
not surprised me, since I have also thought about the same
question. Hence I want to answer clearly 'yes' with a happy
heart." In this decision she was aided by confidence in God's
power, "which will also aid my weakness," and by the fact

Charlotte (Lotte) and Konrad, 1936

"that I have been used to greatest simplicity since my child-hood." Related work interests, long correspondence, and a few meetings inspired the shy intellectual and the impulsive woman to overcome their respective loneliness.[21]

In spite of their contrasting temperaments, the couple's common convictions and shared vocation formed a solid basis for marriage. Lotte was spontaneous, emotional, and outgoing, whereas Konrad was reserved and uptight until inspired by intellectual questions. Communication between such unlike characters was not easy, but "simple mutual trust" overcame most of the differences. Since both had grown up in a Protestant milieu, Christian faith provided a firm foundation for their life together. Although both were interested in history, Lotte's fascination with French culture led Konrad beyond his narrow German outlook. As both

15

hailed from limited material circumstances, they also felt that the life of the mind was more important than amassing possessions. Due to their distant work places, they could merely meet during vacations. Only after the completion of their training and the clarification of Konrad's professional future did they take the plunge into matrimony on December 28, 1933. Their holiday wedding with close family stood under the biblical motto: "Whosoever sows sparingly, shall also reap sparingly; whosoever sows generously, shall also reap generously."[22]

The dissolution of the Weimar Republic hastened the rejection of democracy because it proved unable to provide jobs for the younger generation. Konrad Jarausch's work at the Protestant School Association fell victim to a dispute between the majority who saw the journal as a neutral platform for the exchange of ideas and the minority around Gogarten and Tiling who wanted to push through a more conservative line.[23] In spite of half a dozen applications, Jarausch failed to secure a position in a Berlin high school since the revenue collapse of the Great Depression demanded a reduction of personnel. Many young unemployed teachers were "irritated and embittered," and spoke with resignation "about suicide as the door that always and perhaps alone remains open." Somewhat more fortunate than his associates, Konrad could return to his prior job in Schwedt in May 1933. Dejected, he did not believe that politics could improve the situation: "Sometimes I wonder whether something new does not have to grow out of the great community of those proletarianized by fate." He found the "ever more uninhibited agitation" of election campaigns repulsive. Like other young conservatives, he foresaw a "future right-wing dictatorship," but remained skeptical of "the Nazis' leadership."[24]

Hitler's seizure of power confronted Konrad Jarausch's circle of neo-Lutheran pedagogues with a fundamental dilemma: While they hoped "to use the great possibilities, which National Socialism offers for our work," they also wanted to resist all tendencies "which threaten to falsify or destroy the gospel." Privately, he explained "that joining the German Christians is impossible for me," because this NS-friendly group within Protestantism was using dishonest means and continuing Liberalism's mistakes.[25] But in the volume on "basic questions of pedagogical practice," which he coedited, Jarausch publicly proclaimed "the end of individualism in education," calling for a break with the secular humanism of modernity. In contrast to the republican "dissolution" of a teacher's authority, he saw Nazism as a return to a "genuine state," which might "put the individual into the *Volk*" and lead to a renewal of the church. In trying to define "the tasks and methods of a popular [*volkhafte*] education" one might "perhaps differ on details, but as a matter of principle criticism could and should be silent." Nonetheless, he refused to join the Nazi Party, since he considered "the claim of [Christian] epiphany" superior to the "ties of space, race, and people."[26]

Although Lotte lost her job—only one part of a couple could be employed by the state—the Third Reich advanced Konrad's career because of his advocacy of a national renewal of education.[27] On Easter 1935 the Protestant Church appointed him as "director of the home for teacher trainees at the Monastery of Our Dear Lady in Magdeburg. As theologian and Germanist, he was supposed to provide the trainees, all of whom specialized in religion, with an "especially thorough instruction in methodology."[28] His own goal was to "comprehend the Reformation's understanding of the gospel in a newer and deeper way," but at the same time also

17

Gymnasium teacher, 1938

"to consider the volkish renewal" in an appropriate fashion. Jarausch felt that the training of the next generation of religion teachers was a difficult balancing act due to "the continual discussion about National Socialism, race, [General] Ludendorff, etc., in which one has to weigh every word." The director of the Cathedral Gymnasium appreciated his "intellectual work" with the trainees, because "he had more the

18

personality of a scholar than a teacher"; but he also regretted "certain inhibitions," which made reaching students more difficult. Nonetheless, Jarausch was promoted and given tenure as *Studienrat* in January 1937.[29]

Konrad Jarausch continued to channel his scholarly ambitions into the journal *Schule und Evangelium*, which he coedited from 1931 on. This publication was supported by a small "Working Group for Scholarly Pedagogy Based on the Reformation," oriented toward Gogarten, and a larger and more didactically inclined "Association for Protestant Religious Instruction and Pedagogy."[30] As its de facto secretary he was in charge of planning issues, theological interpretations, and pedagogical decisions while also publishing numerous contributions of his own. Since in his letters he complained about the "devastation of the church" by the German Christians as well as the "systematic resistance against religious instruction" by the party, editorial attitudes toward the "National-Socialist revolution" remained ambivalent.[31] On the one hand the journal pleaded for the voluntary cooperation of the church. "Then whatever is demanded of it will not be an imposition enforced from the outside, but a necessary result of its own character." On the other hand, it inveighed against the "romantic dream" of reviving a Germanic religion, which it deplored as "a special case of heathendom."[32]

The spacious and well-furnished apartment of Lotte and Konrad in the Magdeburg Regierungsstrasse next to the cathedral and monastery became the center of a lively social circle. Its core was the family, brother Bruno and "the little mother" now living in Hennigsdorf, brother-in-law Franz Petri and his wife Lene in Cologne, as well as further relations such as Karl Teich's family, owners of a travertine works in Kehlheim. Next came a professional network of collaborators on the journal, like Pastor Karl Cramer from Gotha,

teachers Irmgard Feußner from Frankfurt, Marga Walther
from Breslau, and Oda Hoffmann from Pirna, who participated in the Festschrift for Magdalene von Tiling in 1937.
Equally close were contacts with the Magdeburg colleagues,
such as Cathedral preacher Walther Ruff and teachers Ruth
Schneider and Magdalene Caspar, who met every second
week at Jarausch's for discussion. Finally, there were also
friendly exchanges with teacher trainees like Arnold Nüßle,
especially during retreats and hiking excursions. Lotte had
her hands full trying to support her husband in his dual
human and intellectual tasks.[33]

During the hardening of the NS dictatorship, the tension between Jarausch's "understanding of the gospel" and
participation in "the common German life" increased no-
ticeably. In his plans for teacher training, the reform of religious pedagogy and an "introduction into the Nazi view
of history" still had the same priority. But when the "plight
of the church" made him aware that it faced "a struggle for
existence," it became impossible to deny that Nazism posed
a "threat."[34] In October 1938, Jarausch therefore warned in-
directly that the church faced "the greatest danger" of a false
direction, "if we let ourselves be captured by the [demand]
that this worldview become ultimately as self-evident among
us as its promoters want." Instead of "revising church dogma
or adapting it to today's views in some way," he held fast to
the priority of the Christian message. Yet he also wanted to
keep working for the volkish renewal of the country, if only
to remain in touch with the Nazified youths in his charge.
"Being utterly serious about the responsibility and obligation
of our national existence" was as important to him as "again
taking seriously the full gospel of the church."[35]

The fact that "'the Christian state' had been finally
buried in Germany with the year 1933" had increasingly

problematic consequences for pedagogical practice. During a meeting of Protestant religion teachers in the summer of 1939, Konrad Jarausch drew up a dire balance sheet, painting "the picture of a field full of rubble." The "isolation of religious instruction within overall education" had led to an appalling marginalization; "the reduction in instructional time" to one hour per week had made regular teaching more difficult; and "the warping of the content" had carried foreign material into the curriculum. The necessary and "comprehensive debate between Christian faith and [our current] time" had therefore become "impossible." While he continued to hope that the NS state would "put the shattered order of our national life onto a new foundation," he demanded "that the state now also grant the church the freedom to carry out its task for the people according to God's will." The ideological claims and dictatorial methods of the Third Reich forced "teachers of religion into a battle," demanding a clear position. "For here only a 'No' to the deification of the *Volk* is possible."[36]

During the last years of peace, Konrad Jarausch matured from a "quiet, shy young man" to an impressive but complicated personality. His small and slender body, which only relaxed through long walks, contained much nervous energy. Since he was willing to treat the young as human beings, his pedagogical charisma had a powerful effect on his pupils. According to a later report, he behaved quite decently toward the Jewish members of his classes.[37] His colleagues were impressed by his critical intelligence, national and religious idealism, and his meticulousness as a scholar. Toward himself he was uncompromising in his mental and physical demands. The result was a psychosomatic breakdown in the spring of 1938 that prompted his brother-in-law to demand: "Either you turn yourself over . . . to an experienced

physician as soon as possible, or you must . . . give up Lotte."
The medical examination in Schallstadt at the edge of the
Black Forest yielded a verdict of "complete organic health,"
only his blood pressure was a bit low. "Analytical conversations" with the doctor, a few weeks of rest, and a reduction of
work eventually restored his health and saved his marriage.[38]

War Experiences

With the German attack on Poland on September 1, 1939,
the rising tension broke as feared and another world war
began. During July, Bruno and Konrad could still hike in
the Carinthian mountains and write home about climb-
ing spectacular Alpine peaks, while their mother and Lotte
took the waters in the health spa Bad Steben. But during
the third week of August, air-raid protection exercises grew
more frequent back in Magdeburg. Lotte expressed her concern to her mother-in-law: "Hopefully all the complications
will resolve themselves without a catastrophe." But her dark
foreboding was confirmed on the 26th. "They have come for
Konrad this morning." Initially the call-up as a member of
the reserves made little difference, since his unit remained
in Magdeburg and his superior officer was the father of one
of his pupils. After receiving his uniform, "he looked quite
dashing," and worked at first as personal aide of the company
commander. "The major takes good care of me [since I am]
the teacher of his sons."[39] But on September 8 the war turned
serious for him as well, when his reserve unit was sent to
Poland. The very the next day he wrote his first postcard.

Conscious of the potential interest of later readers, he
asked that his letters be preserved, following the tradition of
earlier war correspondents.[40] In his descriptions of military

events and foreign sights he wanted both to convey his experiences and make sense of his impressions. Mail was a substitute for a conversation and an attempt to maintain a psychological link to loved ones: "We draw on the things we have brought along from home and also on what we hear from there." Letters were also a method of transmitting small requests for food, clothing, or reading material as well as for expressing thanks for having received news or packages.[41] Generally he wrote quite openly, disregarding military censorship that tried to keep discouraging news from undermining morale on the home front. "I have purposefully written things in a very matter-of-fact fashion, so that this letter makes it to your hands." Since he was cut off from intellectual intercourse, the need to unburden himself sometimes made him commit disturbing impressions to paper with astounding frankness. Yet other veiled allusions to atrocities or references to oral explanations indicate that he also wanted to spare his wife some of the grisly details. It is therefore impossible to tell exactly what he left out.[42]

The actual content of this correspondence, nonetheless, indicates that Konrad Jarausch's experiences in the Wehrmacht were quite conflicting. On the one hand, even an academic could not completely escape the fascination of the adventure of war, the satisfaction over "the rapid victories over Poland and France," or the widening of political horizons through the "enormous tasks" in the conquered East. Also, military discipline, physical exertion, and "good comradeship" could be interpreted as confirmation of his manliness as well as the realization of the national community in uniform.[43] Yet he often felt revolted by the endless "saluting, reporting, standing at attention," the cursing and bellowing during the drilling of recruits, and the unjustified criticism by his superiors. Moreover, he found the "empty chatter" of pointless conversations, the "sexual affairs" of the comrades, or the alcohol-induced sociability of the company evenings difficult to bear. Only if his "duty," a curious mixture of Christian, Prussian, and professional precepts, seemed to have a purpose by posing "educational challenges" could he wholeheartedly identify with the military routine and make the necessary sacrifices without resentment.[44]

For this reason his attitude toward a potential career as an officer remained deeply ambivalent. Of course, he was happy about his promotions to corporal and to officer trainee with shiny "stripes," because these recognized his effort and his leadership ability. But their side effect was a tighter supervision of his actions, participation in tiring courses, and surprise examinations for which he was being insufficiently prepared.[45] Since he was already forty years old, he did not always feel up to competing with younger, more robust comrades. He also lacked the martial bearing, loud voice, and "tone of command" that impressed many superiors. To be sure, he was willing to undergo further military training such as learning how to use a heavy machine gun in order to be able to lead the corresponding platoon. But when he hurt his knee in the fall of 1940 and was stricken from the list of officer trainees in April 1941, he did not put up much of a protest, although this disappointed his wife. Instead he began trying to be declared indispensable at home (uk-Stellung), but this effort was ultimately fruitless because it came too late.[46]

Another handicap that stood in the way of a military career was Konrad Jarausch's fragile health. His body was slim, only of average height; he was not especially athletic due to the time spent at a desk, and his only exercise was an occasional hike. "A little cough and some sniffles" posed no particular problem. But his continual complaints about his "physical tiredness," the going to bed early, and the repeated need for sleep indicate problems of coping with the unfamiliar experiences, the partly frustrating and partly shocking events, which created a "psychological stress" that had physical consequences.[47] Even during peacetime his heart had been none too strong—not enough to keep him out of the military—but repeated chest pains forced him to consult army physicians. Since they could only find a slight enlargement, the doctors prescribed homeopathic remedies like valerian and rest, which indicates a psychosomatic tension rather than a direct clinical ailment.[48] Although there were some phases when he felt up to the tasks before him, the weakness of his heart and his nervous disposition did not exactly help him to meet his military challenges.

To reassure his wife and friends he emphasized in many letters the increasing success of his coping strategies during military service. For instance, he described how well he was protected against rain and snow, how much soldiers had to eat, what opportunities the troops had for relaxation, and how well they all got along with one another. Moreover, he consistently downplayed his smaller ailments. In a positive light he portrayed his human encounters with superiors, comrades, or inferiors, whenever they allowed a genuine exchange of ideas. In the same vein he often reported his romantic impressions of nature, which seem to have served as a kind of neutral ground, connecting him with his loved ones at home and allowing a temporary escape from negative experiences into a peaceful counterworld. Finally, he tried through countless conversations, historical reading, and efforts to learn some Polish and Russian to decipher his visual impressions in order to understand the political subtext of the war. Over time he apparently got better at dealing with the permanent boredom as well as the strenuous physical demands.[49]

In order "to keep his sanity," Konrad Jarausch tena-
ciously attempted to maintain his intellectual life in spite of
the trying circumstances. His favorite source of information
was the *Frankfurter Zeitung*, which contained "a considerable
amount of interesting news" in spite of NS "press coordina-
tion," whereas the "endless radio noise" with its saccharine
kitsch preyed on his nerves.[50] Reading Greek classics like
Plato or Aristotle in the original was another way to overcome his "spiritual loneliness," because he believed that their
"thought forms the foundation of all scientific and personal
knowledge in the West."[51] Less challenging was the perusal
of masterpieces of German literature like "old man Goethe,"
whose aesthetics he considered "fundamentally unchristian,"
or of European authors likes Shakespeare.[52] At the same time
he also read the works of some volkish writers such as Edwin
Dwinger or Hans Grimm and commented thoughtfully on
the historical novels of Hanna Stephan, who was a family
friend.[53] Finally, he also asked for books about Poland, like
The Peasants by Władysław Reymont, and for histories of
Russia, in order to ground his impressions analytically.[54]

For the same reason he continued to contribute scholarly and pedagogical texts to his professional journal, now
renamed as *Unterweisung und Glaube*. "I am thinking how I
can help *Frau* von Tiling in her difficult task of maintaining
publication through the war." This endeavor involved working through the writings of leading theologians like Friedrich Gogarten, who was close to the Third Reich, or reading
"the nice essay" by Dietrich Bonhoeffer, a member of the resistance.[55] At the same time he tried to write his own articles
and reviews, like a long disquisition on "John the Baptist," for
which he needed his wife to check on factual information.[56]
He also corresponded busily with editors and contributors,
even if he could not participate in their decisions from afar.

The "decline" of interest in religious teaching reduced the importance of the journal, so that the already shrunken edition was suspended in May 1941. Disappointed, he fumed: "It does not leave me indifferent when I see how my comrades are even now flooded with illustrated magazines or shallow novels."[57]

Another refuge was his deep, personal faith in Christ, which brought him a sense of comfort and inner peace. The effort to find a community of believers made him attend Sunday services whenever possible, but when a military sermon too strongly equated "soldiership and Christianity" he became distressed.[58] In contrast, the daily reading of the Bible according to the plan of Hans Asmussen, "which distributes the scriptures over an entire year," was an unending source of consolation. "This morning I read a good deal in the Bible and took much pleasure in it."[59] He solved the increasing tension between the "modern world view" of National Socialism and the traditional Christian faith by arguing that the former "is merely right within narrow limits" and that a personal encounter with Christ would yield "those impulses that are hints of a deeper, inner understanding of the world." His existential conception of faith derived from that "disquiet of the heart" that expects a personal "answer of God." By "trusting that the Lord will help and lead us further," he could feel secure and accept his own uncertain fate.[60]

The shrinking resonance of the Protestant Church therefore concerned him greatly. After the initial victories he had still hoped that religious instruction might "stand at the center of the common reality of our life in *Volk* and *Reich*," but would nonetheless be "focused on the gospel." But with alarm he noted a growing disdain of religion by the "younger Nazi generation," which made derogatory remarks about the "priests" and refused to participate in services.

"The news of the cancellation of religious instruction has moved me much," because this measure also endangered his own professional future.[61] Due to the destruction "of an enormous amount of religious custom" by the war, he expected only "a small band" of believers to survive, "gathering in a simple private room in order to hear the gospel and to pray for the church *and the world*." Since he continued to oppose opportunist "adaptation" as well as Christian complacency, he hoped, "After the end [of the war] the field will be open for a radical concentration of the church on its religious task." Hence he sought to prepare this institutional reduction to the core of faith through conversations with comrades in spiritual need.[62]

Critical Turn

As a Prussian patriot, Konrad Jarausch supported the war in principle because he shared many of its national goals. In order to liberate ethnic Germans who had been separated by the Treaty of Versailles and to gain "living space" in the East, he accepted "the necessity that *this* Polish state had to be smashed."[63] Stating that "the dream of Empire is also our dream," he believed that Germany had a civilizing mission in Eastern Europe and should create an order beyond its own nation-state, for which the current war was supposed to lay the foundation. "Will to fight, love and death are our life," he intoned melodramatically. But unlike many Nazis, he thought in historical categories of the Holy Roman Empire because "the eastward expansion could still be understood in connection with a continentally limited, traditionally grounded idea of the Reich." Hence he was skeptical of more far-reaching fantasies of world power and viewed the attack

on Norway as a caesura: "Now Germany is starting the struggle for world domination." Uneasy about this revival of imperialism, he mused about "the strange historical conditioning
of National Socialism in terms of its foreign policy."[64]

Konrad Jarausch's attitude toward the vanquished foes
shared many prejudices of the *Bildungsbürgertum* toward
the neighbors in the East. Based on a historical narrative of
Ostkolonisation and Christianization by force, as well as the
adoption of Magdeburg law, urban trade, and rural settlement by invitation, this outlook assumed a German superiority, entitled to spread the blessings of *Kultur* to the Slavic
people. While describing the "eternal East," he contrasted
German morality, order, and cleanliness with the "pitifully
retarded" character of Polish towns, emphasized the "misery
of Polish peasants" and the monotony of the landscape.[65] In
his portrayal of Jews he reinforced widespread stereotypes of
the *Ostjuden*, by mentioning the "miserable seediness" of the
ghettos in cities like Łódź as well as their "poverty and squalor."[66] Similarly his observations of the Soviet Union showed
a combative anticommunism that sharply criticized the social costs of Bolshevik modernization, Stalinist crimes, and
repression of religion. While some of these impressions were
based on actual observation, they were interpreted in a cultural matrix that justified German domination.[67]

The letters nonetheless depart from conventional enemy
images by showing an increasing curiosity about and compassion for the inhabitants of the conquered territories.
German preconceptions were tempered by a fascination
with the inscrutable "otherness" of the East that stimulated
efforts to understand strange settlement patterns, foreign
customs, and even different politics. In occupied Poland,
Jarausch was quite interested in the strength of the Catholic
Church and attempted to decipher the Slavic mentality by

studying the language and reading its history. In reporting on Jewish ghettos he was impressed by some "single, small faces with burning expressions of intelligence" and condemned the arson of a synagogue while referring cryptically to the consequences of their expulsion: "It is self-evident that this [process] does not take place without victims." In commenting on his Russian impressions, he at the same time betrayed much sympathy for the boundless suffering of the people and the melancholy grandeur of the landscape.[68] For all its initial blinders, the correspondence also demonstrates a critical intelligence that attempted to transcend received stereotypes.

In contrast to the optimism of the Nazified younger generation, he judged the course of the war without illusions since he respected the fighting power of Germany's enemies. Early on he warned that "the Polish victory probably dropped into our lap too quickly" and counseled moderation "so that our people do not suffocate from winning." The stalled decision in the West seemed to him like "an attack on our nerves."[69] Although the "French armistice" raised hopes of peace, the British air raids on Berlin worried him once again. To the attack on the Soviet Union he reacted by issuing emergency instructions to his wife and expressing concern to his brother-in-law: "But we should be allowed to be concerned about the military and political tasks that rise before us even higher. One shouldn't blame the private if he is at first disappointed to hear that the war will last longer." On the declaration of war on the United States he commented clairvoyantly that "now it is really impossible to see the end. I fear that even the fantastic initial successes of the Japanese will have the effect of showing the Americans how seriously they are threatened and thereby only make the situation worse."[70]

Hampered by his pronounced sense of duty, he only gradually developed those moral scruples about the legitimacy of the German attack that might have been expected from an acute observer steeped in the classics. Of course, he did not remain unmoved by the extent of the destruction of the cities, the cruelty of the conduct of war, and the suffering of the refugees or the wounded.[71] His impressions of Łódź were especially shocking: "We shall not soon forget what we have seen there. How poor and squalid is the external appearance of these people." The misery of the Jewish quarter was particularly upsetting. "Three Jews have been hanged in a public square of Łódź—I don't know why."[72] Equally troubling for him was the fundamentally mistaken policy of the Nazi leadership toward the East: "We live at the expense of these peoples and are sucking them dry completely. What should we expect, other than bitterness and an abiding desire to overthrow this foreign rule?" Because he disagreed with these methods, he began to question the purpose of the war: "I don't understand how we can expect anything good to come from these circumstances."[73]

The "untold misery" of the Russian campaign in the fall of 1941 reinforced Konrad Jarausch's doubts about the justice of the war. Since he was responsible for feeding POWs in receiving camp 203, he experienced firsthand the consequences of an insufficient food supply for hundreds of thousands of prisoners from the initial battles. "When they come to be fed, grown stiff from the cold—it has been about minus ten, yesterday minus fifteen degrees Celsius during the day—they stumble, collapse, and die at our feet. Today another case of cannibalism was discovered. At that, the corpses, carried naked to the grave, are emaciated like a late gothic figure of Christ, frozen stiff." Even when the number of POWs in the camp was reduced to a mere two thousand, "every day twenty-five of them die. In the big camps farther west, which hold tens of thousands, there are correspondingly hundreds." Accelerated through the October crisis, this mass death of POWs, which violated the Geneva Convention, shocked him to the core. "If one did not hear on the other hand from the Russians time and again how they had suffered under Bolshevism, one might despair of the sense of the entire thing. Into this situation one is now thrown without being able to do anything but a bit of duty."[74]

The "great dying in the camps" finally awakened his feeling of Christian responsibility. To begin with, it made the elementary significance of the story of the feeding of the ten thousand come alive: "Feeding the hungry really is one of the miracles that God alone can do. When men cry because a comrade who was supposed to share the meager soup with them has disappeared, one understands that fulfillment in the kingdom-come must also overcome this need." Moreover, wanting to help without being able to do so was a psychic stress that he could bear only through metaphysical mystification and artistic reference to the Isenheim Altarpiece. "I must always think of Grünewald's body of Christ and cling to the belief that our dying is related to the death of Jesus in a manner that is incomprehensible to us." For a committed Christian this inhumanity to man could be justified neither morally nor politically. "According to everything I have witnessed, I cannot see an enemy in the broad strata of millions of Russian people. They are for the greatest part the unfortunate victims of a crazy policy, whose roots reach, however, deep into the Russian past."[75]

The enormity of the "suffering and death" inspired Konrad Jarausch to make active, but inadequate, efforts to practice Christian charity. In order to "avert some of the calamity," he tried incessantly "to make available at least the most essential food for the people." On the one hand it was necessary to enlarge the inadequate supplies. "About what they are supposed to receive, there is a continual struggle with the inspectors and pursers who must bring in the supplies— under the greatest of difficulties." On the other hand he had to make sure that available food was distributed equitably. "On some days I had to feed sixteen to eighteen thousand men as much as that was possible at all. We were only five Germans in the administration and kitchen plus eight sentries. You can imagine that one had to bludgeon and shoot. During those times heading a kitchen had nothing to do with civilian procedures. One bludgeons and shoots so as to create order around the kitchen. One looks after the sick so that they don't starve. One plays judge if supplies are stolen, etc." The effort to help the weak and wounded demanded a daily struggle: "My right hand is swollen from the blows I distribute."[76]

Recognition of a common humanity finally led him to feel solidarity with the POWs in general and establish emotional ties with specific individuals. "The best aspect was that we came together with some mature and intelligent Russians in common work" to ease the suffering. His effort to learn the language triggered intensive conversations, enabling him "to hear and see some aspects of the enormous domain of the Soviets." For instance, an opera singer from Moscow sang "Russian folk-songs" as well as "revolutionary tunes," and at his request, "liturgical anthems which the Russians had not heard for a long time," in order to "give him a few hours of relaxation after the excessive duty." In the midst of the horror these were "two hours of most genuine human solidarity, after we had gotten acquainted through other work and knew what we had to think of each other." Another time, he received "a nice likeness that a Moscow painter has drawn of me with charcoal and color pencil."[77] Such expressions of gratitude for his personal exertion on behalf of the POWs created bonds between individuals that transcended all enemy images.

Through such contacts Konrad Jarausch became infected with typhoid fever and suffered as well "the silent dying from exhaustion and disease" in January 1942. During the Christmas celebration with the Russian cooks he had still pointed out that the Son of God "ultimately became a prisoner himself" and that "we Germans do not feel any hatred toward the Russian people." When cases of typhoid fever appeared in the camp, he asked his friend, Werner Haß, not to disquiet his wife with the news: "And of course nobody can protect himself from an occasional louse" crawling on his body and transmitting the disease.[78] On January 11 he fell ill and two days later wrote a few farewell lines to his wife: "I warmly and gratefully feel all the cordial love" that spoke from her letters. "May God bless our wishes for the future. Everything lies in his hands." When he was transferred five days later to the field hospital in Roslawl, he was already so dazed that he was no longer conscious of the severity of his illness. Because his Wehrmacht doctors had no antibiotics, "the progressive general weakness of the heart" led, on January 27, to a "gradual slipping over into a painless release."[79]

The stunned survivors attempted to imbue this senseless death with a higher purpose. The commander of his POW camp, Major von Stietencron, resorted to tried clichés of "his true faith in God" and "his utter certainty of a final victory of greater Germany," but added as a compliment that he had been an "exemplary comrade and capable soldier." The director of the Cathedral Gymnasium found a more personal tone, mentioning that his sense of military duty had prevented a release to the home front and emphasizing that his "pedagogical calling" had kept him from pursuing an academic career. In a similar vein pastor Oskar Ziegner mused "how terribly hard this life has ended" in consequence of its desire "to fulfill itself through renunciation and selfless service, relinquishing any external glory." His colleagues and pupils were "shocked" by the loss and praised the deceased's exceptional character: "If there is such a thing as Christian heroism, then we have seen it in this case." Finally, his wife sought consolation in the conviction: "I think that Konrad has found a consummation, which we ought not to tarnish with our complaints."[80]

Memory Cult

The end of the Second World War made it difficult for our family to mourn for Konrad Jarausch, because traditional nationalist and Christian practices were either impossible or obsolete. With his makeshift grave located in central Russia, cemetery rituals of placing flowers were not feasible, while organized efforts by the *Kriegsgräberfürsorge* remained ineffective since the Soviet Union was not particularly interested in preserving dispersed German graveyards. Moreover, the entire political framework of military, government, and state had collapsed, thereby dissolving those public organizations that had cultivated a heroic memory of the war dead after World War I. At the same time, his former workplace in Magdeburg lay in Communist East Germany, and the colleagues who worked with him on the journal were dispersed, mostly in the West, destroying the institutional and personal supports for maintaining an affirmative memory. Finally, the shattering defeat and the revelation of German crimes undercut the conventional meaning of death in war, making blood sacrifice seem tragically misplaced. These circumstances conspired to privatize pain, leaving the survivors to grieve as best as they could.[81]

For Lotte Jarausch, a forty-one-year-old woman who had foregone her own career, the loss of her husband was a drastic shock, which could only partly be compensated by accepting widowhood. During the Third Reich this was a socially acceptable role, heroized as a woman's necessary sacrifice for the fatherland, but defeat and division robbed it of any transpersonal meaning. Dealing with impoverishment and downward mobility left little time for mourning, because her meager pension was insufficient to preserve her status, and even that was jeopardized by the defeat. Therefore she had to reenter the teaching profession, which turned out to be difficult, since she had not completed her training. She began in a rural one-room school in Lower Bavaria, continued in a private girl's high school in Upper Franconia, and eventually obtained a permanent position in a public girl's high school in the Rhenish city of Krefeld in 1950. With 1.6 eligible women to every available male, the chances of finding another partner, especially of the same social class and education, were slim. Hence, she had to invent her own strategies to remember Konrad as consolation for coping with adversity.[82]

For me, growing up fatherless held different challenges because I had no living recollection, and unlike with POWs there was no chance that he would one day return and put things right. Due to the bombing of the Magdeburg apartment and our frequent postwar moves, only a few physical remains, such as his fine leather briefcase, the Nazi family book, or his military identification card, survived. My father therefore had only a virtual presence in photographs, family stories, and references to his unusual personality that were comforting in an abstract way but provided little help with concrete concerns. Instead of offering protection to a small child, being a role model for a growing boy, or acting as disciplinarian for a rebellious adolescent, there was merely a void. My two substitute fathers were complicated in their own ways, because my mother's brother, Franz Petri, was an opinionated and demanding historian, while my father's brother, Bruno Jarausch, was a nurturing and forgiving trade school teacher.[83] Without a father but with a working mother, I grew up like thousands of others as a "latchkey child," which made my mother and me unusually dependent upon each other.

To keep the memory of my father alive, my mother focused primarily on preserving his written oeuvre. For this reason she made strenuous efforts to keep his two coedited books, all the issues of his journal, other reprints, and also his extensive library, insofar as it could be dug out from under the Magdeburg rubble and shipped to the West. At the same time she retained some of their prewar letters to each other and his entire wartime correspondence, even collecting some pieces from other correspondents. Encouraged by some of my father's former colleagues she began excerpting his wartime letters during the early 1950s. During a vacation at the North Sea, she asked Pastor Nast of Hallig Hooge to create a typewritten transcript of her selections. This more-emotional-than-scholarly effort came to naught, because the religious publishers that were approached refused to print the manuscript. By the mid-1950s the public was no longer interested in yet another set of tragic war experiences, since concerns had shifted from neoconservative attempts to gather the *Volk* to reeducation efforts at constructing a viable democracy.[84]

Another somewhat more successful way to cultivate recollections of my father was personal networking by visiting members of his circle during the 1950s. My mother therefore alternated Christmas holidays with visits to her brother's and his brother's families. The former was complicated, as her sister-in-law, Lene, suspected her of substituting me as an intellectually more promising child for their own adopted son, while the latter proved easier, since Trude had no children of her own and was therefore willing to spoil me. Not surprisingly, all my godmothers were close associates of my father. There was, for instance, the forbidding Magdalene von Tiling in Berlin, still radiating an aura of Old Prussia; the warmhearted and half-blind Bible teacher Magdalene Caspar in Magdeburg; and the professional high school teacher Ruth Schneider in Wuppertal. Finally, my mother dragged me to various friends and acquaintances of my father, like the Berlin Gymnasium director Johannes Dietrich or the widow of my father's star pupil, Ursula Nüßle, in Kiel.[85] This inordinate amount of travel was an effort to bring my father back to life through contact with those who had been closest to him.

A final method of honoring my father's memory was to groom me as his successor. Already giving me the same first name during wartime suggests that I was intended to carry on, should he not return from the front. Magdalene von Tiling's printed dedication of one of her postwar books to his memory goes in the same direction, because she added a handwritten note on the flyleaf encouraging me to follow in his footsteps. Also, the choice of education in a classical neohumanist Gymnasium with nine years of Latin, six years of Greek, and two years of Hebrew on top of English and French indicates my mother's hopes that I would study theology and become a clergyman. This was not quite as onerous as it might sound, because she also sent me to the Protestant scouts, the Christliche Pfadfinderschaft, where I enjoyed camping, bicycle tours, and kayaking trips. But even in the elitism of this group there were remnants of the earlier Youth Movement style that were not exactly democratic in spirit.

Finally, my uncle, Franz Petri, involved me in long discussions and gave me books like Gerhard Ritter's Goerdeler biography in order to create a sense of national responsibility.[86]

The growing discrepancy between such expectations and my desire to find my own way led me to a severe identity crisis during adolescence. Instead of volkish authors my friends and I were reading Albert Camus or Ernest Hemingway and making experimental existentialist films. Instead of worrying about German division, we were devouring the first paperbacks on NS genocide and wanted to shed our troubled past by becoming Europeans. Instead of deferring to our elders, we held them responsible for war and defeat and were determined not to repeat their political mistakes. During my last Gymnasium years, I struggled painfully with my Christian belief until I broke with family expectations, abandoned my leadership position in the scouts, and came down on the side of democratic modernity. When my rebelliousness was punished during the Abitur examination, I decided to get out, gave up my place in the select Leibniz Kolleg at Tübingen University, and embarked to the United States on the steamer *Berlin*. In Laramie, Wyoming, about as far from home as I could get, I finally breathed more freely, pursued American studies, and developed a more critical relationship to my German heritage.[87]

Although my case was perhaps more acute than others, it was part of a broader generational process of rejecting the national legacy. The sociologist Helmut Schelsky called the teenagers of the 1950s the "skeptical generation," indicating that they were unwilling to follow their discredited fathers, while being wary of ideological commitments. Many *Kriegskinder* were in search of new values and authority figures, some admiring the egalitarian Soviet experiment and impressed by Bertolt Brecht, others more interested in

American personal freedom or in humanitarians like Albert Schweitzer. Ultimately, this quest led many intellectuals to switch allegiances away from their own tarnished parents to the victims of Nazi crimes, the Jews, Poles, and others who had suffered from their hands. No doubt, this was a necessary concomitant of the liberalization of political culture that made it possible to accept the recivilized Germans back into the international community.[88] But the personal price was a rupture of memory that contributed to the generational revolt of 1968 and produced an inability to empathize with their forebears. Instead of admiring my father, I came to see him as part of the problem.

This break with tradition was necessary but insufficient since it produced an unstable memory regime. By countering some of the nostalgic portrayals of the Third Reich, still handed down privately within families, this generational shift helped broaden support for the critical interpretation of the Nazi dictatorship that the victorious allies, democratic politicians, and leading intellectuals had promoted since 1945. But its advocates often lacked patience with the errors of their parents and failed to appreciate their difficult circumstances, since in the arrogance of youth they misunderstood how much their rejection was still driven by their personal past. In my case, it was transatlantic distance from the *querelles allemandes* that made it possible to develop a more balanced attitude that combined criticism with sympathy. In the case of my classmates it was growing maturity that blurred the sharp edge of condemnation and increased understanding. Only in searching for their own past did many of the *Kriegskinder* begin to reencounter their parents with greater empathy.[89] The timing and interpretation of this edition of letters written by my father are themselves products of this gradual reconsideration.

Troubled Legacy

How is the "intellectual-spiritual legacy" of such a "life of Christian-German conviction" to be judged by later generations? The key irritant is its complicity with Nazism, typical of wide circles of the Protestant middle class. Even when confronted with "untold misery," Konrad Jarausch clung to his synthesis of *Volk* and faith. "For me one of the strongest experiences of the war has been that in the face of so much hunger, neglect, illness, and death I did not have to renounce anything, which I have lived as German and Christian." Even so, he felt a moral abyss opening under him: "Now to the future. We need an education of European scope in all intellectual respects: languages, history, geography. But what will provide a humane foundation for it?"[90] The enormity of the suffering thrust the crucial question upon him of which values would allow a better order to be constructed. His answer was, "penetrating the riddle of being human ever more deeply in light of the gospel, until in living and teaching Jesus Christ shows himself as the path, which leads right through *our* world and *our* time to God." But precisely this faith's support of duty to the nation and lack of understanding for human rights ensnared honorable people like Jarausch into complicity with Nazi crimes.[91]

As a member of a security division made up of older reserves, my father witnessed key aspects of the Holocaust, because most of the ethnic cleansing and mass killing took place in the hinterland. "The SS is cleaning up terribly," he hinted in October 1941. "Everything Bolshevik is being ruthlessly eradicated whenever it falls into our hands. Ditto the Jewish element." These references show that even those soldiers who did not directly participate knew of the implementation of the "commissar order" and of the "Holocaust

41

by bullets" that murdered about 600,000 Jews in Wehrmacht territory during 1941.[92] However, in the "quiet dying" of the POWs their guards were more personally implicated, though some like my father attempted "to obtain the most necessary provisions for the prisoners." Typical of the nationalist racism of younger soldiers, one quartermaster answered his objections cynically: "Those positions just require tough characters who don't care if a few hundred POWs die." The guard units were unquestionably responsible for the starvation of unprotected, freezing soldiers and civilians. And they did nothing to prevent the even more horrible fate of the Jews. "In that case it is really most merciful if they are led into the woods and bumped off, as the technical term has it. But the whole thing is already more murder than war."[93]

The utter brutality of the ideological war of annihilation ultimately compelled my father to distance himself from the Nazi project of racial hegemony. He had never been enthusiastic about the NS weltanschauung, since he considered the ideologue Alfred Rosenberg "much more confused and muddled" than the philosopher G.F.W. Hegel. Similarly, he warned against blind obedience to Hitler's messianic claims because the Germans would only be able to make sacrifices for the war "if their belief in the Führer and his insights remains temporal and limited."[94] Also, he was appalled by the repression of the church and the spiritual emptiness of the Nazified officer trainees: "Among the younger ones a different attitude prevails, intolerance in every respect toward the church and the Jews." Decisive for breaking with the Nazis was, however, the experience of inhumanity during the mass dying of POWs. "In some weeks we have had hundreds of deaths in our camps. But especially here I have learned again that neither forced contrition nor honest ethical remorse stand at the center of our faith, but solely unfathomable mercy, which outshines all suffering and guilt."[95] Where this return to Christian humanism would have led him we cannot know due to his premature death.

The lasting message of this life cut short is therefore the imperative to overcome enemy stereotyping through renewed humanism, based on Christian responsibility. To be sure, Konrad Jarausch was also politically concerned that German crimes, "when the Jew is eliminated," might once again come to haunt their perpetrators: "I often worry about the thought that all these peoples whom we had to hurt and humble deeply, might at some time band together for revenge." But more decisive for him was the realization of a shared humanity that transcended the ideological hostility against communist Russia. "These people are, after all, human beings like us. Therefore contact with them feels good and awakens sensations and feelings that always return to you [Lotte] and the child." In the midst of the hell of Dulag 203 he realized shortly before his death: "Genuine humanity between peoples and races is necessary if a better world is to arise from the excess of blood and destruction." This hard-won insight that people across all differences share a basic human dignity, which needs to be respected whatever the circumstances, remains an important lesson for later generations.[96]

The effort to come to terms with this troubled legacy that inspired my becoming a historian could not lead to an uncritical heroization but only to a critical appreciation. My father's letters radiate a love for his unseen son that still touches me deeply. "Thus we want to gather this Christmas Eve in gratitude for what God has given to us with this child. That outshines everything else."[97] Nonetheless, I could not really follow my mother's wish to continue his national-Protestant work, but had to find my own way of confronting the aberrations of his generation from a transnational-democratic perspective. Because he might have known better and acted differently due to his faith, his cooperation with the Nazi regime, support of the war, and complicity in war crimes remain abhorrent to me. But a closer study of his life has also taught me respect for his effort to retain humanity under extreme circumstances and his attempt to break with nationalist prejudices through acts of charity. Instead of well-meant wholesale condemnation, I believe that only a renewed attempt at a dialogue with such problematic forebears can liberate later generations from the shadows of their dead.[98]

Part I

The Polish Campaign

The outbreak of the Second World War disrupted millions of lives and plunged Europe once again into a bloody conflict. Hitler's attack on Poland had been long in coming, since the Right never accepted Germany's defeat and the Nazi movement made reversing the "shame of Versailles" into one of its chief propaganda themes. In spite of protestations of peacefulness in order to mislead domestic and international opinion, the Third Reich systematically rearmed, preparing for a second conflict to be waged more ruthlessly and successfully. Hitler cleverly used the reluctance of the victors to grant Germans rights of ethnic self-determination as cover to conquer Austria, annex the Sudetenland, dismantle Czechoslovakia, and demand a transportation corridor to East Prussia. When the West failed to reach an agreement with the Soviet Union and he succeeded in buying Stalin's neutrality on August 23, 1939, war became inevitable. Because German civilians remembered the privation of the First World War, many of them were notably unenthusiastic about another struggle.

Konrad Jarausch was mobilized and sworn in on September 1, 1939, since he was still young enough to serve and not essential enough to the home front to be exempted. Although he had been drafted in June 1918 and trained for the field artillery, he had been saved from going to the front by the armistice in November. Because he had been transferred to the reserves after his thirty-eighth birthday in February 1938, he was called up as a member of battalion V/XI of the Landesschützen (territorial defense forces) from Magdeburg. As an academic he was anything but military in physique or bearing, yet he complied out of a Prussian sense of duty and also because he wished to participate in a historic event that he had missed the first time around. Surprisingly enough, he was quickly promoted to the rank of *Obergefreiter* (private first class) on October 1, 1939, and to *Unteroffizier* (noncommissioned officer) on January 1, 1940. This initial advancement was a result of the Wehrmacht's need for competent personnel as well as of his superiors' recognition of his leadership abilities.

Like many other soldiers, my father observed the rapid victory over Poland with amazement and gratitude. On paper, both sides fielded almost equal numbers of troops, tanks, and airplanes, but in practice the fighting quickly turned into a rout. Britain and France failed to mount a relief attack in the West, while on September 17 the Soviet Union occupied the Eastern Polish territories according to the provisions of the Nazi-Soviet Pact, taking advantage of Poland's focus on the West. The Poles fought gallantly, but the Wehrmacht had better equipment and a superior strategic position, invading from three sides at once: in the north from East Prussia, in the middle from Brandenburg, and in the south from Silesia. With giant pincer movements the German army bottled up the Polish forces around Warsaw and eventually defeated the remnants around Lublin. During the fierce fighting not only the SS but also the regular army began to commit atrocities against Jews and Polish civilians, prefiguring what would become the Holocaust. When on October 6 the Polish army capitulated, Hitler had won his first, perhaps all too easy, blitzkrieg victory, cementing his popularity.

As a member of the reserves, Konrad Jarausch was assigned to security duties during the Polish campaign and its aftermath. Due to reports of guerrilla activity, the Landesschützen were used to secure significant objects like train stations and search the woods for snipers behind the Army Group South in the former Prussian province of Posen. His own unit was ordered to guard POWs, who continued to be captured in large numbers due to the rapid advance. This responsibility involved selecting ethnic Germans who could be sent home quickly, picking out Poles who had to be controlled until the fighting was over, and identifying Jews, increasingly subject to anti-Semitic persecution. Because of his intellectual training Jarausch tended to be assigned to writing reports, giving background lectures, or leading small groups of guards. Repelled by the often rough and alcohol-centered comradeship of army life, he nonetheless strove for a degree of acceptance in his troop. Although these tasks kept him away from the fighting, they brought Jarausch close enough to the front to witness the war's devastating effects.

Unlike many of his comrades, he developed a keen interest in the conquered country and people, wondering how Germans and Poles might be able to live together in the future. To begin with, Konrad Jarausch was fascinated by the east central European landscape in which he discovered many similarities to his native Brandenburg. At the same time, he was appalled by the poverty of many rural towns where he detected architectural traces of earlier aristocratic rule, subsequent Prussian administration, and the new national Polish state. As a practicing Protestant, he was also interested in his own denomination's conflation with German nationality and in the Catholic piety of the Poles, which he saw as one of the sources of their patience in suffering and pride in their own culture. In order to bridge the gap between occupier and occupied, he also tried to learn a bit of the Polish language. While welcoming the return of former Prussian provinces, he was less sure about the success of ethnic resettlement schemes and of harsh Germanization policies. As a historian he sensed that a new order had to rest on more than force and would need to leave space for a degree of Polish identity.

PART I

Konrad Jarausch saw the suffering of the war through the lens of the nationalities' struggle, somewhat tempered by a sense of Christian humanism. His credulity regarding tales of German victimization and gladness over the "liberation" of lost territories show that he shared some of the prejudices that justified harsh occupation measures as necessary retaliation. But his descriptions of the streams of refugees and of the plight of the defeated Poles evince a considerable amount of sympathy for the human cost of the conflict. Similarly, he seems to have been both repelled by and attracted to the Jews whom he encountered because he used linguistic stereotyping along with astute observations in the same description. On the one hand he graphically portrayed the hunger and filth of Jewish ghetto life, but on the other hand he also recognized a superior intelligence that evoked compassion. Only occasionally did he note atrocities, citing their official justifications without making it clear how far he really believed in them. While his letters document the existence of racist crimes in Poland, they also indicate these were still limited, because units like his own were not involved in them.

During the initial stage of the fighting, he viewed the war with ambivalence, alternating between elation about German victories and despair over the final outcome. Konrad Jarausch was willing to put up with a considerable amount of personal discomfort as long as he had a sense of participating in a grand reshaping of history, which would be told and retold as a heroic tale by future generations. Like many of his comrades he was delighted with the speed and extent of the German advance in the East, which had taken years to accomplish in World War I. But he was also concerned that the surprising ease of the victory in Poland would reinforce a set of nationalist attitudes and racial prejudices that might eventually undermine German domination, since it

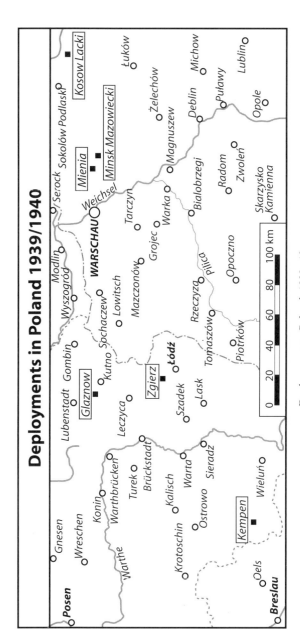

Deployments in Poland 1939/1940

Kosow Lacki

Mienia

Minsk Mazowiecki

Glaznow

Zgierz

Kempen

Łuków

Michow

Lublin

Serock Sokolów Podlask

Żelechów

Deblin

Puławy

Opole

Modlin

Magnuszew

Radom

Zwoleń

Skarzysko Kamienna

Wyszogród

Weichsel

Tarczyn

Bialobrzegi

WARSCHAU

Lowitsch

Grojec

Warka

Lubenstadt Gombin

Kutno Spchaczew

Mazzonów

Opoczno

Opoczno

Łódź

Rzeczyza

Pilica

Piotrkow

Leczyca

Szadek

Lask

Tomaszów

Brückstadt

Warta

Sieradz

Turek

Kalisch

Wieluń

Konin

Warthbrücken

Ostrowo

Gnesen

Wreschen

Krotoschin

Oels

Posen

Warthe

Breslau

0   20   40   60   80   100 km

Deployment in Poland, 1939–40

was likely to foster unthinking arrogance. Especially in the letters to his brother-in-law, he remained acutely aware that the real war in the West had not yet begun and that Poland was at best a first step. Unlike many other soldiers, Konrad Jarausch therefore thought about the war in long-range terms and continued to worry about the unpredictability of its ultimate outcome.

His aims as a Prussian and German patriot overlapped to a considerable degree with the Nazi program of expansion, but eventually also parted ways with the racial imperialism of the SS. Undoing the perceived injustice of Versailles, restoring prior Prussian territories, and even consolidating scattered German settlements in the annexed Warthegau around Posen might still be justified by the precedent of the Holy Roman Empire and a belief in the superiority of German culture. But completely extinguishing Polish identity or murdering an entire Jewish people went beyond his imagination and exceeded his feeling of what would be "right." Moreover, he considered many of the Nazi exploitation measures or SS atrocities counterproductive to the German cause, because they would engender eternal hatred. At the same time, these policies violated his sense of humanism, based on his reading of the Greek and Roman classics, as well as the precepts of his intense, scriptural Christian faith. During his entire service he wrestled with the irresolvable dilemma of wanting to support the war effort, while doubting its moral justification and worrying about its political consequences.

Letters from Poland, September 1939 to January 1940

Arrival in the East

September 9, 1939

Dearest Lotte,

After an eighteen-hour trip we arrived this morning in a very rural and peaceful area right near the German border by Gross-Wartenberg.[1] The trip was tolerable. We now have a seven-kilometer march ahead of us. Where we'll go from there, no one knows. In any case, we are in the East. We traversed the route I've become familiar with, one that I traveled just two months ago as I went on to Oels.[2] Now relax and don't worry too much about me. I have in fact up until now managed to get through everything that was demanded of us in terms of my health and there isn't any danger of battle here. Be well. I'm thinking of you always.

Your
Konrad

Initial Impressions

September 9, 1939

Now we're moving again. We're sitting, comfortably and cozily, in a third-class compartment. The sun is shining on the peaceful, quiet countryside. A German fighter buzzes once over a field. I had an interesting night. I was sent to

[1] A city in the Breslau district (Syców). Place names are given in German when the letters refer to them in that language and also glossed in Polish in order to indicate current usage.
[2] City in Lower Silesia (Oleśnica).

53

do telephone duty; it was a mistake, but because of it I spent a wonderful hour at my post for the first time in a thickly wooded park under a star-studded sky, and I chatted with the housekeeper for fifteen minutes. Today we're seeing real East German vistas and everything that goes along with it—large estates with manors, parks, and halls. Wide swathes of land. Between those, there are woods, deer, and hares. A temporary airfield lies between them. On the roads, steady streams of transports and trucks. Single batteries. Ambulances. At the crossing, a sign announces "158 km to Lodz."[3] We are starting a sort of gypsy existence. One day here, the next, somewhere else. It's easier not to unpack one's things. The experienced infantrymen show us how to pile them up next to us on the straw. I slept well under my coat until it began to get light. At that point we had to get out of our "beds" anyway. In the large hall of the inn where we're quartered, there are over a hundred men. We still have it rather easy in regard to these externals. Since I only got to our quarters at 11:30, I picked out a little corner all to myself.

Even the train trip had at least something gypsylike about it, especially during the night. I fell into a deep sleep right after Magdeburg and woke up only after Rosslau.[4] Then I took turns either standing at the door or eating. It was really lovely that you kept me so well supplied, especially with fruit. There was hardly anything to drink. The trip went quickly, except for the deepest hours of the night; at times it was fully dark in the compartments. Then one couldn't hear a word, only the rattling of the wheels and the clattering of the iron. As it grew dark, I stood with a comrade in the doorway and looked up at Mars, which was large and glowing on the southern edge

[3] Łódź, a large city in Central Poland.
[4] Part of the city of Dessau.

of the sky. These were actually the first hours of reflection I've had in over fourteen days. Then I slept again as much as I could. As we drove through the suburbs of Breslau, it began to get light and the night was over once again. One gets used to going without sleep relatively quickly, at least if one doesn't have to do anything during the day.

Now we're traveling through the liberated areas.[5] The first, yet infrequent, signs of war. Swastikas fly from many houses. Decorated arches have been draped over the streets and the railroad lines, which had been disconnected since 1920 but have been running now for several days. People are at work in the fields. Many greet us with their right hands raised[6] or wave at the train. We're happy that this area in particular has hardly seen any suffering.

Now it seems that we're going to see and experience more than we thought we would at first. But it's really only an inconvenience, and we aren't in any grave danger. And we're happy to take on the task.

Today at noon we're starting a new phase. I'm entering it with heartfelt thoughts of you. When will we hear something from home? But please wait until I send my military post number.

Take care.

Please keep this letter and send it when you can to Berlin.[7] Please get me, if possible, a little Metoula language guide for Polish, and send it to me when possible. I'm sending this letter from an almost purely Polish land—especially in terms of patriotic feeling.

---

[5] According to the provisions of the Versailles Treaty the Prussian province of Posen (Poznań) had become part of Poland after the First World War.

[6] Nazi salute.

[7] This refers to his mother and brother Bruno, who were living in Berlin.

September 10, 1939

Sunday morning in the home of a Polish railroad employee. The inhabitants have fled, naturally. The furniture has been pushed toward the walls. Straw has been spread throughout the rooms. Above it all, the pictures are still hanging on the walls. Everyone takes what he needs at any given moment, according to military custom. Nothing is being destroyed willfully. But of course, things will get scratched or damaged when people put their weapons on polished furniture or drip coffee on the upholstery—these things are typical behind the front. Field kitchens and supply wagons are in the courtyard. Across the yard is the only well, at which hundreds of soldiers (including comrades from the lower Danube[8]) do their morning ablutions. Now it's dry again. I write to you from a vine-covered garden shed. The sunflowers are in bloom. I can hear the bells from the village. Sunday morning.

The Shabbiness of Polish Life

September 12, 1939

In the meantime we've had a chance to get acquainted with the town where we find ourselves. Everything is somewhat shabby here, especially in comparison to, say, Schwedt. There's hardly any industry. The only thing here is a mill, and its owner has had to let us use his car. That was an interesting transaction. Our company leader tried his best to be polite. And at the end of it all, Jan signed as Johann. There's also a creamery here at the train station that is in German hands, and there one can now buy lovely cream and butter. Otherwise there aren't many stores. In the

[8] The National Socialist term for Lower Austria.

bakery where I bought my Sunday ham there was a photograph on the wall from an apprenticeship in Dresden during
the prewar days, and the woman's German was quite good.
Otherwise only the broad, market square gives an impression of urbanity. Even in the Marshall Pilsudski Street[9] the
houses are all of differing heights. Hardly any of the window frames are painted. The curtains are dirty and full of
holes. Spider webs hang in every corner.[10] The only beautiful building is the baroque Catholic church, a simple structure surrounded by greenery. We got to know the area quite
well yesterday in an official capacity; I unfortunately saw it
only from the outside, because I had to keep watch—with
my weapon clamped under my arm—in front of the Dom
Katolicki, the Catholic club house. I had ample time to
think about this new affirmation of the old relationship between the terms German=Protestant and Catholic=Polish.[11]
Unfortunately, I didn't get too far in my reflections, because
if you wear a steel helmet for a couple of hours in a row, it
begins to press upon your head. Notably, the Protestant pastor has been named the acting mayor of the place, and the
area around the Protestant church is the only place where
swastikas hang in somewhat larger numbers. Even the population doesn't make a particularly sympathetic impression.

---

[9] Józef Klemens Piłsudski (1867–1935) was the leader of the Polish Legion in
the First World War, the founder of the modern Polish state, and the president of
the Republic.

[10] Stereotypes about lack of Polish cleanliness were widespread among the
German middle class.

[11] In 1910 the province of Posen had per 1,000 inhabitants the following:
307.9 Protestants, 677.3 Catholics, and 12.6 Jews. In the administrative region of
Gross-Wartenberg, of 100 inhabitants 58.2 were Protestants and 41.8 Catholic. In
1910, 6,400 people lived in Kempen. Kaiserliches Statistisches Amt, ed., *Statistik
des Deutschen Reiches*, vol. 240: *Die Volkszählung im Deutschen Reiche am 1. Dezember 1910* (Berlin, 1915), 135, 139, map no. 5.

The girls are really only pretty if they're young. The women in many cases have sunken and washed-out faces, and the mixture of shabby elegance and slatternliness reappears in every facet of life. Overall, the poverty and meanness of things is alarming. Even in the men, who hold themselves back more and who only appear in large numbers on the streets at dusk.—At night by the way, the entire civilian population is not allowed on the streets.—Yesterday there were a lot of farmers' carts in the city. Simple wagons with small horses; the farmers sitting in the wagons on bundles of straw. Many of them greeted us. Supposedly about one-third of the surrounding population is German. The city has become almost purely Polish.

The trains are gradually starting to run again. Yesterday the first trains went to and from Breslau, naturally not for civilian use. Our people are spread out at the smaller stations. So the nightly shoot-outs will probably also slowly stop. A lot of horror stories are making their way into the city. In the future it will be just as difficult to ascertain the truth as it was in Belgium in 1914.[12] For me, these things have resulted in a nighttime drive between 2 and 3 a.m.; the hours were more romantic than dangerous as I had my steel helmet and a loaded weapon. If we hadn't received the first news from the West toward evening, we could have almost completely forgotten the war here. The prisoner transports are still not very numerous. The ethnic Germans and Ukrainians among the prisoners are being sorted out from among the Poles.[13]

---

[12] In World War I, the army in Belgium was fired upon by militias and countered with brutal repressions that in turn served as Western propaganda. See John N. Horne and Alan Kramer, eds., *German Atrocities 1914: A History of Denial* (New Haven, 2001).

[13] Nazi ethnic policy aimed at a reconsolidation of the German *Volk* and the exploitation of the local Slavic population. See Götz Aly, *"Endlösung."*

Now and then infantry troops come by, completely covered in dust and with strained faces and burning, overtired eyes; naturally everyone is fully motorized.

I take part in the normal company duty, and have the advantage that I don't have to participate in regular sentry watch, and must occasionally do other things, when the others are here. Today, for the first time, I could sleep in absolute peace from 10:30 until 5. But it seems that we are to stay here for a while and to get things in order and become more "civilian" until the next wave carries us forward.

I have purposefully written things in a very matter-of-fact fashion, so that this letter makes it to your hands. [. . .]

The Plight of Refugees

September 14, 1939

Now we are slowly starting to put down roots. That is, for the time, being rather nice. Last night the weather, which had been so wonderful, suddenly took a turn for the worse. It rained in buckets. Hopefully the Polish fall, with its mud and damp, isn't about to set in. But I still have the shelter of the orderly room where I can keep dry; it's very comfortable and I can always stay in there. We had hardly any duties yesterday. In the morning we went for a shower in the surprisingly lovely city baths. The swimming pool was still being cleaned and should be available for us to use for the first time this afternoon. Hopefully the sun will break through during the course of the afternoon. My impressions of the people and landscape here are slowly both taking

---

Völkerverschiebung und der Mord an den europäischen Juden, special edition (Frankfurt am Main, 1999); Peter Longerich, *Politik der Vernichtung. Eine Gesamtdarstellung der nationalsozialistischen Judenverfolgung* (Munich, 1998), 243–72.

shape and becoming more stable. When one drives out of the city, one is struck by the expansiveness and emptiness of the landscape. Because there are so many large landed properties, the villages lie far apart from one another. There are so many trees and wooded areas that the villages are almost hidden. So much of what one sees looks like it was settled during the last century. Most buildings are made of brick; many still have straw roofs. But the original clay buildings are already disappearing. We saw only a few on our way. We did see one new, half-finished school building and an almost-completed church. The impression of shabbiness and backwardness is stronger in the cities, of which we saw one with more than a thousand inhabitants, unfortunately too quickly to get an impression.

The thing that makes the war most visible here is the suffering of the refugees.[14] They march along the side of the road; if they're lucky with a horse and a wagon, with bundles and straw, with children and cows. The poorest among them have only a goat tethered and their belongings on their backs. They have left in part out of their own free will; mostly they've been forced to move. My comrades maintain that some of them said that the preachers in their pulpits have been saying, "The Germans cut off women's breasts, etc." Hence an antipathy to everything that has to do with the church is growing here in the East. People had traveled hundreds of kilometers toward the East. Now they're moving back. German troops support their own when necessary.

---

[14] For this widely held impression, see Field Marshall Fedor von Bock, *Zwischen Pflicht und Verweigerung. Das Kriegstagebuch*, ed. Klaus Gerbert (Munich and Berlin, 1995), 46; Hans Umbreit, *Deutsche Militärverwaltung. Die militärische Besetzung der Tschechoslowakei und Polens* (Stuttgart, 1977), 215f. The Jewish population in particular fled before the advancing German troops.

Yesterday we spoke with a family from Kattowitz.[15] The woman broke out in tears as she showed us her sick infant. The poor, so say the locals, are fairly happy that the Germans are back again. Only the landholders and the bureaucrats have fled. The fact that the Catholic Church is harping on the same subject doesn't surprise me, but it makes the situation even more difficult. Hopefully things will end quickly here in the East. Otherwise, the number of victims among the Polish people will be enormous. Certainly the encirclement battle is causing a great number of losses on the other side. The Jews flee toward the East in front of the advancing troops.

In the city there is much suffering. Most of the shops are closed. Some of them, along with their inventories, have been seized to provide for the troops. In the last few days I was in the back room of a large grocery store. They were letting people in up front in batches. Today everything in there will probably be gone. Matches, flashlights, batteries, etc., aren't to be had. No tobacco, either. At noon, long lines formed in front of the NSV[16] on the avenue to get food. Ragged children begged for food in front of our post.

The greatest danger facing us is being here in the "rear echelon" and everything that goes along with that. Yesterday we had such a strong prelude to this that I hope that this tendency will be countered more resolutely. One experiences the strangest things: the day before yesterday hour-long repairs on the road; then yesterday throwing out drunkards or putting them to bed. One learns a lot about human nature. [. . .]

---

[15] Kattowitz (Katowice) is a large city in the East Silesian industrial area.

[16] Nazi welfare organization. See Herwart Vorländer, *Die NSV: Darstellung und Dokumentation einer nationalsozialistischen Organisation* (Boppard, 1988).

Tales of German Suffering

September 16, 1939, Sunday noon
I'm sitting here in the kitchen of Frau Kasprzikowie, or whatever her name is. I'm sitting on a chair I've taken from the dining room and am thinking about you and about home. The officer in charge of munitions is tampering with a gas flame over his weapon. Another is having his breakfast; still, it's quiet here, and I can at least collect my thoughts. Yesterday we had another beautiful afternoon of Indian summer, but it's been raining hard since last night. Our courtyard is now a small lake, and everyone has crowded together in these cramped quarters. The men are resting, playing cards, or sleeping. Everything is the way it always has been on such days during wartime. Wallenstein probably didn't lie down in straw any differently.[17]

The last few days have left many strong impressions and have demanded some effort, as well. [Adding to] the misery of the Polish farmers who are fleeing from the East we now have that of German refugees. Yesterday evening we were returning from reviewing the troops quartered at the train station and I was sitting with our driver in the bar of the German hotel on the main avenue. At a neighboring table, someone I couldn't see was going on in an irritating and excited manner. All at once he interrupted himself with the question, "Yes, what else should we talk about? Should we talk once more about the filth that we come from?" I don't know if this remark was the reason, but in any case, the conversation moved from table to table. There were six men of differing ages and rank. Almost all of them had remarkably

---

[17] Albrecht Wenzel Eusebius von Wallenstein (1583–1634), commander in the Thirty Years' War, famous because of a play by Friedrich Schiller.

open faces and the large, open eyes that one sees in those who come from the "front," those who haven't yet been worn down by fatigue. I won't tell you everything they told us. Maybe you've already long since read about it in the newspapers. They were from Bromberg[18] and had made the march over Thorn (until there they walked in pairs with their hands tied) to Lowicz. Those who spoke had an enduring hatred as a result of their experience. "They aren't animals, that word is too good for them." And who's to blame? "The priests and the Jews." They were standing with 5,000 others along the long church courtyard wall in Lowicz. The machine guns had been set up. Then the first grenades hit. The German troops knew about these people's fate and moved their attack up a day.[19] "It wasn't an accident; our dear God had mercy upon us." Among the victims of this attack, in which anyone who for any reason had stayed behind or stepped out of line was shot down, was the dean of Bromberg [cathedral].

The next morning I found myself in the city on duty. There I watched as a long line of German refugees filed out of the Protestant church where they had spent the night. It was an image that brought home to me all the descriptions that I have ever read of such misery. People were grouped according to their city or region of origin. At the head of each line, small plaques decorated with swastikas announced each individual group. The west Prussian city of Strasburg headed

---

[18] City in Pomerania, now called Bydgoszcz.

[19] At the beginning of September 1939, between several hundred and one thousand ethnic Germans were killed in Bromberg, and exaggerated accounts of their deaths were spread by National Socialist propagandists. See Hugo Rasmus, *Pommerellen Westpreußen, 1919–1939* (Munich, 1988), and Włodzimierz Jastrzebski, *Der Blomberger Blutsonntag—Legende und Wirklichkeit* (Poznań, 1990). After German troops secured the city, several thousand Poles were imprisoned and several hundred communists or members of the intelligentsia were "liquidated." See further, Alexander Rossino, *Hitler Strikes Poland* (Lawrence, 2003), 62–74.

up the group, and made a strange impression. There followed
the names Thorn, Graudenz, Hohensalza, Schwetz, Briesen,
etc.[20] Here as well there is no point to picture the details of
suffering. There were some young people present, some of
them still in various pieces of Polish uniforms. Everyone tried
to pull themselves together and show off Kempen's pride and
poise to the Polish population. I don't think that I have ever
been greeted with "Heil Hitler"—a symbol of everything
German here—with such blazing eyes. Again and again a
song sprung up, as the group trudged toward the train station;
actually it was just one song: "We'll see each other again on
the shores of the Weichsel." No one at all knows how those
who stayed are doing or how the other refugees who've been
hauled someplace else are faring. It's just good that the war
has moved so quickly through this area. [. . .]

Yesterday we sat for hours outside in lovely warm weather.
The hills rolled in bending waves toward the West. It's going
to be a moraine landscape like the Uckermark.[21] To the East
lie deeper hollows and forested sand flats. Fields, upon which
lupine and buckwheat bloom. We traveled for miles through
a forest that was varied and well tended. Hares started up
and the blue jays scolded us because we were disturbing the
deep peace. No one bothered *us*, only our feet were aching as
we waited for the trucks to take us "back home."

One gradually becomes accustomed to carrying a rifle and
wearing a helmet and boots. If I ever go out with an empty
belt without a sixty-round load of ammunition, I feel quite

---

[20] Strasburg (Brodnica), Thorn (Toruń), Graudenz (Grudziądz), Hohensalza
(Inowrocław), Schwetz (Świecie), and Briesen (Wąbrzeźno) were West Prussian cit-
ies with considerable German populations that became Polish after the Treaty of
Versailles.

[21] Region in northeastern Brandenburg.

unencumbered, although my sidearm is heavy enough. I'm also sleeping really well, if I don't have to go out on duty at night. But on the other hand, my nighttime walks and drives belong to some of the most beautiful experiences we've had. [. . .]

Reassurance for Home

September 21, 1939

Unfortunately we still didn't get any mail today. Today marks the second week since we left Magdeburg. Our time here will be over tomorrow or the day after. At that point the squad replacing us will arrive. We still are having a rather easy time of it; dry quarters without vermin, enough straw, regular provisions, the ability to buy additional food. We're anxious to see how things will be farther east, where there's more destruction. The other company in our battalion has had to endure many more inconveniences than we have. Apparently people in Magdeburg have also already heard about this. You shouldn't worry about this if you hear of it. I'm still in good health. I'm not terribly concerned about our departure. I hope everything is all right with you. Have you already started work at the Alumnat,[22] or have you been put to other work? All's quiet here now; the depots and the support commandos have already left. Only regularly scheduled trains are running at the train station. But yesterday morning, a train with wounded soldiers was sent here to relieve traffic on the main lines. Hopefully tomorrow when we leave the train will be running through to Lodz. The large bridge

---

[22] Boardinghouse for students at the cathedral high school. See *Vereinigtes Dom- und Klostergymnasium Magdeburg, 1675–1950. Gedenkschrift.*

over the Warthe River near Sieradz[23] was destroyed so that trains couldn't go any further. [. . .]

Signs of Impatience

September 22, 1939

Another day. We're getting tired of waiting for our replacement. Hopefully there's more for you to do there. Because this last week has really been starting to make us feel superfluous, it's getting harder to stand being so homesick. But I think that's going to change soon. Otherwise, I'm doing my best to find a way to work at least a few hours a day. The gossip is endless. Today's topic of discussion is Daladier's declaration and what will happen next.[24]

I can barely stand to listen to all the mindless chatter. But I have to stand it, and it will work out one way or another.

I gave a postal worker who was going to Oels a package with about a pound and a half of butter. He was going to send it tomorrow. I hope you get it. A pound costs .90 Mark here. So I wanted to try it.[25] If you don't get it, we won't have lost much. Eggs cost four to five pfennig each here. On Sunday, each of us paid .15 Mark for a portion of roasted goose. Prices are slowly starting to rise. The civilian population has limited access to groceries, matches, etc. But on the other hand, stores are slowly starting to open. People are switching

---

[23] City on the Warthe (Warta) south of Łódź.

[24] Édouard Daladier (1884–1970), French prime minister. France declared war on Germany on September 3, 1939.

[25] In the province of Poznań a pound of butter cost 2 zloty in September 1939; in November 1939 a price ceiling was set at 1.10 Reichsmark. See *Verordnungsblätter* nos. 1, 5, and 7, issued by the Chef der Zivilverwaltung beim Militärbefehlshaber Posen und des Reichsstatthalters Warthegau on September 21, October 21, and November 18, 1939.

over to speaking German. All the elderly men tell people that they served at the front in the German army. These are great lessons that help to judge the nationality struggle and determine who belongs to which ethnic group.

I hope you're fully well again! Love and kisses.

I'm wondering a great deal about how life and work will continue after what's happened. But it's difficult to come to any kind of conclusion, given the incessant restlessness, which remains despite the fact that we don't have orders.

Ethnic Selection

September 30, 1939, West of Kutno[26]

Dear Franz, dear Lene,

I wanted to send you at least a few lines. We are now in the middle of Congress Poland in a lovely manor. The extensive stables house 1,700 prisoners, mostly from former Prussian lands. Our task is to find the ethnic Germans among them so that they can be released early. I've gained some interesting insights into the fluid boundaries between languages and peoples. Of course everyone wants to be a German now.

I've also gained a good sense of the Polish landscape from some long wagon drives. This has helped somewhat to deal with the other great tasks we face. For that reason alone it might be good for you to go and do some harvest farm labor. You'll quickly adjust to the physical labor and the discomforts that weigh upon people like you and me more heavily than our more primitive comrades. Take a few toiletries with you that you're used to for your more sensitive needs. The medical care here is bad; the medics are careless and listless.

[26] City in the district of Łódź.

67

Hopefully Lotte is healthy again. I was very sad to get your news.[27] I would appreciate it if Lene would visit her for a few days. Please send a few lines when Franz leaves. I would like to know at least in general terms where you are and how you're doing. One can get through a lot if one can focus one's thoughts on clear goals. [. . .]

Comradeship

September 30, 1939

Five weeks! I've had a reprieve; yesterday I spent the whole day on the sofa, well cared for by my comrades. (Not in the orderly room; they are rather selfish.) Today I used the morning to write the enclosed report. Please keep it safe. Up until now I've always had to sleep on straw, and it wasn't easy to take off my clothes. Whenever possible I did it and put on my pajamas. A prisoner washed our laundry yesterday. Socks? I need black thread; please remember nail clippers and some kidney-belts[28] when you're back on your feet. If the kidney-belts are too heavy, you'll need to send them in two packages.

As far as comradeship goes, that's hard to explain. Especially the better-educated ones are also the ones with higher standards. They fill their free time taking care of themselves and try to make their lives more bearable. Added to this is the fact that I actually am unattached and don't really belong anywhere. And soldierly comradeship grows out of group membership. [. . .]

---

[27] Reference to his wife's stillbirth in August 1939. See "Familiennachricht," 95a.

[28] Wraps to keep the kidneys warm.

Military passport, 1939

Eastward Journey

As I stepped out of the house on Sunday morning at around 4:30 after too little sleep and too short of a night, I was startled by an astonishing picture: toward the East a hole had been torn out of the dark night sky. A piece of the morning sky, sharply delineated, had broken through into the night with broad streaks of brilliant color. It's the green-blue of the morning that is always reminiscent of the ocean and the infinite expanse of space. Did the chill that made me shudder come from it and its cool brilliance, or from the dark recesses of the night? Light from the East—a shining prelude to our journey.

At 7 a.m. everyone was sitting comfortably on the train, pleased that the boredom of Kempen would soon be behind them. Shortly thereafter our train rolled out of the station—slowly, but steadily, we passed by the sites of our heroic deeds—Hanulin = Birkenfelde,[29] then past the beautiful forest near Domalin. The forest, which we patrolled, is also haunted by a wood nymph armed with a rifle, and is also the site of what will be the famed "Battle of D."[30] Wanda Forest is what it's called on the map. Isn't there a Polish story about a beautiful princess named Wanda? We've added a new story to the old ones. In the first few exhilarating days and nights, we would dream that our comrades' throats (or our very own) might be cut through—now all that lies behind in the quiet of a fall Sunday morning. "It is a truly beautiful day, by heaven! A day created by God, the great Ruler of the universe, for gentler things than war."[31] [. . .]

[29] Polish and German name of a city near Kempen (Kępno).

[30] This likely refers to Domanin (see the letter of October 17, 1939).

[31] Heinrich von Kleist, *The Prince of Homburg*, trans. Diana Stone Peters and Frederick G. Peters (New York, 1978), 26.

We're continuing on our long journey, which leads through Kalisch[32] and Sieradz. We all crowd the window seats. Because now the war is finally visible outside our windows. It's true that on the left and right of the tracks things are still undisturbed. The object of the battle was the train tracks themselves and the road that runs parallel to them. The Poles tried to destroy both as they retreated. We are traveling over demolished bridges, provisionally repaired by our sappers. It looks as if the train is floating over the water, as everything that holds it up seems as if it's been washed away. On the other side, the tracks have also been blocked by a train. The Poles shoved the cars toward the blown-up bridge. It's torn in half. The cars are burned out. Telegraph poles are partially sawn off. The wires are hanging in a confused tangle. Debris and jumbled wires cover the streets, where the antitank defenses, which have been removed, still bear witness to Polish activity. On the other side, burned-out train stations, sheds, and factories show signs of German air attacks. And so we move on slowly. Sometimes our train uses the tracks on the left, and other times, those on the right. Near Skalmiercz we cross the old German-Russian border. Large switching stations here and there with rusted rails and empty halls. They've been decaying for over twenty-five years! The German border station is a fine brick Gothic structure with elaborate decorations, practically a historic monument. At the somewhat larger stations there are German troops. Labor service men. Overall, however, these signs of German rule are overwhelmed by the vastness of the landscape. Only Kalisch shows more signs of life. Freight and prisoner transport trains arrive and

---

[32] Now Kalisz, large city in central Poland.

depart. German soldiers. Refugees perch on their bundles and wait for a connection.

The closer we get to Sieradz, the more numerous become the signs that intensive work has been done on the rails. Machines. Materials. Work has already ended. It's almost evening. The sun is setting as we arrive in Sieradz.

What does the night have in store—that's the question? The lieutenant, who drove ahead in his car, was expecting us much earlier. The bridge over the Warthe is still not passable. He has ordered a train to take us farther on the other side. In between lie eight kilometers that must be crossed. The supplies are removed from the train, horses are harnessed. They set off into the night. In the meantime, it has started to rain, hard and steady. We are protected somewhat under the roof of the supply hall. Nonetheless, we're tired and freezing. The mood varies according to temperament.

On the road, officers with radios stand in the rain, stopping traffic. Eventually they turn up a truck. The brigades depart one by one. I'm finally crammed into the lieutenant's car and try to find some room there between the rifles, helmets, and pieces of baggage. Everything is wet, and difficult to make out. We're the last to leave. To the right and left are illuminated quarters. We start to climb toward the bridge. A vast flood plain, with one bridge after another. German sentries are standing watch at the guardrails. Behind them the water is wide and deep.

We finally reach the loading area. A paved path turns off into the darkness. Upon the road there is a lively traffic. A truck has hit a hole in the narrow track and has turned over. The troops have lost their way in the dark, despite the sentries, and are only just now arriving. The loading ramp is much too steep. It's quite an effort to push the wagons and supply kitchens up onto the lorries.

The first lieutenant intervenes. Gradually, our efforts become more orderly. We unload the stuck truck. Then the wagons are arranged one by one in place and are fastened down. The horses disappear into the closed freight cars. Now the troops can also disappear one by one into the lorries. As I walk wearily behind the first lieutenant, I can for the first time allow the magic of the night to sink in. We're in the middle of a field. The rain slackens. The moon breaks through the clouds. Ahead, a windmill stands still in the shadows. At its feet our people move about busily. Flashlights and lanterns. Large horses. Fully loaded cars. Off to the side, our train.

Midnight. Our work is done. The whole lot is loaded. We have worked everything out. We climb into the train carriage. Dead tired. Frozen through. We sit tightly cramped together. The train rattles and shakes. Our eyes close; our heads sink forward.

Incessant, hurried jolts. We are making good progress. I sit in the farthest corner of the car on my knapsack. On my right sits Lieutenant Schulze, to my left the first lieutenant is sitting on a carton of hand grenades. We help keep each other warm. The lantern casts a weak light upon us. Occasionally in its glow one can see one of the three horses that have been placed in the back part of the wagon so that their warmth can make the night a bit easier for us. Every now and then one of them stamps against the wooden floorboards, making a thunderous noise. The harnesses clatter. Someone moves. But not a word is spoken. What an hour! But clear thoughts escape me. The first lieutenant leans against me, deep in sleep. I slump over him. The train rattles on.

Morning breaks. Leczyza, our destination. The locomotive driver, who has been holding the train for us since three

73

o'clock, drove too far on the line, with which he was completely unfamiliar, so he had to push us back. Cold, tiresome hours spent waiting. Then we march from the train
station into the city. We were dog-tired. Finally, we reached
our quarters. The large prisoner camp is located in a new
schoolhouse that has been hit by grenades. Our comrades
are located in a building close at hand and in neighboring
houses. I look to make myself useful and accompany the first
lieutenant on his round of the houses. I am confronted with
the sorrows of the inhabitants. One woman stands crying
at the entrance to her home, which is billeting yet another
set of troops (this makes how many now?). It is too much for
these people. I slink back to my quarters, throw myself onto
the straw. Sleep. Quiet. Warmth. And then the first letters
from home. [. . .]

I doze in the straw, covered by my coat, my head on my
pack. I hear voices and noises around me. My comrades are
getting settled. Prisoners assist them. My thoughts are far
away. Fever, chills. I sleep on.

The next morning, as we await the doctor, we learn that
we have to decamp in the afternoon. I won't take the castor
oil I was prescribed after all. The doctor warned: "Make sure
that you can keep up with your company." Now I'm sitting
on a miserable wooden cart trying gain some impression of
the city, although my insides are aching from the jarring
caused by the unevenly paved streets. "There isn't a Polish
city on the other side of the old Prussian border." The setting is an East German one: a broad square; straight avenues
leading up to it. But the Jews have filled the scene with their
miserable seediness. How squalid and pathetic. How sordid
they are in their wretched humanity. At the moment, I cannot offer more than that semi-aesthetic judgment. Maybe
the future will bring clearer impressions. In such a setting,

churches and cloisters serve (differently than they do at home) as islands of the spirit, as symbols of a higher world. If one cannot be a manorial lord in Poland, one can only be a priest.

Or a farmer. Because now we find ourselves happy beyond the gates. The road cuts through a broad, swampy flatland. Stacks of turf and deep cuts in the moor attest to the fertility of the fields. Fresh graves, however, line the road—a small hill of dark peat. A rather sad crucifix made of two pieces of wood and some fresh flowers. Refugees move along with us: newlyweds; the woman is carrying her child in a cloth at her breast. They march along bravely and move almost as quickly as we do.

Polish hamlets. The farms lie far apart; they have no clear boundaries to hold them together. Individual families live slightly apart from one another, but their worlds do not extend beyond their own courtyards. At least that is what it looks like when one travels, as we do, at such a slow pace. The farmsteads have plants around them to protect the homes from the weather. Poplars are the trees of choice. Their greenery stands out in narrow stripes against the bark and emerges above in broad crowns. Thick, wild shrubs grow along the fences, sometimes covering them completely. Such signs of human activity as expressed in the farmsteads are practically overwhelmed by nature. Our own familiar image of the village as a place with a church and tiled-roof houses has no corollary here. But the landscape is overgrown with these green islands. Poplars and willows lining the road forge a link between them.

Where there are larger farms, there are fewer trees and the fields extend beyond, with the manorial house—as it was meant to be—centrally located surrounded by the stables and parks. As one travels for hours through the landscape, it becomes evidently clear how overwhelmingly agricultural this place is and how much these people are still the same as they were when they entered history: they are *polanie*, people of the fields, inhabitants of the plains. Imagine the work the young [Polish] National state could have done here! During such travels one feels strangely close to the beginnings of the volkish movement—Herder! The life-giving Mother Earth. One feels safe and protected by nature. But instead of beginning there and moving forward, nationalist thought has, as it has done everywhere else, taken a wrong turn. The young National state ambitiously set out to establish hospitals and schools in the larger cities and then hoped to pursue power politics toward the outside. The result: The country has now become an object of economic development within the [German] Four Year Plan. A foreign industrial culture will "develop" the land. Its sons will go off as workers far away, rootless and homeless, happy if they can become part of a foreign people within two generations.[33]

Evening in Krosniewice.[34] Rain. Cold. Temporary quarters in train cars on piles of straw. Sleep.

In the morning, a short brisk march along the road connecting Posen with Warsaw. Then a field. We've finally arrived at our goal for now. The manor Glaznow.[35] We're beginning a new chapter.

---

[33] This echoes National Socialist "blood and soil" theory. See Anna Bramwell, *Blood and Soil: Richard Walther Darré and Hitler's "Green Party"* (Abbotbrook, 1985). For the economic exploitation of Poland, see Umbreit, *Militärverwaltungen*, 222–72, and Robert Seidel, *Deutsche Besatzungspolitik in Polen. Der Distrikt Radom, 1939–1945* (Paderborn, 2006), 87–169.
[34] Krosniewice in the district of Łódź near Kutno.
[35] Three kilometers from Krosniewice.

Polish POWs

October 2, 1939

It was such a joy to receive mail on a bleak and tiresome Sunday evening. We had a lot to do. Plagemann[36] and I had selected over eighty prisoners who were to be released. We asked each one of them about their homes, occupations, etc., in order to determine whether they could speak German. We also got our typhus vaccination.—The dentist from Magdeburg, Rusche, did his work decently and discretely—I have hardly felt any side effects. In the afternoon I filled out the paperwork for the identity cards for the people to take with them. The day thus took its course. It was, by the way, a beautifully warm and clear fall day. I walked a while in the park and enjoyed the dahlias and chestnut trees. It didn't feel at all like a Sunday. On the radio we listened to pieces of a beautiful English service with hymns and psalms. [. . .]

I wrote today to Ahrbeck about the books, and also contacted Dr. Schmidt,[37] so that I can keep in touch with the teachers-in-training and their work. Your letters are arriving regularly now. That makes me happy and helps me feel more secure in our relationship. There's a lot of activity here today, and on the road the troops are returning from Warsaw. The place is swarming with officers. We welcomed a new officer today, Lieutenant Sachse. He was a teacher at the Victoria School,[38] and he (as is his wife) is a follower of Ruff.[39] We have already had a long talk with each other. [. . .]

---

[36] Colleague from Magdeburg.
[37] Magdeburg bookstore and Protestant teacher.
[38] A high school for girls in Magdeburg.
[39] The cathedral pastor, Walther Ruff, in Magdeburg.

I'm sitting at a mahogany table on a stool. For my view of the Polish prisoners, who are lined up in front of me in long brown rows, I am framed by two white Doric columns flanking the stable entrance. I have to keep pulling my coat over my knees. It's cold today, and the prisoners are also freezing from having to stand so long. Comrade Plagemann is questioning them very thoroughly. I can study their fearful and embarrassed faces. Many break out in a sweat when they have to speak German, and they stumble to find the right words: *rolnik* = farmer; that's the word on everyone's lips. "How many acres [do you have], how many cows, horses; are you married, do you have children? Did your father serve in the war? Did you attend a German school?" Those are the things we ask. Many of them who have learned the most important answers by heart get stuck when we ask them their occupation and are sent back. If anyone passes the questioning, they come up to me and tell me their names and occupations, so that tomorrow they can receive their papers.[40]

Meanwhile, life goes on. The size of the manor has proven to be something of a handicap for its owner. The prisoners are kept in the stables in close quarters on piles of straw. During the day, they lie about the courtyard. [. . .] Of course the prisoners are responsible for keeping things orderly, and they are called upon to do all kinds of work. But their situation is tolerable. Their health has been good up until now. Imprisoned Polish doctors look after them. Ethnic

---

[40] Maike Sach, *Die "Volksdeutschen" in Polen, Frankreich, Ungarn und der Tschechoslowakei. Mythos und Realität* (Osnabrück, 2006). For the fate of Polish POWs, see Rüdiger Overmans, "Die Kriegsgefangenenpolitik des Deutschen Reiches 1939 bis 1945," in *Das Deutsche Reich und der Zweite Weltkrieg*, vol. 9/2 (Munich, 2005), 743–55; Edmund Nowak, "Polnische Kriegsgefangene im Dritten Reich," in *Kriegsgefangene des Zweiten Weltkrieges. Gefangennahme-Lagerleben-Rückkehr*, ed. Günter Bischof et al. (Vienna, 2005), 506–17.

Germans are in charge of the companies and groups to which they have been assigned. And so life is easy for the prisoners and guards. During the first couple of days, some non-commissioned officers appeared with whips. But they have long since disappeared. In comparison to Dwinger's "Army behind the Barbed Wire,"[41] German camps are orderly and run with good intentions. Our first lieutenant is a model of both qualities.

Market Day in Krosniewice

Our field drills are done. We have half an hour free. With my weapon slung over my back I go to visit the market. Today is a big day in Krosniewice. Early in the morning, one cart after another has rolled along the streets to the market square. There are many women present. Most have large, often quite colorful shawls draped over their heads and shoulders; when the wind blows from the East, it is easy to understand why. They often have one of the colorful ducks of the region (alive) tucked up under their arms. This gives the soldiers who are standing around an opening for their jokes. And Bianka, or whatever her name is, doesn't take offense at national differences and smiles back kindly in return.

Numerous carts mass in front of the ugly Gothic church. The unharnessed horses chew at the straw upon which the farmers and their *matkas*[42] had sat. On the other side of the square, the farmers and their wives crowd around their ridiculously paltry wares. [There are] some baked goods, some

---

[41] Edwin Erich Dwinger (1898–1981), in *Armee hinter Stacheldraht. Das sibirische Tagebuch* (Jena, 1929), described the suffering of Germans in Russian captivity during World War I.

[42] Polish for mother.

gingerbread, a pile of bonbons on one side. Across the way (and here the crowds are thick) there is a pile of woolen stuff, from which the women reach in and pull out some knickers, a shawl, or a sweater. The farmers huddle at the side of the road with their ducks. Of course they also have hens and geese. The white down feathers fly through the air. A few soldiers have ventured into the fray and receive the appropriate respect—they are looking for butter. There is none to be had. But those who know their way around and who are willing to pay a few pennies extra can still find some.

Lining the market are some modest buildings, in which the business life of the village takes place. One of the more respectable-looking ones has been hit by a grenade. But someone is already on the roof trying to save the rest of the tiles, and down in the cellar, which remains unharmed, business goes on as usual. Surprisingly, the cramped, seedy shops are full of life. The pharmacy is the only building that isn't a narrow hole in the wall; many of the windows have been blown out. The closed shutters make everything seem even darker. "A cup of tea?" "A piece of soap?" But the tea is horrid, and the asking price for the soap is already far too high.

So I turn away to study the architecture. Across the square stands a real log house. The blacksmith on the main street still has a storefront. Anything with any sort of style is vaguely classical. How long would the classical period have lasted here? It was followed by a horrid art deco period. That was superseded by the Pilsudski era; here it is embodied in the large, simple elementary school that bears the general's name. What future age will determine the architectural style of this place?

Guard Duty

Glaznow, October 4, 1939

[. . .] Life here unfolds with a certain regularity; that's always a bad sign in the army. We get up at 6:30. Our work, as I recently described it to you, starts an hour thereafter. Today I devoted myself almost exclusively to paperwork. In the morning we interrogated twenty-five prisoners about the supposed massacre of wounded [soldiers], but of course no one knew anything. I took notes.

[. . .] It's warm, we're fairly comfortable, and have no reason to complain—except for the fact that we're not at home. That's the subject of our daily discussions. I don't know if that's a good thing. The day before yesterday, Lieutenant Sachse reminded us of Rudolf Koch's war memoir.[43] I guess one should always be ever more brave and full of resolve. But of course it's natural that when we do this paperwork we feel we might be doing more useful work back home. But you shouldn't think that we're despondent. If we have work to do, the time does go by. And one day is followed by the next. If it stays as quiet here as it is now, I would be grateful for some books. [. . .]

I received a note from Magdalene von Tiling[44] with some news about the journal ([it is down to] eight pages per month!) and greetings. By the way, I asked Ms. Osterloh[45] for some remedies for circulation, colds, and indigestion. I also

---

[43] *Die Kriegserlebnisse des Grenadiers Rudolf Koch* (Leipzig, 1934).

[44] Magdalene von Tiling (1877–1974), religion teacher, politician, Landtag deputy of the DNVP, and editor of the journal *Schule und Evangelium*. See Gury Schneider-Ludorff, *Magdalene von Tiling. Odnungstheologie und Geschlechterbeziehungen* (Göttingen, 2001).

[45] Likely a pharmacist or doctor.

received a packet with candy from Franz and Lene with a lovely warm note from Franz. It is really good news that he can continue his important academic work at least for now. If he were to be called up to serve at home or here in the rear he wouldn't be happy, and he would be overwhelmed by his desire to return to his studies. [. . .]

Hope for Peace

October 7, 1939

Before the mail goes out today I wanted to send you a note. We've had many quiet days. Life is as regular as in peacetime. My health isn't that good. I can't seem to shake this cough and runny nose. The weather turned colder yesterday, after we had enjoyed some beautiful days. We listened to the Führer's speech yesterday.[46] We were disappointed that there was no news of a decision. But it did leave open the possibility of a peaceful future. [. . .]

Doing Paperwork

Glaznow, October 9, 1939

I'm very pleased to hear that you are enjoying the Harz mountains again. [. . .] I work the whole day long in the orderly room. We have double windows and a great tiled stove, from 5 p.m. on the electric light shines. All the work here is done by a prisoner: he shines our shoes, gets our wash, cleans the dishes, tends to the fire, so that our lives are pretty easy. I'm getting along well with the others in the orderly room.

---

[46] Hitler's speech to the Reichstag, October 6, 1939, in Max Domarus, *Hitler. Reden und Proklamationen, 1932–1945*, pt. 2, vol. 3, 4th ed. (Leonberg, 1988), 1377–93.

[. . .] In the past few days we have had some pretty serious discussions. Unfortunately, Plagemann is a rabid Nazi.

Yesterday I didn't have a particularly good Sunday. In the morning we received our second inoculation, and it took its toll on me. I had a fever all afternoon and could hardly sleep at all. The medic said it's a good sign when one's body can react with such strength. But it's fairly hard to have to go through. I was pretty wiped out today but did manage to complete my most important duties. We identified eighty prisoners [as ethnic Germans], and in the afternoon I wrote up their I.D.s. And that was my day. Our time here is unfortunately about to come to an end. We are going to be stationed at a village nearby, where our quarters will be cramped. Naturally everyone is talking now about going home. But it's just idle gossip. [. . .]

Facing Winter in Poland

Glaznow, October 10, 1939

I hope to use this quiet evening to answer your sweet greetings, which arrived today in different installments, as soon as possible. I received the card from Thanksgiving Sunday,[47] and the two packages with the socks, the kidney-belts, and the darning thread. I will need them because according to everything that we hear, and after today's speech by the Führer,[48] there is little hope of peace in the West. That means we'll spend the winter in Poland. It's *extremely* unlikely that we'll be moved to the western front. Instead,

---

[47] In Germany, this is a harvest festival in which people take offerings to church to be blessed and then celebrate a meal.

[48] Hitler's speech, marking the opening of the "winter aid campaign" on October 10, attacked England. Printed in Domarus, *Hitler*, pt. 2, vol. 3, 1395–99.

everything will be done to find more officers and NCOs. The others will continue to serve as guards here, either watching prisoners or serving as occupation forces. Active troops roll farther East along the broad Posen–Warsaw road. When we leave in the next couple of days, we'll likely move thirty kilometers northward from here. Hopefully the weather will improve somewhat by then. We had our first snow flurries today. [. . .]

We're releasing more of the German-speaking prisoners, which means twice as much work for me at the typewriter. The others will be transferred wherever we hope to be stationed.

I've read a little in Hegel. That should last for months. Some variety every now and then wouldn't hurt. Hanni's book[49] is probably too heavy to mail. If you have an extra copy, you should divide up the unbound pages and send them to me in pieces. But that can wait until I figure out what our new quarters will be like, and whether we'll have relatively quiet, warm evenings.

We received the V[ölkische] B[eobachter] today.[50] Our comrades are happy to get it regularly. I was very grateful for the *Frankfurter Zeitung*.[51] It contained a lot of interesting news. Please buy the Sunday edition and send me the interesting bits once you've read it. I don't have any other requests. We have enough food, even though we miss fresh things. But even with all the love and care in the world, that can't be pulled out of the thin air. We do have our daily glass of milk here.

---

[49] Hanna Stephan was a friend who wrote historical novels. The book in question was probably *König ohne Reich* (Munich, 1939).

[50] Nazi party paper.

[51] A leading, formerly liberal, newspaper.

Tell me more about what you're reading in English when you have a chance. I always warn people about underestimating the British. The others here place too much hope in the supposed weaknesses of the British Air Force and the possibility of rebellion in the colonies. [. . .]

Shots in the Night

Zgierz,[52] October 17, 1939

[. . .] Our move yesterday was bearable. We were on our feet all day with the usual long delays. But we didn't have to march much, and it was a beautiful, mild fall day. On the way here I could only spy out of a small slit in the door of the cattle car. As we switched over to electrical mainline in Czortkow it was already dark.[53] Our quarters are located in a very modern school: double-glazed windows, electricity, central heating. We have iron bedsteads and are supposed to receive straw and sacks this evening. Last night we slept like logs and didn't hear anything of the nightly visit to our office. Our windows look out on small houses, gardens, and fields that stretch down to the forest, which lines our view on all sides. This city is supposedly the nicest suburb of Lodz. I haven't yet seen any villas. But I've seen many gardens and parks. There are factories and some chimneys, but they aren't all that obvious. After our recent experiences we're skeptical that we'll stay here long. Under the major's supervision we follow the rules more carefully. No one is allowed to leave barracks after dark, etc. [. . .]

I've just read the instructions regarding officer training. I don't see any way to be promoted (it should be people who

---

[52] Town in the district of Łódź.
[53] Czortków junction in the district of Tarnopol (now Chortkiv, Ukraine).

have served for two years and have proven themselves on the battlefield).[54]

During our last evening in Glaznow (a part of our division had already departed) we had a little adventure. At about nine—I was speaking with the lieutenant about the suffering of a poor beautiful horse that had broken its leg a while back and it was in the stall, shivering, covered in sweat, with the saddest eyes you've seen (it was to be slaughtered immediately)—when suddenly we heard a series of rifle shots. All hell broke loose. I had just washed my feet and didn't have any socks on. So I had to pull on my shoes and run out into the night. Our patrol down to the pond didn't turn anything up, even though we crept around in the dark like Winnetou.[55] We searched the neighboring manor, where the SS are stationed. Lieutenant Sachse, a sergeant, and three others, followed by me. Steel helmets, loaded weapons. We were right behind the park. Behind us, we heard another shot. Then absolute silence. Gradually, our eyes grew used to the darkness. But we couldn't see anything more than the trees at the side of the road and the darkness beyond. [. . .] Then we saw something moving off to the right, and spied a sentry box. The night watchman. As we followed him, the relative brightness of the lawn stretched out into the darkness, where we could see a man in a much-decorated uniform and two-cornered hat. What a picture in the night! What kinds of stories could one associate with the weakly lit manor windows. But this was no time for dreams. The "comrades"

[54] On September 20, the Army High Command issued an order on "Offiziers-ergänzung während des Krieges und bei besonderem Einsatz," *Allgemeine Heeres-mitteilungen* 6 (1939): no. 786, 342.

[55] A character in Karl May's (1842–1912) popular novels about the American West, this Apache chief befriends the first-person narrator, called Old Shatterhand.

SEPTEMBER 1939 TO JANUARY 1940

from the SS were already at hand. It was an awkward meeting insofar as we hadn't yet been addressed by the SS in front of others. They gave us their report: three of them were stationed in a building nearby. They were making their evening rounds when they heard a suspicious cough. So they fired their weapons. One of them saw two figures run away—thus the hubbub and excitement. Of course the woods had to be searched yet again. We stayed where we were. The flashlights disappeared into the night. Cigarettes appeared, and the conversation turned to the usual topics. Then, suddenly, another shot. This time it was clear and loud—a revolver. We crouched low and listened. Our people returned. None of them had fired a round—it was a mystery. Luckily, Lieutenant Sachse kept his cool. (I don't need to emphasize that we of course were fine—what did we have to be afraid of?) So the riddle remained unsolved and we marched back home. Our eyes grew ever more accustomed to the night. Off to our right we could see the bright lights of Krosniewice. The view reminded me of our Sunday evening walks from Rosenthal or Senzig to the train station. I thought of the war years when we would walk to Niederschönhausen.[56] The night was the same; we walked under the same stars.—We reached Glaznow without further incident.

The place was in an uproar. Every man was at his post and the lookouts were at their stations. An old sergeant (decorated with the Iron Cross) had heard the shots in the park. We unfortunately disappointed him with our report. One last search party was sent out, of which I was a member. Then even more men were posted on watch duty. We were allowed to go to bed. Our evening had been shortened enough anyway.

[56] Various Berlin suburbs.

87

So our battalion has added yet another victory to a string a victories. The battle of Domanin [. . .] has been joined by that of Glaznow-Beilice. Hopefully our future battles will all have similar outcomes.

And the mysterious revolver shots? Probably one of our guards fired, and then was too afraid to admit it. [. . .]

Dreaming of Love

Zgierz, October 21, 1939

It's Sunday evening. I can hear the raindrops beating against the windowpanes. Otherwise it's relatively quiet. [. . .] Our days are quite long with all the running around in the or-derly room. And whenever work isn't quite so demanding and when one isn't under constant pressure (as we were yes-terday and today), then one feels the stress even more. The place is buzzing with activity now. Some are on sentry duty; the drivers and detail troops are on the move, but the rest of us are drilling, doing lessons, cleaning our weapons, etc. We no longer have the pleasure of interacting with Poles as in Glaznow. I was therefore even more grateful for the two Shakespeare volumes. I keep being swept away whenever I have a chance to read undisturbed. I was especially moved by *Richard II.* I'll try to convey my impressions to you, but I think it will sound banal if I write them down. I'd be grateful for *The Tempest* if you could send it.

Lieutenant Sachse just came in to talk about theology and philosophy. So I'll need to close before it gets too late. But I want to tell you one more thing. I had a lovely experience recently right before falling asleep. Do you know how when you close your eyes you sometimes see shimmering? This time I saw a wonderful, bright blue. Suddenly the blue turned into a beautiful field of forget-me-nots. [. . .] Then you were there in a bright summer dress and a large straw hat, and you were picking the flowers. Your white dress and hat were shining in between the blues. I couldn't see your face, because you were leaning too close to the ground. Then everything disappeared. Only the blue shimmered in my dreams.

I want to hold onto that forget-me-not, even if it was only a dream.

The Lodz Ghetto

Zgierz, October 22, 1939

This Sunday is much quieter than yesterday, so I want to answer your rich and joyful greetings as soon as possible. [. . .] They're calling up the younger cohorts after all.[57] What a war. [. . .]

I had a real soldier's Sunday today. We had service on the market square; we wore our helmets and stood before mounds of weapons. The service was for both Catholics and Protestants. The "deists" could stay at home, even though the "morning celebration" (that's what they were calling it) would have helped them more than others. The moralists among us, like our sergeant [or] the company leader, were happy to hear so much about soldierly virtues and duties. I was freezing both on the outside and on the inside, because we arrived forty-five minutes too early and had to stand in the cold rain; the text was all about knighthood, belief, and a clean conscience. Then two hours of work at the typewriter, followed by a Sunday lunch: roast beef with carrots,

---

[57] For the call-up of the 1929 cohort, see Bernhard R. Kroener, "Die personellen Ressourcen des Dritten Reiches im Spannungsfeld zwischen Wirtschaft, Bürokratie und Kriegswirtschaft, 1939–1942," in *Das Deutsche Reich und der Zweite Weltkrieg*, vol. 5/1 (Stuttgart, 1988), 727.

potatoes; a short nap and then the big event of the day: led by a freed prisoner I went with fifteen comrades to Lodz for a few hours.

We won't so easily forget what we saw there. How pitiful and sordid these people are in appearance! The Jewish quarter is located near Zgierz, where our train lines end.[58] There wasn't a ghetto, just one shop after another with signs announcing Abraham and Chil, Lajb and Szeml. The shops were closed, of course. But the masses pushed their way past us on the narrow sidewalks. The Jews held themselves back, casting sideways glances at our uniforms. In the alleyways they group together, like at home in the Münz- und Hirtenstrasse, yet here more fully themselves. Among them one finds single, small faces with burning expressions of intelligence. Every now and then one sees some elegance. But overall, there's just poverty and misery. There is very little of that quiet composure that must come from one's convictions and belief, especially important for this people (more than any other). Lodz still doesn't have a sewage system. Our throats seized up with the smells that came out of doorways and from fetid waters in the gutters. As night fell, the fog rising from the ugly, uneven facades took on something of the grotesque. And then the constant pushing and shoving on the streets. The only good thing was the number of swastikas hanging from the houses of the ethnic Germans. The flags fly from the villas of German industrialists as well as the one-story homes of German workers and artisans.

Lodz also naturally has streets lined with European shops. They are the goal of officers and troops, buying up

<hr/>

[58] A large ghetto was established in Łódź in 1940; see Andrea Löw, *Juden im Ghetto Litzmannstadt. Lebensbedingungen, Selbstwahrnehmung, Verhalten* (Göttingen, 2006).

everything on hand, just as they did in Austria and the Su-detenland. [. . .] We drank coffee with whipped cream and ate cake in a nice cafe. Prices are going up even though strict laws are in place. Food is getting scarce and no one knows how people will survive the winter without some serious measures. Perhaps the very poverty of life here will be an advantage. We expect that a lot will need to be brought here from the Reich.[59] This whole spending frenzy isn't particu-larly dignified. Many people have their families send them additional funds. [. . .]

A First Promotion

October 27, 1939

[. . .] The evening was nicer than I expected. I was especially interested in the ethnic Germans from the men's choir. It's odd to see how nineteenth-century cultural forms continue to live on here. Everyone related to middle-class culture was present: master craftsmen, merchants, and a few academics. I wasn't able to speak to them because they were sitting with the major and the staff officers.

The evening also brought news of our promotion. Our sergeant got two new stripes. There are so many privates first class in our company that no one got a special acknowledg-ment. But the kicker came this morning. The first lieutenant has given me the command of a machine gun troop. I was so flabbergasted I could barely mutter my reply of "present"! In

---

[59] Hitler's plans for the German-administered part of Poland were dreadful: "He would only need working slaves from there." In contrast the annexed districts of Poznań and West Prussia were to become "flowering German lands." Helmut Groscurth, *Tagebücher eines Abwehroffiziers, 1938–1940. Mit weiteren Dokumenten zur Militäropposition gegen Hitler*, ed. Helmut Krausnick and Harold C. Deutsch (Stuttgart, 1970), 381.

the meantime, I've come to terms with the fact that I know about as much about machine guns as an African about an automobile. But one can learn. It will be more difficult for me to leave the office and its somewhat dignified atmosphere. I've put off moving until tomorrow so that I can write a little in peace. Tomorrow a new life can begin. I've already had command of the group during parade exercises. The deadlines for officer training courses have already passed, so we can have some quiet for a while. I'll be able to get used to the whole thing and figure out how to command sentries or understand topography. The commander of a machine gun squad is responsible for twelve men. That's what makes exercises so interesting. This means that in terms of service I now belong to the NCOs. I don't know whether or not these military details interest you. But I have to busy myself with them. In addition to myself, one other man has been named to squadron leader, a somewhat older veteran. I thanked the lieutenant this evening for his trust in me and asked that he bear with me at first. He seemed pleased that I asked. "When God gives someone a task, he also gives him the knowledge [to do it]," he said in closing. I'll take some comfort from that. When you get this letter, I will have already had a chance to get used to things. Such is life now. We always live a little bit behind each other.

We recently heard Ribbentrop's speech from beginning to end.[60] We thought things would go quickly against England. But instead, there is this strange silence. The *Frankfurter Zeitung* gives some insight into many things. Overall I am gaining the impression that there will be no quick

---

[60] Joachim von Ribbentrop (1893–1946), German foreign secretary, gave a speech on October 24, 1939, in Danzig, accusing England of starting the war. Cf. Michael Bloch, *Ribbentrop* (London, 2003).

First advancement, fall 1939

decision. In Poland, we now have a Governor General.[61] More reserve police battalions, SS troops, and others are arriving in Lodz, and we are becoming superfluous. But where to?—that's the question. [. . .]

Many kisses to you and Bruno. Please write soon. And you, dear little mother, don't worry too much about me. I'll get through this, and eventually will even become a real soldier. That will be a good thing in many ways. [. . .]

---

[61] Hans Michael Frank (1900–1946) was named governor general of Poland on October 12, 1939. Since he was responsible for the brutal exploitation of the country and the conscription of hundreds of thousands slave laborers, he was executed in 1946. See Werner Präg and Wolfgang Jacobmeyer, eds. *Das Diensttagebuch des deutschen Generalgouverneurs in Polen, 1939–1945* (Stuttgart, 1975), and Martyn Housden, *Hans Frank: Lebensraum and the Holocaust* (New York, 2003).

Watching POWs

Sunday, October 29, 1939

[. . .] Just as we had finished our morning's duties and were looking forward to the weekend, we received the order that we were to relieve the watch at the prisoner camp. They weren't able to deal with the Poles any more, and they had let too many of them get away. So we packed up quickly and washed once more. Then we went out to the edge of the city, where the Poles had been building a large base for a tank regiment when the war broke out. There were around 1,500 prisoners there. There were fifty of us there to bring them to reason. But it turned out to be quite harmless. We had to exert ourselves a little though. I wasn't on duty, but stood in for a sick comrade in my group and kept watch for seven hours between nine at night and nine-thirty in the morning. By then most of the prisoners had been cleared from the camp and we had some peace. Every six hours I spent two hours at my post. I sat in an enclosed wagon behind a bench, upon which the machine gun is mounted, and I could have covered the entire courtyard in an emergency. But there are only 250 prisoners left, and they're busy cleaning the empty base. They won't cause any trouble.

Something strange happened last night. I was standing at the doorway. The night was fresh and dry at first. Toward morning, it was foggy and rainy. Woods ringed the square before me in dark strips. A few imposing shadows cast by mighty pine trees, accompanied by the softer shades of a few birches. I could have been in Rehfelde or in Möser.[62] When I turned around toward the door, I was almost floored by

[62] Towns outside of Berlin.

the oppressive odor. What must it be like upstairs, where hundreds of men are locked up together! The door to the upstairs stayed closed the whole night long. Every once in a while someone came needing to use the latrine. No one is allowed to leave wearing a jacket or coat, so that their shirts will gleam in the night—on the other side of the barbed wire is a wooded area [in which they could easily disappear]. That's my main duty. There's always a gown, a jacket, or a sweater on the ground at my feet. Many of them are stiff with dirt; the worst part is the smell clinging to many of them. I often gag. But there are many prisoners who are amazingly clean, given their circumstances. Whenever they approach me I have a chance to study their expressions for a moment. Many are exhausted and worn out. Some chat me up in Polish and are in a good mood. From the other entrance I could hear someone being pistol-whipped. I can do my job just fine without having to resort to such measures.

Morning breaks. 1,200 [prisoners] are assembled in the courtyard. They receive coffee, bread, and some margarine for their journey. Almost all of them are freezing, and stomp around to keep warm. Once again one can see how different individuals accept their fate. Men of all ages are here together. Young men are wrestling for the fun of it. A father has a photograph album and shows it to his comrades. Most of them have lost their luggage during the retreat and look awful. Still, a few have managed to clean their boots for the trip to Germany. When the food arrives, almost everyone forgets everything else. A few fights break out, especially when a container of margarine has to be divided in ten portions. Deprivation causes mistrust, and surely not without reason. Over night a few have entrusted me with all their belongings (coats, bread, canteens, or cooking utensils) instead of leaving them with their "colleagues" (that's what the Poles call their comrades). But camaraderie still exists. More than once I saw men sharing cigarettes.

A few hours later, a large cloud of blue smoke rises from the courtyard, obscuring the pines. They're burning the filthy straw. The remaining prisoners are leaning out from the windows, cleaning the panes. A few more days, and the "tank camp" will be just a memory. [. . .]

Target Practice

Zgierz, November 1, 1939

As you can see, I'm still writing from Zgierz. Things aren't moving along as quickly as it seemed they would yesterday.

I overreacted yesterday when someone from the company came and told me the bad news in confidence. I hope I haven't worried you. The thing is—at least, the word here is (and take it with a grain of salt) that the area around Lodz will be incorporated into the Reich, as the district Kalisch.[63] I can't believe it yet. The area is supposed to be under civilian control, and we are to be moved to the "Polish Protectorate."[64] Blaskowitz[65] has issued an order in his

---

[63] These formerly Prussian and Polish areas were combined on October 28, 1939, into the Reichsgau Posen, later called "Warthegau." Cf. *Reihe historischer Ortschaftsverzeichnisse für ehemals zu Deutschland gehörige Gebiete, 1914–1945*, vol. 8, 5.

[64] From October 26, 1939 on, the central Polish territories were known as "General Government" and were put under civilian administration. See "*Führererlasse" 1939–1945. Edition sämtlicher überlieferter, nicht im Reichsgesetzblatt abgedruckter, von Hitler während des Zweiten Weltkrieges schriftlich erteilter Direktiven aus den Bereichen Staat, Partei, Wirtschaft, Besatzungspolitik und Militärverwaltung*, compiled by Martin Moll (Stuttgart, 1997), 103f.

[65] General Johannes Albrecht Blaskowitz (1883–1948), commander in chief of the eastern front, was removed because of his protests against SS crimes in Poland. Cf. Richard J. Giziowski, *The Enigma of General Blaskowitz* (London, 1997).

capacity as commander in chief in the East that all soldiers should now return to military duties. So it's a given that our battalion will be removed from the regiment and used as a "field troop"—that doesn't mean we'll be front troops. We are to improve our military capabilities. We had shooting practice today as a result. It was a lovely afternoon. [. . .] We shot at a range of one hundred meters, and I was the best, getting three head shots and leading overall by five shots. I was very pleased, because there's been a lot of talk about our promotion. Many in our company missed completely five whole times. It was a pretty miserable result. Such are our worries. Yesterday we cleaned up the prisoner camp and then turned it over to our replacements. I had night duty, naturally, because it seems that I am the one who always gets sent on special details. This morning I stood behind the target range and tried to get used to the noise of the bullets as they hit the targets. But I've been off duty since four-thirty. I haven't had it this good in quite some time.

[. . .] Today I noticed with some dismay that I'm slowly losing my intellectual abilities. I received the last section of her book from Miss Stephan, along with a friendly and informative letter. But the first time through, I couldn't understand a thing. I'm happy about the book though. I'm still reading the Shakespeare volumes with pleasure. [. . .]

NCO Duty

November 3 [1939]

[. . .] Your letters have left me feeling rather low. I was especially struck by the news of Engler's[66] death. [. . .] You know what he meant to me in my work. [. . .]

---

[66] Colleague.

97

The gossip in our NCO room, which is not particularly reliable, as well as the continuous radio playing is getting on my nerves. [. . .] But I'd rather not speak of that. We have to hang on, at least until we get our new orders. The day after tomorrow I'll be duty officer for the first time.

There's no need for you to worry about the weather. On bad days we stay inside. I'm sleeping well enough on a straw-filled sack on my cot. Our laundry is being done by a clean German woman. She comes to the base and that makes it easy for us. We went swimming again today. We'll probably stay here for a while, which would be good in a lot of ways (our quarters, for instance). Wild rumors about our future continue to circulate. [. . .]

Germanizing the Warthegau

Zgierz, November 5, 1939

I don't want Sunday evening to go by without sending you a note, even though I can't relax because of the unfamiliar pressure that comes with being the duty officer. The weather is so nasty that the only good place to be would be in front of a fire in a cozy café in the city. But that actually wouldn't be very nice, because no one has any coal and all of Poland is freezing where there's no wood to burn. It's a lot nicer in the base, and we have thirty-six men here tonight in case of an alarm. [. . .]

Zgierz is now a city in the German Reich, at least that's what they're saying here. There are lots of rumors that we'll be sent home in a few weeks. I pass them on, without knowing whether they're true or not. They're saying that those born in 94/95 and earlier will be sent back first. We live in some uncertainty. Our duties remain the same, but our work doesn't seem particularly significant. We went to the shooting range again. Standing at one hundred meters. I had three bull's eyes again. [. . .]

My reading has been limited to the *Frankfurter Zeitung* and *Henry IV*, in which I'm constantly interrupted. I don't have a chance to concentrate on anything. In any case, reading is seen as "disturbing" the *Volksgemeinschaft*. Reading is something that sets one apart.

The package to Trudchen[67] was sent to your address today in Hennigsdorf. I also sent a package with some soap. Only people with special connections can buy butter—dealmakers and their friends. And I don't have too many friends. Since I've been promoted, I don't have the natural support of a group of comrades. [. . .]

When one walks through the city streets, one can easily forget that this was only just recently enemy territory. Yes, people speak Polish. There are a lot of Jews.[68] But everything is so completely in German hands; [one sees] German troops and construction units; swastikas; Hitler Youth armbands all over the city. The factories are now being incorporated into the German economy and using German methods.[69] Our shooting range is located on the grounds of a chemical factory with excellent facilities—playing fields, swimming pool, etc. Our people all agree that the Poles were making good progress in their young state.

And finally, I don't want to conceal from you the fact that even if we were to return to Germany, we won't be

---

[67] Gertrud Kauba, wife of his brother Bruno.

[68] About 2,600 Jews still lived in Zgierz at the beginning of 1942. See Frank Golczewski, "Polen," in *Dimensionen des Völkermords. Die Zahl der jüdischen Opfer des Nationalsozialismus*, ed. Wolfgang Benz (Munich, 1991), 449.

[69] Hans Umbreit, "Auf dem Weg zur Kontinentalherrschaft," in *Das Deutsche Reich und der Zweite Weltkrieg*, vol. 5/1: *Kriegsverwaltung, Wirtschaft und personelle Ressourcen, 1939–1941* (Stuttgart, 1988), 3–345.

released from duty and there is no chance we'd be together in peace. The overall political situation is such that intense diplomatic efforts are underway to determine the final front-lines. It's not clear where the fighting will be taking place. That's the reason for this military indecisiveness. In such a case will anyone willingly give up troops that have just barely been brought together? I doubt it.[70]

I hope you're all well. The more uncertain the future, the more we must hold each other close in our hearts. [. . .]

The Power of Literature

No date [November 8/9, 1939?]

Your letter of November 4 has occupied me so that I need to answer it straight away. I don't know if I'm too late, and it's not fair to try to intervene from far away. But I think it would be a shame if H[anna] St[ephan] thought she were in competition with Bäumer.[71] I don't think the publisher's offer is all that attractive. Miss St[ephan] should go her own way in these things. I think alternating between academic and prose writing is confusing in any case—for the author and her readers. Even though she looks to the past in her work, she must remember the present if she wants to write real literature. If a book is to engage thoughtful readers, it needs to express something eternal about the human condition. The dream of empire is our dream. Ambition, the will to fight, love and death, those are our dreams. An academic

---

[70] At this time Hitler was already planning the attack on France. At the beginning of the war about 1,200,000 men born prior to 1900 were drafted. The shift to younger recruits proceeded slowly due to lack of trained personnel. Cf. Kroener, *Ressourcen*, 824f.

[71] He is referring to Gertrud Bäumer, a liberal feminist who was also active in the Third Reich.

description of womanhood asks us to consider something that exists beyond our experience. Its value is in letting us sense things that lie outside our own lives. Academic discourse dispels the spectral otherness of the past. But popular writing is nothing more than a concession to the masses who cannot bear poetry because it touches them at their core, at the place where individuals are truly themselves. Academic discourse can't abide this either, because it attempts to circumscribe that which is foreign and unknowable and ultimately describes that which is most personal. In between these two poles lies an indistinguishable mass that is neither poetry nor prose. It allows the reader to disengage. The reader isn't challenged, just busied. It's just like our radio here—it's on all day, without saying anything; like the movies, newspapers, magazines. I now understand this from my own experience. Who can help defend us from this maelstrom, if not ourselves?

I've just now read the chapters on Hadburg.[72] As you might imagine, I found them very moving. I don't see how they will unfold. But I think there is a piece here that could be developed to become the first great German epic of the East, just as A. Miegel's work on the seven knights served as a starting point.[73] Stifter's Witiko had asked the same questions.[74] Having said that, I realize it's too academic; or, to put it another way—too Catholic-universal, too secularized. In the few chapters that I've read, I've run across a great deal that we've experienced here on a daily basis. And not just as an academic exercise, but as reality. Does the whole

---

[72] Hadburg is a medieval women's first name. This likely refers to a chapter in Hanna Stephan's book.

[73] Agnes Miegel, *Kirchen im Ordensland—Gedichte* (Königsberg, 1933); this East Prussian author (1879–1964) was a favorite of NS elites.

[74] Adalbert Stifter (1805–1868), Austrian novelist.

thing—*Frau Oda*[75] or "the King without a crown"—need to find some conclusion at the end of the book? The East, the German Reich, the unity of tribes, the crucifix. Doesn't this need full and undivided attention? [. . .]

Attack on Hitler

Zgierz, November 10, 1939
We're all still in shock from the attack in Munich.[76] It's quieter here in the duty room than it's ever been. Everyone is aware of the earthly and heavenly forces at play that thwart even the most determined individual will. At the moment it's clear to each of us that there is no telling what the future will bring for anyone. And the news spread in no time at all around the entire world! We can hear the faint echoes of the event everywhere. Our own tension happens to coincide with the long-awaited Polish holiday celebration of national independence in 1918.[77] We're on special alert tonight. The streets have been empty since five. We've scheduled innumerable foot patrols for tonight. We don't expect anything awful to happen, just a few demonstrations. Some posters were put up by the Poles, but we've already caught the culprits. Three Jews have been hanged in Lodz's main square—why, I don't know.

I'm still doing fine personally. We're outside a lot with the lovely, mild weather. We're starting to do more field

[75] Hanna Stephan, *Frau Oda. Verheißung und Geschichte. Buch der Ludolfinger* (Berlin, 1937).

[76] On November 8, 1939, the carpenter Georg Elser detonated a bomb in the Munich Bürgerbräukeller, which just missed Hitler. Cf. Helmut G. Haasis, *"Den Hitler jag' ich in die Luft." Der Attentäter Georg Elser. Eine Biographie* (Munich, 2001).

[77] November 11, 1918. Armistice Day was celebrated in Poland as Independence Day.

maneuvers. I've also been on horseback, and rode through the city streets as pleased as punch. [. . .] Afterward we went to a speech for officers that we had to attend. The major spoke of the victory near Brzeziny in November 1914.[78] [. . .]

Meaningful Duty

Zgierz, November 12, 1939

Dear Lene,

Yesterday I heard from Lotte that Franz has been called up "for special duties" since the beginning of the month. I wanted to let you know that I hope that these special duties are in keeping with Franz's knowledge and abilities. Because at our age, grunt work in the military is only bearable if one is at the front, where the sense of urgency and importance trumps other feelings, and where the most basic elements of life and the need to prove oneself make everything else seem much less important. I hope Lotte will report soon about some worthwhile activity. Some opportunities do exist: for instance, a Magdeburg official (who had previously had to deal with Poles and Jews at the local level) was sent today to Posen to a central office. And how are you doing alone at home? As long as Franz is nearby, I assume you'll stay in Cologne. We find ourselves in a strange limbo. On the one side, we are faced with new directives. Every few days we have to integrate new troops into the unit: light and heavy machine guns; grenade throwers; cavalry, bicycle troops; anything else that needs to be done. All kinds of things that take time to do really well. And much of the

---

[78] This World War I battle involved a successful breakthrough in the area of Łódź under General Karl Litzmann. Hitler mentioned it in his Reichstag speech of October 6, 1939, in Domarus, *Hitler*, Part II, vol. 3, 1379.

company is constantly called up to take part in sentry duty and foot patrols. On the other hand, for some time now we've been faced with the possibility of being sent out of Reich territory (that now extends beyond Lodz) into the General Government. We have now become a unit for "special duties." That will likely mean that we'll be leading a rather mobile existence. My own NCO service suffers under the same conditions. My machine gun group is always somewhere else; they are never around for proper training, and in these circumstances I personally find it difficult to find the energy to familiarize myself with the weapon.

Those are very specialized military things, but perhaps as a wife of a soldier you can understand that they determine the larger part of our lives. I've kept up my attempts to carve out my own personal space—even in the face of barbs from my comrades and their inability to understand me (I am now living in the NCO quarters). In order to lighten my backpack (just in case the general's[79] visit on Wednesday means that we really will be on the move soon), I've been reading my Poland book. I couldn't go into the city in any case, because the anniversary of Polish National Independence day (November 11, 1918) has resulted in special measures and curfews. It is a statement about ruling Polish circles. After what happened to ethnic Germans at the beginning of the campaign, one can hardly doubt the facts. I think that even the "great general" (whose portrait is still hanging in the corridor) didn't end up looking very noble.[80] We'd like to know the details. In any case, Soviet policies now seem more

---

[79] Friedrich Wilhelm von Rothkirch und Panthen (1884–1953), major general and from November 1, 1939 commander of the 13th Division. BA-MA, MSg109/10851.
[80] Probably a reference to Marshall Piłsudski.

comprehensible. The tasks that we Germans face—should it actually come to a cease-fire—are really quite unbelievable. Last night here the Jewish synagogue was set on fire. Today the Jewish meetinghouse is in flames. In Lodz, Jews and Poles have been strung up in the market places, because they were putting up anti-German posters. And now we are expecting the arrival of Germans from Wolhynia.[81] Those are just a few random examples. What do they say about individual and national destinies? [. . .]

The Meaning of the War

Zgierz, November 12, 1939

Dear Joachim Müller,[82]

[. . .] We should be allowed to ask our God that He not always make us and others take the most difficult path in regard to this world. So many people today have been torn out of the security of their existence. If they only all knew of the force that can provide help in such situations. If I look out the window to the left, I can see a tower of fire over the city. The Jewish baths are burning, and the synagogue was burned down last night. The fires were set by the ethnic Germans who live here, against the will of the military authorities, who were able to thwart an earlier attempt fourteen days ago. And so each of us is affected by the strange tumult of our times. But I often wonder how most people can just ignore such things

---

[81] On the basis of the Hitler-Stalin Pact of August 23, 1939, ethnic Germans from eastern Poland were to be resettled. In Zgierz the Volksdeutsche Mittelstelle had established several camps for about 10,000 people from the Baltic states and Wolhynia. Cf. Stephan Döring, *Die Umsiedlung der Wolhyniendeutschen in den Jahren 1939 bis 1940* (Frankfurt, 2001); Markus Leniger, *Nationalsozialistische "Volkstumsarbeit" und Umsiedlungspolitik, 1933–1945* (Berlin, 2006).

[82] Joachim Müller was a colleague who worked on the journal.

and protect themselves with cheap explanations. Most of my comrades act as if our destinies were nothing more than the result of a mere accident—the authorities should have just called up the younger generation and let us stay at home. Our victory in Poland has just been too easy and too quick. Only some of us, like our own 13th Division, have encountered the Poles as serious opponents.[83] The enormity of the task facing us in the East (not to mention in Russia) is slowly becoming apparent. The Munich attack has revealed momentarily the otherwise hidden facts of our existence. Over the past few days, all the chatter about our imminent return has died down. In fact, we reservists are gearing up at the moment. We're slowly starting to grow accustomed to the gray uniforms that we've been wearing for almost three months now. It's becoming clear who among us isn't up to the task. The past few weeks were almost like basic training: shooting practice, drills; slowly we're starting to ride. The strong impressions of the first Polish weeks have now faded. We're living in a city of the Reich that stretches beyond Lodz. Because the city is becoming more German (helped in large part by the relatively large numbers of ethnic Germans here—I went to a German Protestant service last Sunday)—it's easy to forget how dangerous this place still is.[84] Yesterday was Polish Independence Day—November 11, 1918! We doubled the watch and sentries. Posters were up, and there were public hangings in Lodz. Overall the strength of our political will can put down any enemy activity. It could seem that everything is already over,

---

[83] During the Polish campaign, the division lost 84 dead, 226 wounded, and 121 MIAs. Dieter Hoffmann, *Die Magdeburger Division—Zur Geschichte der 13. Infanterie- und 13. Panzer-Division, 1935–1945* (Hamburg, 2001), 83.

[84] For the Germanization policies, cf. Heinemann, *Rasse- und Siedlungshauptamt*, 187–303; Valdis O. Lumans, *Himmler's Auxiliaries: The Volksdeutsche Mittelstelle and the German National Minorities of Europe, 1933–1945* (Chapel Hill, 1993).

and that we just have to count the days until we can return to our families and jobs. But in reality, over the next few weeks we'll be moving into the General Government. Today saw the arrival of an entire regiment of young Germans from the West—recruits here to relieve us.

And so it is that those of us born in 1900 have to make up for what we didn't experience in 1918; and those born in 1899, '98, and '97 must now also make up their missing service years. In many ways, we'd have had an easier time of it, if in 1918 we had been more active in terms of politics and military service. We probably all believed that we could accomplish whatever we needed to with our intellects and our faith alone. It's difficult now to start anew from the ground up and at the same time to be without any responsibility. And rightly so: even as the leader of a light machine gun squad I still don't know how to use my weapon properly. It would help if I could cover up my deficiencies with a sense of energy and purpose, but I'm often too tired to do that! Our military duties aren't so all-encompassing that they can banish all thoughts of civilian life. And when I think about how difficult it was for soldiers to return from the front in the winter of 1918/19, I think it best not to break off all ties to my past life. And so in my spare time I'd rather pick up a book than a training manual.

And so now in closing let me thank you very much for the reading material. Your article[85] was very moving and reminded me of much that is still unclear to me. I've learned a few of the poems by heart as I sit at my machine gun post in this prisoner camp, in case the book gets lost during one of our many moves. [. . .]

---

[85] Perhaps he is referring to Joachim Müller, *Gott schweigt nicht* (Wernigerode, 1939).

Ethnic Revenge

Zgierz, November 13, 1939

Today I'm writing to you from a sentry post. I'm to be on watch. It's not much fun to be shut up in one room for 24 hours; the only way to get a break is to go out and do the rounds, as I just did. [. . .] A general is coming to inspect us on Wednesday and we need to demonstrate our machine gun. Because I can't shoot with the light machine gun as a leftie, I don't need to be present and hope therefore not to attract notice. Those are our newest problems. I'm sure they are starting to bore you. [. . .]

The major is also suddenly ill (kidney complaint and a heart problem) and was sent to the infirmary in Lodz. Maybe the tension of the past few days was too much for him. The Poles have been pretty quiet. Just the ethnic Germans were a problem; they set the synagogue on fire on Sunday and then the prayer house; this happened without the blessing of the military, because they don't know where to put people any more. We have twelve companies here and are expecting the Germans from Wolhynia that were hoping to use those spaces. We've set a curfew for 5 p.m. Our sentries and patrols are doubled up. So I'm in charge of twelve men tonight.

We had beautiful weather again today during our practice. [. . .] I had peace and quiet yesterday and could rest my tired bones. I got the Polish book that Franz and Lene sent and wrote Lene after I got the news of Franz's conscription. I got your sweet letter from last Monday and the training manual. Thanks very much. And for the nice package, which I could share with my comrades straight away. We're packed pretty close here. We sometimes talk more seriously about home and women. Now they're nodding off and starting to snore. We only have three cots for eight people; I can hardly stretch out. Please don't take offense if this letter doesn't have anything else of interest in it.

I wonder if you're dreaming of me because I'm spending this time meant for sleeping thinking of you?

Now it's morning. We got through our watch in one piece. I slept an hour. I had to report someone because he was AWOL until 2 a.m. He had been sleeping with his "bride." That was a bit of a conflict—should I have let it go because we're comrades?

Jewish Women

November 15, 1939

Thank you for your last letter from the ninth. . . . I'm happy you could use your time in Berlin. [. . .]

I'm starting to get used to life here with the NCOs. It's amazingly clean in our quarters. Jewish girls and women have to scrub the barracks and clean our windows. Many were from good families. The comrades behaved themselves. The Nuremberg race laws can perhaps serve to protect Jewish women. Things are pretty bad here with the Polish women. [. . .]

Bouts of Self-Questioning

Zgierz, November 19, 1939

[. . .] Yesterday's lecture was very well received. I'm to give more of them and am already thinking of the next topic. Please remember those Polish books. [. . .]

Now all the Jews in the Kalisch district must wear yellow armbands,[86] and Lodz's streets are crowded with them.

---

[86] After November 14, 1939, Jews in Kalisz had to wear the yellow star. See *Enzyklopädie des Holocaust. Die Verfolgung und Ermordung der europäischen*

The Wolhynian settlers are to follow us as residents in this school.

You'll have gathered from my letters that we've had a rather comfortable and regular existence here. We haven't had any great experiences or gained any special impressions over the past couple of weeks. Perhaps I had let myself be carried away by them. I'm continually confronted with the question of what kind of soldiers we are or can be. Everyone talks about this a great deal. Our battalion is considered tough and that's why we've been attached to the reserves. We are therefore no longer members of the Landsturm;[87] we now have heavy machine guns, and are going to be attached to an infantry division next week. But our company is considered the weakest in the battalion. That has to do with how we've been divided up (for instance the first company has a lot of old veterans in it); but our officers don't exactly provide us with shining examples of soldierliness. Our first lieutenant, for instance, has been away for almost two weeks. Our sergeant rarely leaves the office. He's a bureaucrat at heart. My comrades are mostly just nostalgic for their homes and jobs and feel more strongly every day that they are militarily inept and superfluous. Accordingly, the long hours spent with them during our watches are really quite insufferable. Our mood gets even worse when we think about the young men still at home and about the fact that we aren't part of any decisive action. Maybe I need to step up; not that that would change anything. But we can't be seen as trying to avoid our duties in any way. Please there-

---

Juden, ed. Eberhard Jäckel, Peter Longerich, and Julius H. Schoeps (Berlin, 1993), vol. 2, 750.

[87] Prussian militia, similar to the National Guard.

fore don't send anything for me to read—except for those books about Poland, or anything otherwise that will assist me in my duties. I want to wait and see how things turn out near Minsk. I want to use our free time up until then to become more familiar with our rules and with our new weapons. I think you'll understand that.

In addition, it's often impossible, given our lives, to lose oneself in a book. I have felt this way even with the Shakespeare you sent. It's not surprising, given that I read between 3 and 4 a.m., to try to stay awake. But Shakespeare is too precious to use for that purpose.

Maybe I'm just moody. Likely a result of my loneliness. Lieutenant Sachse, who came back to Zgierz after being gone for a while, said to me today in a friendly way, "How are you doing? I mean physically. Because morally, that goes without saying." But it's not that self-evident. Even knowing that I'm secure in God's hands doesn't mean that I can feel sure of what I'm to do here; it doesn't protect me from feeling exhausted in my body and soul. And especially in times of relative quiet it's easier to feel that way more than at other times. Perhaps I should focus more on the Bible. But that would require some quiet and some reflection.

I hope that last line doesn't make you sad. I had to say it. I can get it off my chest, and start the next week, one that will be determined by preparations for our departure. [. . .]

Feeling Lonely

Zgierz, November 20, 1939

[. . .] I presented a lecture to our company for the first time last Sunday. If I'm to continue, I need to get the books I asked you for about Poland as well as that volume about Poland and

Germany edited by Brackmann.[88] If you read something interesting in the *Adelsblatt*,[89] please clip it.

Plagemann's duty is up, but the people are keeping him here longer. I would ask him to visit you, but he is so skeptical and negative about our existence here that I just don't feel like it. Inwardly I struggle against his view that everything that we're doing—indeed our very existence—is meaningless. He also believes that we would have long been released or in Blankenburg[90] if it weren't for the personal ambitions of our regimental commander. [. . .]

Did you get the card of yesterday evening?[91] I had just written you a philosophical letter about comradeship and loneliness and was taking it to the office when I ran into a party filled mostly with NCOs. I drank at least five schnapps but stayed completely sober. We all wrote letters to our wives. And I thereby solved the problem that had plagued me so. [. . .]

Our departure depends on when the trains are available. Our regimental commander just received the Iron Cross for the work of our battalion and another.

Just now I heard [Zarah Leander singing] on the radio, "The Wind Told Me a Song." My stomach is churning. [. . .]

Giving Lectures

November 25, 1939

It's Sunday evening. Tomorrow we shall have been soldiers for a quarter of a year. It's a long time, if we think about

---

[88] Albert Brackmann, ed., *Deutschland und Polen. Beiträge zu ihren geschichtlichen Beziehungen* (Munich, 1933).

[89] Paper of the German nobility.

[90] German city in the Harz Mountains.

[91] Konrad Jarausch and his comrades to Lotte Jarausch, November 20, 1939.

what happened in those three months and yet this is probably only the beginning of great political decisions. As I was preparing today's report about German naval strategy, I was struck by the uniqueness of this war and how it determines our own personal destinies.

Our company's make-up is changing daily because people are being released. When their replacements arrive, we'll seem to be the knowledgeable and experienced ones. But we still have a lot to learn. Today I fired the first few shots on the heavy machine gun. I should look at the weapon manual now, but I'm too tired. Not only from my work, but from yesterday evening. [. . .] The food was excellent. We didn't drink too much. In Mienia,[92] thirteen kilometers east of Minsk, they're building the first barracks for our winter quarters; at least that's what we heard yesterday. [. . .]

Lieutenant Sachse is leaving for furlough in Magdeburg in the next few days. Unfortunately, he's not coming back to our company. We exchanged a few words with each other yesterday. But otherwise, there's no one here with whom I can have a decent conversation. I'm happy at least that things are going smoothly with my comrades. Most of them are interested in my lectures; today was the same. Yesterday everyone received a little couplet. Mine ended with "our most efficient lance corporal." I don't think anything will happen with officer training; our service here is not considered as one's having been tested at the front.[93] [. . .]

---

[92] A village on the rail line to Brest, south of Minsk.
[93] Troops proven at the front were promoted first.

113

Belonging Here

November 29 [1939]

The landscape here is draped in the same colors that you described. There seem to be little climactic differences [between here and there]. Eastern Europe really does start on the other side of the [river] Bug. That's where Russia's natural border is. We had a nice outing today. But I couldn't look around much, because I wasn't on a camel, but had a horse on a halter. I was the leader of the equipment train and had to advance three carts filled with machine guns behind the company, always keeping the same distance. Whenever we stopped, we had to hide behind houses and disappear into the woods so that we wouldn't "come under enemy fire." It was a lovely game, especially since the horses always had other ideas. But we got back home in one piece. One comrade wanted to ride, but fell in somersaults from the horse. That was a nice morning. Especially since the day before wasn't very pleasant. Drunk colleagues; the first lieutenant yelling that the non-coms didn't take their duties seriously; missed shots during our practice. That was enough. Today a comrade from Mienia came back to take the place of someone who's to be released. What he tells us is that everything is still up in the air. It's odd that a lot of troops are now being massed along the demarcation line. We're following the situation in Finland with some interest.[94] The major is back, and he will decide our future.

Your sweet letter of the 25th came in the mail today. [. . .]

---

[94] On November 30, 1939, the Soviet Union attacked Finland. The troop movements had to do with shifting forces to the west. See Hitler's speech to the commanding officers, November 23, 1939, in Groscurth, *Tagebücher*, 414–18; and Karl-Heinz Frieser, *Die Blitzkrieg-Legende. Der Westfeldzug 1940* (Munich, 1995).

It's nice that you would like to help with the company wives' dinner. In general please remember that it is true, as I've always said, that you shouldn't gossip. When Frau Plagemann says something like that it's hard to understand exactly what she means. If she means that many things here are hard to bear (drunken officers, the gossip, the Polish women as "brides," etc.), she's right. She's also right to say that I'm often exhausted and tired when my duty is done. But I still think that I belong here.

For us, the past years have been difficult because those of us born in 1900 didn't get the chance to experience the world war. Those who don't take part in today's experiences will belong to the generation that no longer has a voice in determining the future. You can see this in young people's attitude. If you have a chance to speak with Frau Schulze or Frau Leopold,[95] you can mention that in passing. Also that I'm grateful for the attention of my superiors. I don't want to play the role of the unhappy and ungrateful one. I don't have any reason to do so.

Suffering Warsaw

December 1, 1939

Now things at the Finnish border are developing in a way that's shameful for us. Who knows what kind of crisis this will lead to, at least morally.[96]

Today a comrade told us in graphic terms about Warsaw, where people were trying to grab anything of use out of

---

[95] Wives of superior officers in Magdeburg.

[96] Although the Soviet attack on Finland created international outrage, German intervention was precluded by the Nazi-Soviet nonaggression pact and Hitler's further war plans. Gerd R. Ueberschär, *Hitler und Finnland, 1939–1941. Die deutsch-finnischen Beziehungen während des Hitler-Stalin-Paktes* (Wiesbaden, 1978).

the almost fully destroyed houses. Along the roads and parks there are graves of civilians. The wind carries the smell of corpses through the streets.

The survivors flock to the soldiers offering things to sell, and the women offer themselves because they don't have anything to eat. This is a solemn Advent we're celebrating. And yet many here feel that everything isn't all that bad and these things don't touch them personally. It is like in 1914 and the years thereafter. When the wives' evening takes place, please don't chime in with the others who set the tone. Many of the others don't have it easy and have to work a lot more than their husbands here. But you wouldn't do that in any case.

The new trend now is grenade throwing. I began the appropriate crash course today. That's a weapon that I don't find particularly sympathetic. But I have to be everywhere; it appears that nothing will work without me. I'm interested to see what will happen with our first use of live rounds. [. . .]

Planning a Leave

December 3, 1939

On this decidedly most nonfestive first Sunday of Advent, one of your red candles is burning before me. How odd everything is around me. The mess in our room; my comrades who are still hungover from yesterday; the radio with its endless kitsch—and yet: how can I reach you? How bankrupt these people are. I can't even judge or condemn any of them when they come back at 9:30 in the morning still drunk; I can only feel *sorry* for them. But that isn't a pleasant word; it has such a false sense to it. There were many people there—ethnic Germans. I danced a lot with one of them, a young woman from the Bund für deutsche

Mädel.[97] We danced one dance after another, from 8:00 to 11:00, and then suddenly her boyfriend was there, and I left the young people to themselves and sat with the comrades, ate a few crepes, and then went home at 10:45. I brought the drunken comrade (whom I had thrown out in Kempen when he had had too much to drink), and we talked—in loud voices that could be heard everywhere into the stillness of the night. [. . .]

I spoke a bit with the sergeant today about my furlough plans. [. . .] The first lieutenant has to approve this tomorrow. The people here (sergeant and first lieutenant) are far too kind and considerate with me. The sergeant greeted me with compliments, instead of just saying yes or no.

I think if it works, we'd have a few days for us in Magdeburg and could leave for Berlin on the 15th. I'll write as soon as I know more. You could invite some people on the 12th if you'd like. But it should be modest. Please, don't go to any lengths preparing the food. A few light dishes that we can't get here: vegetables and the like. But nothing elaborate; no roasts or anything that would take up too much of your time. I'd rather go for a walk with you in the Kreuz forest, if the weather permits. If there's a good concert (chamber music or choral music), then please get tickets; the same goes for the theater.

Now I need to close. [. . .]

Coming Home

December 4, 1939

I received permission to leave on the 10th. The major talked with me about it today, as he was visiting us during our

[97] Nazi girl's association (BDM).

grenade throwing practice. His son writes him that you'd really very much like to see me soon. Well, it's time. [. . .]

I'll be sending a few packages of books, so that I don't have to carry too much. Otherwise, please don't expect too many presents. There isn't anything left here to buy. [. . .]

I'll keep this short, so that I'll have something to tell you [when I see you].

December 10–18, 1939: vacation leave for his brother's wedding

Return to Duty

Undated, incomplete [likely December 18/19, 1939]
I wonder how you made it back to Cologne?[98] [. . .] I first went to Lodz and asked if the company was still there; then I bought a blanket for Trudchen. I'm not all that crazy about it, but I think it will please her. You can try out the colorful one in our living room. I was welcomed here with the same sense of uncertainty that reigned when I left. Are we leaving tomorrow or next year?

It's so nice that I can take memories of our vacation into the holidays. They'll accompany me for some time. I hope then we'll have more to do here. [. . .]

Reports of Atrocities

December 22, 1939
Let's see if I can write a more reasonable letter today than the day before. That won't be easy, because our group is now in a great state of agitation. We start tomorrow morning. We'll

---

[98] For the holidays Charlotte Jarausch visited her brother and sister-in-law.

arrive in Minsk on Christmas Eve after an eighteen-hour trip. You can imagine how people are cursing about the news. Whatever we had saved to make Christmas special in terms of food and drink went down the drain. We've emptied our packages; the bottles have all been drunk. And so we have already "celebrated Christmas" with an ethnic German couple last night. I kept my bottle hidden away in a crate, and managed to put away my books. I sent a package with two books, a piece of soap, etc. to Magdeburg today. [. . .] I had brought [Ernst] Jüngers "Marmorklippen"[99] along as Christmas reading. But when I heard on my first night back how unsure our future here was, I read it right away on the train. It's wonderful, with powerful language. It might be a little too crass for your taste, but read it, once you're back in Magdeburg.

When I returned on Wednesday with the others who had been on leave, the first lieutenant invited me to a cup of tea with the lieutenant from the second company. It became clear to us during our conversation that the infighting in the battalion is in full swing. Our departure here is payback for his hesitation in Kempen;[100] at least that's what it looks like from below. But it's also possible that the higher ups wanted to bring the troops together. It's still not clear what will happen tomorrow. We're done with our packing for now at least. But we couldn't start loading the larger pieces. [. . .]

My trip didn't offer any lasting impressions. [. . .] I made my way through Lodz on foot. [. . .] The yellow armbands for Jews have been replaced by a gold star; it must be displayed on the right chest as well as on the back.[101]

[99] Ernst Jünger (1985–1998), *Auf den Marmorklippen* (Hamburg, 1939). Jünger's description of a decadent society and the establishment of a new order under the leadership of a "master forester" was seen as a criticism of the Third Reich.

[100] Apparently the different companies quarreled about their reassignment.

[101] Different types of identification were now made uniform.

The mood here seems to have become tenser. Strict orders forbid soldiers to have any contact with the Poles. We are to be armed everywhere, in the cafés, etc. Our evacuation is making things worse. Since the Wolhynian Germans are to arrive over the winter, the Jews are being driven out in large numbers. There's a concentration camp on the road between Lodz and Zgierz that holds almost 5,000 Jews of all ages. On the roads you can see the trucks heading off. Of course all of this doesn't occur without victims. And then there are rumors that can't be confirmed: the USA is going to intervene. Large round-ups are taking place.[102] An officer recently told us that according to official records, 300,000 civilians and 60,000 soldiers have died in Warsaw.[103] So of course we need to avoid the city. It's also understandable that our unease is growing. Whether or not it's well founded, no one knows.

Most recently everything depends on the West and the war at sea. If you hear something in Cologne about that, please write.

Holtermann sent the reading plan from Asmussen; it divides the Bible over the whole year.[104] I'm going to see if I can follow it, even if I won't always be able to read everything. [. . .]

---

[102] The expulsion also removed Christian Poles. Jews were crowded into ghettos and driven into Soviet territory, which resulted in many victims. In 1939, 385,000 Jews lived in the Warthegau; they were almost all murdered. Cf. *Enzyklopädie des Holocaust*, 1559; Golczewski, *Polen*, 423–32.

[103] According to the *Enzyklopädie des Holocaust*, 1525. Twenty thousand people died in September 1939, while another 32,000 were shot.

[104] Hans Asmussen (1898–1968) was a Lutheran theologian and leader of the Confessing Church.

Christmas on the Move

Minsk in Masovia, December 24, 1939
It's Christmas Eve between five and six. My thoughts are with you. I'm glad you're with Franz and Lene. Here (at least outwardly), things are anything but lonely. I've managed to withdraw into a relatively quiet corner. But now the whole company is here in the barracks. Twenty-four in each room, and these are linked via large open doorways. In our hearts we can feel the spirit of Christmas, even if we are lonely. When we lit the stall lanterns in our rooms yesterday and buried our wet feet in the straw, I thought: a manger, just like in Bethlehem. He comes in poverty; He visits us in the deprivations of our bodies and souls. That is the joy of Christmas, and no sadness or hubbub can take that away.

When we awoke yesterday in the early hours, we discovered that the weather had taken a radical turn: it was thawing, and rain was followed by sleet. We had to fill wagon after wagon. Finally, around noon the last wagons could leave the base, and we left with them. There was snow at the train station. We had to wait some more, but then our train arrived. I was one of the last people to leave the base. I had to make do with a place on a wooden stool in the second-class car with the noncommissioned officers. But I wrapped myself up in my blanket. And I spent the time rather comfortably, even though the compartment wasn't heated. We didn't see anything; once we saw some lights—Warsaw! I would have had to climb up over my sleeping comrades to get to the window. Most of the time I napped. We arrived around five, but we slept until seven before we got out and took a look around. Vodka was distributed again for the journey. Others had brought along some rum. A few of the fellows in our car

121

were completely drunk. Boisterousness was followed by sickness and then sleep. Some of the enlisted men in particular really let themselves go. The second company, which was loaded with us but has taken up quarters a bit farther in the forest, was even worse. There the enlisted men were in really bad shape. Of course that meant that they didn't have to report to duty, and the others feel that they're the dummies, since they have to do their work. We had to unload the train in Minsk and load everything onto the wagons. We drove through the town to the base. It was a dreary day. [. . .] Sleet and rain. The houses are one-story high and made of wood. The stores are decorated with colorful placards that testify to the illiteracy of the population that is apparently more widespread here. The Jews are being used to clean the streets.[105] The Poles gather in large crowds in front of the church with two towers and look at us with some derision; they certainly have some reason to do so.

The base is located on the other end of town. There are new large buildings for the generals, their staff, and other officers. Then rows of barracks. From the outside, they look like log houses from the Russian era. Inside, our commandos have done great work. Everything is freshly painted. There are new floors. Wooden bedsteads, where we put down our straw sacks that we've brought with us; tables and benches have been constructed out of raw planks of wood. The large ovens heat the space. There are even electric lights, although rather dim ones. Only water is in short supply, and it's difficult to bring in. We'll need to send out our laundry.

As we entered the barracks, we were greeted by wreaths of evergreen. We were also pleasantly surprised that everything was so clean and orderly.

[105] From October 26, 1939 on, the Jewish population was forced to work.

Finally we had arrived and could get some rest. But then we received less welcome news: Lieutenant Graf's luggage, along with that of some of his men, had been stolen along the way, and our quarters were searched; naturally nothing was found. That ruined whatever sense of holiday cheer we had managed to scrape together. There's nothing left but for the first lieutenant to give a short speech in front of the tree: then we'll get our mail and the drinking will start anew.

We're at a real military base with stables, parade grounds, shooting ranges, and whatever one might wish. From here we'll exercise our rule over the quite foreign city. I hope the depressing images of this Christmas Eve don't stay with me. But I think I won't easily forget the sight of drunken brawling soldiers among the Poles and Jews, some of whom were being evacuated and sitting there with their pitiful belongings. The maudlin holiday cheer of the radio doesn't do much to dispel those images. And yet: it's Christmas Eve.

And our first holiday evening. Everything went pretty much as I thought it would. No one really cared much for the little gathering. We struggled through a few songs. Then more rowdiness and drinking. I read some today in the Brackmann book. I also read Braem's sermon[106]—I need to thank him. Then I took a short walk through the town. It made a more favorable impression than yesterday, because of the snow that had fallen overnight. [. . .]

Back in the barracks, things were getting out of hand. I took refuge in a corner with a Polish reader but couldn't avoid my destiny. I had to intervene between a lance corporal who is an SS member and one of the workers who watches over the Polish prisoners who work as tailors. "As a member of the SS I won't allow someone in a gray uniform standing up for a Pole!"

[106] Dr. Braem, cathedral preacher in Magdeburg.

Kluge came and got me [. . .] so that I could listen to poems with his friends. I had to explain to him what a sonnet was, but he was too drunk to understand. Nonetheless, I got along well with everyone. Drunken desperation was mixed with an odd sense of the carnivalesque. It was unnerving to see such existential emptiness. But in such moments you can't do anything but be friendly to them and just sit down next to them.

[December] 26

Today I was the only person in the company who went to church. The place was embarrassingly empty, and if there hadn't been a few rows of ethnic Germans there it would have been even worse. The sermon was hearty, not evasive. [. . .]

Tomorrow we are going to have our first real Christmas celebration. We're as afraid of that as we are of thinking ahead to New Year's Eve. The war veterans among the NCOs say that they've never seen such drunkenness. They blame it on our lack of discipline, our high salaries, and the willingness of the women.

I'm going to close now. You'll understand this letter. We all want to share these difficulties. You'll hopefully notice that I'm not despairing. Gather as much strength and warmth in Cologne as you can. [. . .] Please be careful with the contents of this letter. These things shouldn't make the Magdeburg gossip rounds. [. . .]

The Weakness of Humanism

December 28, 1939

Dear Franz,

I have a chance to send a letter with someone going on leave, so I wanted to write you a few lines; greetings to Lotte as well. We had a company evening yesterday during which so much was drunk that everything is very quiet tonight. I couldn't have a better opportunity to write, yet I'm tired from the emotional exertions of the past couple of days and this morning's march. But I did have time to read. I am very interested in the Brackmann book. What I find most fascinating is his attempt to appreciate Polish developments without giving up any German claims. In his chapters on the nineteenth century, it's clear how the best spiritual achievements live on and how today's politics are not much rooted in the past. It's obvious that 1933 is a clear historical caesura. One keeps coming back to the fact that this intellectual tradition has been too weak to give shape to Germany's destiny. Will there be a role for it in the future? I'm thinking about this more than I ever did back at home over the past few years. "An eagle on the chest is good, but an eagle on the armband is bad"[107]—that's what the people here say. The past can provide helpful explanations for a few observations. [. . .]

We're not allowed to leave the city. So what we see of the villages is the little that we can glean during our exercises. But some typical details stand out: the strange way in which the villages stand detached from the roads; the manner in which the farms face away from the road. [. . .]

Our daily lives are marked by the fact that we've received twenty-five new men, some of them young ones, but many of whom have such physical disabilities that one has to wonder how they could have been sent here.[108] [. . .]

---

[107] German army soldiers had an eagle symbol on the front of their uniform, while SS units had it on an armband. Perhaps this allusion also refers to the ethnic vigilante groups, identified by an armband, who were responsible for many murders in Poland.

[108] The conscription age and physical requirements had already been lowered during mobilization. See Kroener, *Ressourcen*, 729.

I'm now the squad leader of our three grenade launcher troops, and I'm now in "charge" of eight men. Duty is apparently becoming more strenuous. But of course I can practice or march outside only for a few hours. The snow is freezing harder. The days and nights are mostly clear. The stars are twinkling but dim in the light of the rising moon. During the day, crows, sparrows, and titmice come to our doors. But we haven't heard any wolves yet. [. . .]

Bolstering Morale

New Year's Day, 1940

The company didn't get much mail today; but I received your two Christmas letters from the 24th and 26th. They were very moving. So much love and a sense of home spoke from them; they warmed my heart. I'm also pleased that you had a holiday, surrounded by love and care. I'd like to learn your lovely Christmas verses by heart. [. . .] I did hear Brauchitsch's speech,[109] but just in the background, as I was unpacking and settling in. The speeches that I heard today were objective and without any false notes.[110] Over the past few weeks I've made my peace with the radio. There's been less pop music and faux childishness; there's even been some Christianity. Today we heard some beautiful organ music. [. . .]

I was envious of your walk in the woods. We're almost prisoners here, because the city doesn't offer us anything

[109] Walther von Brauchitsch (1881–1948), commander in chief of the army, 1938–41, said in his Christmas speech: "The day shall come when the Greater German Reich, which the *Führer* has created, and the living-space of our nation of 86 million will be secure. Therefore we are firmly convinced that justice is on our side." *Deutschland im Kampf*, ed. A. J. Berndt und Oberstleutnant von Wedel, vol. 2, Dezember-Lieferung (Berlin, 1939), 15f.

[110] This is an allusion to the various end-of-year messages by Hitler, Göring, und Himmler. Cf. *Deutschland im Kampf*, Januar-Lieferung (Berlin, 1940), 32–39.

other than a cinema and a few cafés overflowing with soldiers. But we do have winter all around us. [. . .]

The sparrows and the crows come to our windows and doors; there are a few crested larks and titmice among them. Everyone wants to live with us now, even the Polish children, who come in ever-greater numbers at lunch, and the Jews, who work for us here in the morning.

[. . .] There was quite a party on the 30th; Stempel, who was an ordnance sergeant became a master sergeant, and he paid for his stripe. Yesterday everyone was pretty tired and many slept. At nine we went over to the other barracks. The corner where my people were sitting was pretty quiet, and we had a nice conversation. There are a few thoughtful ones among the new men. Overall they were quiet and thoughtful. More so than at Christmas. Around midnight, many of them started crying. A few lay on their bunks and refused to get up. Most of them were loud and drunk, but didn't get out of hand. At midnight everyone was shaking hands and there were a lot of heartfelt confessions. The staff sergeant waxed poetic about my abilities (a role model for the company; the best comrade, etc.). I went to bed, but didn't get any sleep, because we still had visitors with us. This morning I was tired, too. I've been using the last few days to read Frau von Tiling's brother-in-law's book on "Heimat as the Foundation of Human Existence."[111] When I was done, I wrote the author, at Frau von Tiling's request. It's a very well written and clear book, based on the love of his home in Latvia. I now understand why Stavenhagen broke down. I wrote him, and told him that it was important that his work be part of the creation of a new order in the East; I said that if the Baltic

---

[111] Kurt Stavenhagen (1884–1951), professor of philosophy from Latvia, wrote *Heimat als Grundlage menschlicher Existenz* (Göttingen, 1939).

peoples could realize this, their losses wouldn't be in vain.[112] I'm supposed to give another lecture. Perhaps I'll choose "Poland's Economy." [. . .]

Tougher Duty

Minsk, January 5, 1940

[. . .] It's always a joy for me to read your rich descriptions of landscapes, art, and people in the West. Here the changing face of winter is the only thing we have. [. . .] In terms of our work, we can tell that the major is back from his leave and has brought along his criticisms of the fourth [company]. That puts a damper on things and makes it difficult to enjoy our duties. I tried to strike up a conversation today during my lecture, but that didn't go well. The major was unhappy with the state of our quarters. But it's difficult to keep things orderly, given how primitive things are. It's good that we could all go to take a shower yesterday. I sent out my laundry yesterday, but the woman can't speak a word of German, and it's not always possible to get one's own laundry back. I would be grateful if you could send twenty tags with "KJ," so that I can mark everything.

There are new postal regulations regarding packages. We're only allowed to send one kg per month, regardless of content. So we can't send our laundry home. If I send home the books that I read over Christmas and New Year's, I've already reached my allowance. I'm looking forward to reading the book that Franz ordered for me.

---

[112] This refers to the 1939/40 resettlement of the Baltic Germans into the Warthegau, since the Baltic countries were declared part of the Soviet sphere of interest during the Nazi-Soviet Pact of 1939. Cf. Lars Bosse, "Vom Baltikum in den Reichsgau Wartheland," in *Deutschbalten, Weimarer Republik und Drittes Reich*, vol. 1, ed. Michael Garleff (Cologne, 2001), 297–387.

Otherwise, the prices are so high here that it's hard to buy anything. In Warsaw, butter is selling for 7 Marks per kilo; cloth costs 30 Marks for one meter. Overall we can sense in many ways how much hatred there is for us here. Recently two staff sergeants were shot as they were brawling in a bar. Hopefully the new year won't be too difficult for our people. [. . .]

New Challenges

Minsk, January 8, 1940

I'm so grateful to you for the lively reports from the first and the second. I also am grateful that you understand it when I have the feeling that we need to persevere here, even if our work often seems pointless. When you write about your conversations and your lives together and I compare it to the way that I spend my time here, it's hard to repress the feeling that I've wasted months and that it would be best to wipe them from my memory. But that's foolish. And I'm grateful to you and also to Franz and Lene for your support. It helps. Yesterday I was faced with the question of whether I should spend my time reading and writing or if I should go with the NCOs to visit an antitank company in Mienia. I would have stayed, but because the sergeant made it into an official duty (not the sergeant major but another man who was promoted in October), I didn't protest and went along. Mainly the visit consisted of pointless drinking—punctuated by bad jokes— and everyone exclaimed they'd never had such a lovely time with their comrades. The sergeant major asked me my opinion, and I gave it to him straight up. But it's not like most of the people here have the ability to understand me. It was obvious to me that there is an inner emptiness that leads [these men] to act in this manner. The Hitler Youth could be doing wonderful things here. It's just not enough to be ready to spring into action and maintain discipline. One must also be ready to lead and to demonstrate something.

It's not out of the question that I'll be asked to do more of that soon and then I'll have to stop reading and writing. Our company is being disbanded and we're going to be divided up among the others. There will be groups of ten enlisted men, and lance corporals are supposed to take over a new replacement company meant to train those new recruits born in 1906.[113] It's still not clear who will be chosen to do this and whether or not Leopold[114] will take over. In any case, we won't be together anymore. So everything really is up in the air at the moment.

If I should be a part of this—and I'd be really happy if I were, because then we'd have a real task—I would then move to Mienia. That's a village on the rail line to Brest fourteen km east of here with a manor, a sawmill, and a St. Joseph's Hospital. The second company is there now; that's where we would go. Across the street there's a former children's home in the forest where the antitank division now is (we were their guests yesterday). We drove over by car. It was bitterly cold with a cutting wind from the east. The sky was covered with gray, so the frost lay on the ground without glistening at all. The trees stood with an eerie lifelessness on the side of the road, upon which the snow was frozen like granite . . . [. . .]

In these conditions, we're grateful for technology that allows us to enjoy warmth and light. It was 31 degrees below Celsius last night out in the open. Today it's clear and cold. We took a short half-hour walk and then had to participate

---

[113] This cohort was called up on October 5, 1939. See Kroener, *Ressourcen*, 727.

[114] Head of the company, First Lieutenant Leopold.

in an exercise in which changes to the training manual were introduced. Up until now I haven't suffered and I also haven't gotten a cold. If we do go to Mienia, I may ask you to send that sweater, because we'll need to be outdoors more. But up until now I'm getting along fine with what I have. Our rations are also better here. I've even managed to lay in some stores from my Christmas packages: a pound of honey; some liverwurst. [. . .]

Pride in Promotion

January 9, 1940

A freshly promoted Prussian corporal introduces himself: The stripes shine, the second step is accomplished. Unfortunately this promotion—two others were also advanced—occurs during a tense time. The changes before us illuminate how problematic our existence is. It's not clear whether Leopold will be sent to the training company or not; whether we'll be soldiers or not. Leopold is trying to make up for what was not done before. But things are really unclear. Today the enlisted men and lance corporals met the major. He was pleased and agreed with Leopold's suggestions. But now the general is here and who knows? [. . .]

Trying to Understand Poles

Minsk, January 11, 1940

[. . .] Today for the first time the mail train didn't arrive because of the cold. It was 38 degrees below zero. The nights are strangely dark. The days are bright, clear, and beautiful. We only spend about three-quarters of an hour outside, because so many men get frozen ears. [. . .] Otherwise we're trying to repeat our military training. We work mornings on standing,

131

turning, etc., and in the afternoons the NCOs and lance corporals in training are taken to train even further. So at least we're busy. In every other way they're tightening the reins. Last night I began the interesting and engaging book Franz sent. It's entertaining and not too strenuous. In reading how Polish folktales and Polish poetry have continued to pass on certain stereotypes of the Germans, I can now understand some of the problems that arose during the beginning of the war. I've just ordered Völker's[115] history of the church in Poland, and then I'll be finished with that kind of reading for a while and dedicate myself to learning the language. But we are increasingly warned to stay away from the Poles.[116] Now we aren't even allowed to have Polish women do our laundry. [. . .]

It's odd how politics become less and less important. We rarely read the newspapers; they come irregularly in any case. [. . .] Our world now consists of: our duties; food and drink; card playing; beer and schnapps; and then there's vacation time (the trip now takes more than twenty-four hours). How much more interesting and full our lives were in Zgierz. But we have to grin and bear it now. [. . .]

Intellectual Frustrations

January 14, 1940

Dear Franz,

[. . .] I've been reading Lück's book[117] with great interest. I'm very sympathetic to the author's assumptions. Having to live

---

[115] Karl Völker (1886–1937), Protestant Church historian who published a history of the Polish Church in 1930.

[116] Many orders attempted to limit contact with Polish civilians. See Umbreit, *Militärverwaltungen*, 72, 155, 198.

[117] Kurt Lück, *Der Mythos vom Deutschen in der polnischen Volksüberlieferung und Literatur* (Poznan, 1938).

together in the same space won't go away in the future, even if the situation is now completely different. It's something grand if someone doesn't become bitter in the face of hatred and argues that popular opinions aren't a result of some underlying metaphysical rejection, but rather arise from a particular problem. That is why I appreciate the book's realism. Perhaps the author could identify those forces in earlier periods (particularly the Middle Ages) that formed folk beliefs. I'm missing something (hypothetically, I'm not an expert here): perhaps a clearer depiction of the role of the aristocracy in shaping these views. It's clear that since then the clergy, followed by poets, artists, and scientists, has become the most important force in shaping popular opinion. And you're right when you write that intellectuals appear in a special light. I'm grateful for your news about Brackmann's position. The quote from that article by Brackmann really is refreshing for us, because we see the human side of this collapse right in front of our eyes. I'm not denying the necessity of the fact that *this* Polish state must be destroyed. I'm not talking about the future, and you are certainly right that our future will be determined in the West. I'd like to talk to you in person about what you say regarding the future of our people. [. . .]

Slowly it's starting to become clear to me what it means that all of 1940 will stand under the sign of war. What of the tasks and relationships that it took me from; what will remain? Will I have to start anew at another place, or will I finally be able to start a normal career as a *Studienrat?*[118] That question busies me the longer the war continues. But I don't have any clear goal toward which I could toil to shape the future. If I wanted to work toward a particular literary goal, I would have to give up proving myself on a daily basis. And so

---

[118] Teacher in an academic high school.

I have to console myself with my NCO stripes over the fact that months have gone by, and I've made no progress at all toward a career *in literaris*. Younger men will come and write the book that demands hours of dedication, and I shall only be able to add critical footnotes and feel that it would have been better if I had written it. [. . .]

Polish Winter

[. . .] The afternoon of January 16 We notice daily that we occupy the border between two worlds. That's what geography tells us: the Bug marks the boundary between Eastern and Central Europe. "This far extend the effects of the maritime climate." Over the last few days, the temperature had risen from −37 to +9 degrees. The melting snow turned into a horrible freezing mess. Things were melting everywhere, but meanwhile snow was still falling. Today another hard frost set in. A cold easterly wind sweeps over us. It's −30 degrees. Between the barracks one is protected from the wind, and things are all right there. But the wind was so biting out on the parade ground that we had to give up our exercises right away, because everyone was getting frostbitten noses.

The general visited our quarters today and was pleased with how orderly and clean things were. Hopefully Leopold will be named head of the training company. He's taking this really personally. This afternoon he talked to me about designing more lectures. My health is all right, now that I have a bout of sickness behind me (GI tract virus and a cold). The Tamalbin worked well,[119] and I'm eating figs and dates in the morning. [. . .]

[119] An antidiarrhea medication.

Intellectual Aspirations

Minsk, January 17, 1940

[. . .] I spent three and a half hours with the first lieutenant yesterday. We talked about politics and the church. While I was there the sergeant came and gave us an update. No one has made a decision yet about who will take over the officer positions. Leopold takes it personally. He believes— and he's probably right—that things will also be unpleasant for me if a certain other person took over. If that were the case, he would rather take me with him wherever he might end up. But those are the kinds of feelings that don't really apply to our situation. He tends to analyze situations and then speak from the heart. We're to have some clarity on Sunday evening. We are all not looking forward to moving in this weather. [. . .]

I'm so pleased to hear that Cysarz[120] made such a good impression. It was also nice that you told him so. I remember hearing him lecture in Vienna about the literature of the late medieval period. Hübener[121] lectured on the same subject in Berlin. But Hübener's lecture was so dry; he just presented different works. Cysarz on the other hand made it clear that what was at stake was a battle about life's most important questions. I remember that he also spoke of the apocalyptic nature of the times. He fought in the world war, and was badly wounded. Perhaps at some point I can read his book on Schiller.[122] I do often wish that I'll have important intellectual and artistic work in the future. There are so many

---

[120] Herbert Cysarz (1896–1985), Austrian professor of German literature, supported the Sudeten German "independence movement" in Prague.

[121] Arthur Hübener (1885–1937), Germanist, taught in Berlin.

[122] Herbert Cysarz, *Schiller* (Halle, 1934).

beautiful, wonderful things of which we should take note. Yet I'm afraid that such wishes will remain unfulfilled. We'll be lucky if we can bring ourselves back home in one piece. Maybe you overestimate what we're doing here. So much human potential remains unused.

[. . .] I was surprised to discover that my comrades here really don't know anything about the larger dimensions of the Polish campaign. They seem to forget that we are fighting for *Lebensraum*, for generations to come. [. . .]

A New Superior

January 19, 1940

Our future is decided. We're losing our dear little lieutenant. He's going to be replaced by Lieutenant Herrmann, the major's adjutant. He is a stickler for details; not exactly my type. But we'll get through this. Leopold is giving a small going away party tomorrow evening. We're also losing the replacements we received over Christmas. [. . .]

I'm sorry we're losing Leopold. It's strange that my fate now lies in the hands of such an old soldier. I'm going to have to pull myself together and make sure to keep moving. I won't be able to do any more reading. It's nice that Lieutenant Sachse is coming back to our company. We're also getting a bunch of people who have aspirations to become noncommissioned officers. Leopold is being sent to higher staff for special duties. He'll probably go on furlough and then soon become a captain. [. . .]

Even if I can't write so many letters to our acquaintances, things should still be all right. I don't want to give up my Polish reading altogether. The pieces are interesting and varied. I've got a lot to do in the first volume. Yesterday I read a short allegorical story by Sienkiewicz;[123] Poland is depicted as a ship in great danger that is saved by its crew—they return to the land and start work there.

Recently another farmer here was shot because he had an illegal weapon. We've heard that people are stealing weapons. Things are boiling just under the surface.

When we're gone, the only people who'll miss us are the Jews who bring our coal—I often gave them a few cents. They're poor fellows who were previously carrying sacks in a factory that burned down. They also lost a lot in the fire, which destroyed a corner of the city. We've always gotten along pretty well.

I just came back from the city. It was a relief to move freely among civilians. But everything is covered in snow. [. . .]

---

[123] Henryk Sienkiewicz (1846–1916), famous Polish author and Nobel Prize winner for literature.

Part II

Training Recruits

The transformation of a series of short campaigns into a pro-tracted military struggle required a difficult adjustment from soldiers and civilians. To be sure, the "phony war" in the West gave way to a quick conquest of Denmark and Norway. Also the long-awaited battle with France resulted in a sur-prisingly rapid and complete German victory in June 1940, surpassing all gains of World War I. But the submarine cam-paign remained inconclusive and the air attacks on Great Britain were a strategic failure, since the Luftwaffe's change of targets and the tenacious resistance of the Royal Air Force blunted the German assault. While the initial Nazi victories had followed the blitzkrieg script of defeating one opponent at a time and then using his resources to subdue another, the stubborn British defense turned the war precisely into what Hitler had wanted to avoid—a prolonged conflict. When the euphoria of the early successes wore off, German soldiers were faced with the prospect of an endless struggle, stripping the war of its heroic appeal.

The manpower needs of the Wehrmacht kept Konrad Jarausch in uniform while changing his assignment from guarding POWs to training new recruits in January 1940. Even the Polish and French campaigns had exacted a con-siderable price in dead and wounded, requiring soldiers and officers to be replaced in order to continue the fight-ing. Therefore, the reserve army sought to upgrade its com-bat ability by issuing light machine guns and field artillery. On March 30, Jarausch's unit was transformed into a "field recruit company" for training fresh draftees while remain-ing stationed in Poland. On May 31, it became a *Schützen-Feldersatzkompanie* in infantry regiment 660 as part of the combination of such outfits into *Landwehr* divisions. In early July of 1940 the unit was shipped back to Germany and dis-solved, but he was assigned to the "Infantry Replacement

Battalion" in Bernburg in central Germany on October 9. Successive entries in his *Wehrpass* (military identity card) show that he was busy training recruits during most of 1940 and the first half of 1941.

Due to the experience of actual combat, the training process became increasingly arduous for the NCOs and draftees involved. It took considerable effort to shape a diverse group of civilian recruits, some of whom resented being in the military, into a fighting unit of soldiers who would obediently carry out orders, even if they did not immediately understand their purpose. The German army sought to accomplish this goal through instilling routines, keeping men busy, and frequently checking their performance so as to break the will of individuals and meld them into a coherent group. In contrast to the customary practice of only drilling in weapon presentation and marching in formation, new orders emphasized shooting with live ammunition as well as field exercises, based on combat situations. The former required long hours of target practice while the latter consisted of deep forays into the countryside, sharpening orienteering skills and engaging in mock battles. While the troops found outdoor exercises simulating combat diverting, they resented the mindlessness of more traditional training routines.

The graphic descriptions in the letters show that the training of recruits was exhausting, since it demanded considerable physical stamina and psychological resilience from the instructors. The lengthy field exercises tested the endurance not only of the draftees but also of their officers, because the latter were supposed to master the relevant skills and lead by example. Especially in the winter with subzero temperatures, deep snow, and chilling wind, drilling outdoors proved painful and often had to be broken off to avoid frostbite. In spite of the new orders, the attempt to instill military discipline continued to involve more "reporting, running back and forth, bawling out and threatening" than weapons' training or fieldwork. Moreover, the short time to get recruits ready for the front, limited to four weeks, rendered it impossible to establish lasting forms of comradeship. Finally, many draftees resented the toughness of their training as excessive, since after the victory in France they hoped that the war would be over soon. My father seems to have enjoyed those aspects of the training that resembled his teaching, but he loathed the prevailing barracks tone.

Konrad Jarausch was, nonetheless, pleased to be considered for officer training due to his leadership potential. On March 9, 1940, he was selected as "reserve officer candidate" with a few others, and a couple of days later invited to attend a "course on defending against espionage, sabotage, political disinformation, punishment, and penitentiary during the war and on special assignment." On May 1, he was promoted further to staff sergeant. This advancement came in recognition of his sense of responsibility, organizing talent, and capacity for teaching. But ultimately he failed to become an officer for several reasons: Due to his age, his health was not robust enough for active duty, turning it into "a struggle to get through from day to day." Since his superiors had not prepared him properly for the test, he flunked a surprise examination in "soldierly knowledge." Finally, his "soft approach" to leading men lacked that stentorian voice and arrogant bearing considered necessary for advancement into the officer corps. Although this outcome disappointed the social aspirations of his wife, he was too bookish and independent to fit well into the Nazi war machine.

On October 31, 1940, he had "a little accident" that ended all hopes for further promotion and began to alienate him from military service. Already beforehand, the training of ever-younger recruits had become increasingly onerous, since his ambitious superiors set too high a standard. But then during exercising in a hall he fell down an unsecured stairway and thereby ruptured a meniscus, incapacitating his right knee. Since the military physicians opted for noninvasive treatment, he spent the next two months in an army hospital in Wernigerode without really improving much. This was not only a boring time of bed rest, which could only be passed by resuming his classical reading, but it also got him out of touch with what was going on in his unit and made him subsequently more vulnerable during physical exertion in the line of duty. Moreover, the three months of convalescence also increased his psychological distance from the service and made him cast about for alternative assignments. When he was stricken from the officer candidate rolls on April 28, 1941, he no longer protested, since he had already given up on this ambition.

Due to this disenchantment Konrad Jarausch increased his efforts to be reassigned to reserve duty at home or declared "indispensable" for the war effort so as to be released from military service. However, both alternatives were complicated by the more stringent requirements for transfer or exemption of battalions that had served in Poland, since they were now considered part of the field army. As long as he was still toying with the idea of an officer career, he did not want to be transferred to the home guard since further promotion would then be impossible. Exemption from service was also difficult, because teachers were not included in the list of "essential occupations" such as postal clerks, metal workers, or farmers, and his health was not bad enough to keep him out of uniform. Moreover, the procedure required an emphatic request by the director of the Cathedral Gymnasium who first had to be persuaded to support such a move.

144

When all the paperwork was finally assembled in the summer of 1941, the impending attack on the Soviet Union canceled all plans for release, and another application during the fall of the same year was also turned down.

As a result of such frustrations, the letters commented more acerbically on the military and the war during the second half of 1940 and the first half of 1941. While still in Poland, he considered the "watch in the East" necessary, but during garrison duty in the Reich he found the endless grinding of recruits increasingly tiresome. Konrad Jarausch grew quite critical of "the completely mistaken kind of education" that sought to eradicate individuality and foster "blind obedience," because it clashed with his own Prussian ethos of internalized responsibility. In contrast to the boisterous racism and nationalism of many comrades confident in victory, he preferred a quiet humanistic patriotism and was less sanguine about the eventual outcome of the war. While back in Germany he enjoyed his leave time to visit with his wife, he also felt increasingly cut off from intellectual developments and peaceful pursuits. No wonder that during this indecisive period of the war the tone of the letters grew more irritated, because he was trying to find a way to make these months meaningful so as to solve his personal problems and reassure himself about the future of the country.

Letters from Poland and Germany, January 1940 to August 1941

Watch in the East

January 22, 1940

Now we've really begun our watch in the East. We've never been so cut off from all bourgeois, western ways of life. It's too bad we don't have the inner freedom to fully experience the world around us. It really is like a dream vacation. The surrounding countryside is quieter than I've ever experienced it. There are unending vistas of snow. The silent forest serves as a backdrop to the scene; in the foreground is the manor with its large barns and stables. [. . .]

The day had started off all right. It was clear and beautiful. We got our things onto the wagon quickly and they took them to the train. At noon we marched through the city to the train station. The comrades had done their work well. Everything was ready for us to climb into the cattle cars. But then the torturous waiting began. We were to start after the Warsaw train, but it was horribly late. After we had stood there for an hour in the freezing wagons, we were allowed to go into the waiting room. Finally the Warsaw train arrived—terribly packed, soldiers, Jews, Poles; everyone was trying to squeeze in there, fighting over space. It took at least ten minutes before the last Jew with his bundle was shoved in and things could continue. I wonder if it's any different at home? Then we could get in quickly enough. In Mienia the containers and boxes were stacked up on the rail platform. But the wagons still hadn't arrived. We settled in as best we could and waited. It got dark, and still the wagons weren't there. Then we had to go back out, at least to bring in the backpacks. Finally the baggage wagons arrived. It had taken them four,

146

long, miserable hours to work their way from Minsk through the snow, and they kept getting stuck, even though they were empty. Then they had to get to the train again as quickly as possible, loading and packing. I don't think I've ever experienced winter as I did during those evening hours. The easterly wind kicked up again, bringing icy, fine-grained snow along with it. It's not like when you're out taking a walk in winter. Then, if you're tired, you can just stop. Here you have to keep at it and are happy when the wind isn't blowing directly in your face. I was finally sent back alone to headquarters with an assignment. I'll long remember that fifteen-minute walk. I trudged and stumbled along. All around me was a white barrenness with a few small black patches and the lights lining the path. It's amazing how alive a tree can seem at its edge, standing alone in its organic wholeness amid the really quite overwhelming and deadening emptiness. [. . .] We were all exhausted when we were finished.

We just learned about how the training is to proceed. We will be on duty from seven in the morning until seven at night. Within four weeks the training should have progressed enough so that they can be sent to the army. That is not quite correct, since we now also belong to the regular army (field recruit company). Supposedly we're the only reserve formation in the army that has been given charge of training recruits. [. . .]

Learning about Training

January 25, 1940

This letter is arriving later than usual. But yesterday we had to drive by car to Minsk to the theater, and so I didn't have a chance to write last night. First, thanks for your last package: razors, nametags for my wash, marmalade. [. . .] It really makes a difference whether one is done at five or seven and if one then still has to read training manuals. We're progressing systematically to cover everything: starting with basic training, then rifles and machine guns—everything down to the last detail. Leopold left today, after he'd made himself pretty scarce the past couple of days. Tomorrow Lieutenant Herrmann will take over the company. [. . .] Everyone in our room is studying very hard, and I'm glad to be away from those constant whiners. [. . .]

We've already used our free time to check out the neighboring village. I can't agree entirely with all the lamentations about the Polish economy. But that's probably because I'm too skeptical about the term "progress." These wooden houses with their straw roofs appear to be the natural result of the landscape; the fact that people rarely do anything in such cold circumstances is really quite understandable. [. . .]

I'm including a rough translation from my newest Polish reading, about "Mr. Thaddäus" by Mickiewicz.[1] Certainly some things are unclear and I don't have the energy to try to make every word read like poetry. But there's a lot about the countryside in these few lines. It's too bad that there's so little time to read. [. . .]

A Rough Start

January 27, 1940

It's Sunday evening. Some of my comrades are in Minsk at a show; some others are drinking beer with the antitank unit in their quarters about a half a mile down the road. It's pretty quiet; only one other person is here. And last night

[1] *Pan Tadeusz*, an epic poem by Adam Mickiewicz, was first published in 1834. It is a classic of Polish literature.

we all talked about home so much that I felt I had to chat with you a little bit, even though [writing] is a rather meager substitute. And I really have to thank you for your long, lovely letter from Halle. Our week ended with a big event. Our new company commander is here and he treated us today with the natural self-confidence of a man who has spent twelve years on a base and has been training ever since. In a way that's somewhat liberating in comparison to the old insecurities, but it also pretty much gets on our nerves. Things started early this morning with an alarm. Then we practiced with our guns; that meant we were to show how we would train recruits. When it was my turn I didn't do too badly. Things are now going to have to be much better organized and more straightforward than they were when we practiced with Lieutenant Sachse. Then, we needed to understand each step thoroughly and be able to exercise individual judgment. Now what matters is that we learn each technical step quickly and thoroughly. After the lessons, we exercised quick marching, practiced shooting, and other nonsense. It was bearable and all happened without any bullying, but it was really quite difficult. Since we're supposed to prepare new training lessons for Monday, we hardly had any work in the afternoon. I slept, sewed my tags in my wash, prepared for duty, and read a bit.

Once again I've started to sketch out plans for my [book] on religious pedagogy so as to get an overview. At least it keeps me connected to home and distracts me from my worries and sorrows here. It's hard to avoid thinking about the present and the near future. Everyone keeps asking why we reserves are being called upon to carry out such unusual tasks. If our health holds up, then these weeks will be a really good experience for us. We'll be able to feel like real soldiers. Whether or not we will be tested in earnest is a

question that remains a constant concern for the younger
men among us. [. . .]

Worries about the New Arrivals

January 31, 1940

Dear Hans-Lothar [Dietze],[2]
It's already the last day in January, and I'm just now thanking
you for your friendly New Year's greetings. Up until now, the
year 1940 has started out tolerably enough. We got through
the cold, and that's now the most important thing. [. . .] At
the moment we're all somewhat on edge. Our outfit has become a field recruit company. During the next few days we're
to receive 120 "recruits," all of whom are already thirty-three
years old. We're to make real soldiers out of them in four
weeks' time. Before that, we ourselves have to know our
stuff. We haven't even received any regular basic training in
peacetime, because we're all war recruits. Soon I'll be educating recruits instead of [teaching] young men like you. I'm curious to see what they'll be like and what we can achieve in
four weeks. We can't complain anymore about being bored.
Our days are filled from beginning to end. [. . .]

With best wishes
and Heil Hitler

The Recruits Arrive

February 4, 1940 (*Esto mihi!*)[3]
Our people finally arrived today after a 100-hour journey
from Kempten in the Allgäu. I spent almost all afternoon

[2] One of his students in the Cathedral School in Magdeburg.
[3] Name of a Sunday in the pre-Lenten period.

with them. Now at 9:30 they're in bed, and we can rest. To-morrow is going to be so busy with training that I have no idea how these exhausted men are going to stand it. [. . .]

Send me good thoughts over the new few weeks so that I can get through this. It was actually pretty nice with the wild Bavarians. Most of them come from cities (Munich, Augs-burg, Lindau, Wertach) and are workers or businessmen. But they are a pretty crude bunch. I hope I can find the right mixture of exacting authority and solidarity. Twenty-two men are in one room. Because of all the things hanging off the tops of the bunks, the air for those below is pretty stifling. If you could send some detergent or cleanser, that would be good. Otherwise I have all I need. [. . .]

Training as Teaching

February 6, 1940

Just now, at 7:30, we've returned from bathing over at the quarters of the antitank unit. It was a lovely walk through the night, and even the others found it enjoyable. You can imagine how exhausted we all are. We are awakened at 6 a.m. now. Then from 7:30 to 8:45 there are the lessons, and we haven't had to participate in them yet, which has been the only break we've had. We then had to drill for three hours, but we did get a respite. Yesterday we could only spend an hour outside. When we got back in I could have wept from the pain in my fingers. As long as one can take part in the drills oneself, one can stay warm. However, when you have to stand in front and hardly move, things are different. I have to spend the whole time speaking at the top of my voice or screaming, really, and all the cold air streams into [my lungs]. Today it was only 10 degrees below. So we thought the three hours were pretty tolerable. In the afternoon, we have at

151

most a half an hour to lie down. Then we have another hour and forty-five minutes of drill outside. After that, we practice with our weapons and then spend time cleaning or sewing. Those hours are also filled with other things, or otherwise we couldn't get through them. Nonetheless, I'm happy. It's a little like my job. I can teach and instruct again. I have personal contact with others once more and do it in a manner that I think is right (in my tone and in the whole way I interact with these men), even if [these men] often don't (and never will) look particularly smart. Many of them are already worn out and have stiff joints that really only get loose after a lot of exercise. But they do follow orders and exert themselves. It's really quite a difference in comparison to the years during the world war. Their attitudes have changed and one can see how education has brought that about. If only the whole thing didn't have to be put to such a serious test. Franz wrote today very upset about the looming decisions of world-political importance. I'm very grateful to him for the insights about what lies ahead, because we tend to see these events more from our own personal perspective.

Everyone's talking a great deal about how one of our superiors has exceeded his authority and expanded our military duties too far. A reserve battalion shouldn't be in charge of heavy machine guns, grenade throwers, cavalry units, etc. [They're also complaining] about how we're now a "field unit." Supposedly that will change soon. And in fact we've seen some adjustments along those lines. We wonder what will happen to our "field recruiting company" then. Perhaps that won't last much longer either. But don't talk about this in Magdeburg, and don't mention it to the Leopolds. Personally, I'm happy that we don't have to endure those miserable guard duties any more or the deadening life

On guard in Poland, February 1940

at the rear. I think I'll be able to make it through. Even if I don't win any more laurels, I can bring some comfort to these men during their first weeks of being soldiers. Because our reserve officer candidate hasn't arrived yet, I'm the NCO in charge of the whole room of twenty men and don't need to share responsibilities with anyone else—at least for now. [. . .]

Reserve Officer Candidacy

[February 12, 1940]
[. . .] Today's work is now also done. [. . .] The work itself isn't actually the exhausting part. What's bad is having to be in constant contact with others in one room, from which there's no escape. And we have it relatively good. Over at the antitank unit the NCO's get pulled out of bed at night when the sergeant thinks it's a good idea to have a few more drinks. But here we really notice the lack of any sort of common room. That means that everything plays out in our sleeping quarters. [. . .]

It's strange. No one here has told me yet officially that I'm a reserve officer candidate, and I hardly have any more contact with the officers than the others. Hopefully it's not necessary to ask one of the women each time. If I tried anything with the unit commander that would probably have the opposite effect. Still, I'm happy of course that you have found nice people there. Here I'll just have to get through the first two and a half weeks of the first training. Then we can see if H[ermann] will keep me here, and if I can make it through here, or if I'll be sent to another unit. It's six of one, half a dozen of the other. Here, the intense stress and there, total isolation. [. . .]

False Cheer

[in February 1940]

Dear Franz,

I send you my warmest greetings on your birthday.[4] [. . .] We're still in the pedagogy business. I can say that we've made great strides during the past fourteen days. You know it hasn't been easy. When I have to drill (as I do now), it takes a lot of effort because I lack any kind of soldierly precision. The result is that even here I'm experiencing some doubts that go to the heart of what it means to be a soldier. To put it bluntly: [I doubt] the value of drills in the case of a real battle. One of my Bavarians said to me quite openly: "I'm a pacifist and I've always been one." He draws attention to himself because of his laziness and lack of discipline. But that's not so much the case with me (he likely trusts me) as it is with the other men in our quarters. The most fundamental questions facing our generation crystallize around the smallest issues. But no one ever talks about them. And in this regard I'm completely alone. There's a false sense of cheer in our NCO room. They're creating a sort of artificial world with their jokes and ironic tones, because they can't bear reality. But their jokes fall flat and really grate on one's nerves. It's easier to have more reasonable conversations with the simpler comrades. But with them our topics stay within rather narrow confines. Because I regularly go to bed at 9:30 or 9:45 in order to keep up my health, there isn't much time to read. That's why I especially appreciate the *Frankfurter* [*Zeitung*].

---

[4] Franz Petri's birthday was February 22.

That's enough about me. At the moment we're not getting much news about more general or important things. In the back of our minds we all wonder whether this whole training exercise and the weapons drills will help us progress from being reservists and if it will have readied us for other assignments. Rumors continue to fly. Perhaps we'll still experience many adventures. That is, if the battle lines are extended. But happily there seems to be little chance of that.

So we try to get through, one day at a time. Sometimes things go well. Then there are those days when things are horrid and oppressive from the moment one gets out of bed. The idle chatter of the others, half of whom are sick; the constant repetition of the same distractions; the concentration needed to carry out the exercises; the difficulties running in knee-deep snow and yelling out commands in the cold air. But it's been going all right so far, and God will help me further. [. . .]

A Setback

The Evening of Reminiscere[5] [February 18, 1940] Sunday evening. The men are still having a few beers over at the antitank unit. I'm alone in our room, and the only sounds that reach my ears come from the hallway and the room next door and they combine the sounds of war and peace: heavy footfalls, a harmonica. Something just happened—a soldier from my group (the black sheep, the one who always stands out because of his laziness and lack of discipline) came up to me and said, "Sergeant sir, everyone here has decided that we must have a picture of you!" I spent this afternoon with them again over at the antitank unit. Before that, we spent more

---

[5] The second Sunday of Lent.

than one and a half hours trudging through the snowed-in woods. I hung back a bit with the lance corporal and told him about our school days. He was in charge of the German Gymnastic Association's youth group and so he understands quite a bit. Last Sunday he kept telling me (he was slightly drunk) how hard it is for him not to be able to influence his students with his own ideals especially now in these most horrid times. I'm not telling you that to make him look bad. But that's just the way things are. Over at the antitank unit I tried to lend an ear to each of the recruits. They have so many questions— about the war, about Poland; we even spoke about religion. One of the stiffest and most awkward members of my group told me that an old friend of his, a priest, has also now been called up. Another told me about some moving services that his brother had held at the Westwall.[6] The officers had requested them, he said (and here his voice faltered), after they had originally been more or less forbidden. A few tables down our NCOs were sitting without our men with the antitank unit leader. Now they'll complain again about how I didn't join them. But my conversations were so much more rewarding than their beer-induced bravado. [. . .]

Yesterday I experienced another small setback in the development of my military pride. At around noon we were sent to Minsk, and as we got there, frozen through (I'll tell you a little more about that in a moment), we had to take a written exam with ten others. We sat there at our desks like schoolboys and chewed on our erasers. "If you talk once more I'm going to take away your test." The two of us from the 4th company were completely taken aback while the others knew all about it and had talked about becoming officers the previous day—maybe even earlier than that. In any case,

[6] German defensive line in the west.

neither of us distinguished himself. The whole thing had to do with proving our soldierly knowledge in order to be confirmed as reserve officer candidates. So that should answer your question from your last letter: first we're recommended, but not confirmed. If I don't get the approval, I won't be disappointed. The impression I got about the whole thing yesterday wasn't all that great. But please don't talk about this in Magdeburg. The major was *not* there. [. . .]

A Sleigh Ride

Everything around us is so gray and empty. The lack of any light in the sky belies the existence of the sun. A dull half-dome extends above us, and the snowflakes around us are similarly without light or color. Even the woods and the houses on the horizon can't break the monotony; their colors have been drained away and completely dimmed. Every now and then a raven will patrol the path we have just made, and its dark color stands out against the mind-numbing dullness that surrounds us. In the sled no one says a word beyond the bare minimum needed to lead our horse or find the way. The animals have to fight their way out of a snowbank, and they pull us out, stuck in the snow up to their flanks. Now we find ourselves in the forest. The way is clear. But in the bridle, treated carelessly and patched sloppily, a knot has come undone. We stop. The driver swears, trying to find some wire to fix it. Otherwise, all is still.

Only then did it become apparent that there is in fact something alive here around us, living and yet also horribly torpid. It's there: a dark green, and looms out from under the snow. It sees without eyes and reaches without hands. But it doesn't search or seek the forest, even less the few firs and birches that line the path to our left and right. It's destiny itself.

How can I put it into words, to make it real for you? The sled continues on. We glide by trees and houses. The wide street. There are Poles shoveling the snow to the side looking after us with large eyes that betray nothing. The cold has long since been a companion with us in the sled. It makes our faces burn; it stings our knees. Mostly it sits right in the middle of our feet. It seems as if these were in fact no longer even there. It's a beastly, meaningless cold, from which one can't protect oneself. [We need to] get out, just get out, walk around, wave our arms. [We need] a warm room; it doesn't matter where, or with whom.

Toward evening it has grown warmer. The day comes to an end. There's no dramatic dying flash of light, no flourishes or grandeur. Instead, there is an unnoticeable transition. The gray slowly loses its color. Now we can see in the darkness the bright squares of snowed-in houses. They also then disappear. We see only shadows. But that can't be right, since shadows live in the light. But where would that come from?

We're sitting on the long sideboards of the sled that brought us here. It's not a terribly comfortable seat, but it's ok. Our knees are pressed up against the sacks filled with mail; the coffee cans and snow shovels clatter away. Our conversation has long since died down. Each of us is alone with his thoughts; we doze. It's Sunday evening. The evening before Reminiscere. This has always been such a special day. Images flash before my eyes: in my childhood—grandmother is there, and we are being bathed. Bible circle on Sunday evening. Long conversations with Martin Hatje,[7] and so the years pass. Once—in 1918, around Pentecost, a Sunday in Flinnsberg.[8] I was about to be drafted, and took a lonely walk

---

[7] A school friend.
[8] Likely Bad Flinnsberg in the Silesian mountains.

along a mountain path. Where does it begin, where does it end; where is the origin, what is the goal? How to make sense of the day's events? What was the important event, what was the insignificant one—the sleigh ride, or the possibility of becoming an officer?

In the meantime, our surroundings have changed. Above us we see light, for the first time today. The clouds have started to move, and the moon shines, a crescent above us. The forest ahead opens like a gate. We get out of the sleigh. Ahead of me a comrade is stomping around the sleigh in a long, white fur coat. To the right and left are the horses. There's a new kind of magic. But now everything is free and clear, and like a fairy tale. Snow-covered firs. The sleigh glides with its mute-colored load between the straw. The man in a fur coat. Just like Saint Nicholas walking through the forest.

But the cold returns. We've left the forest. The wind is in our faces and cuts through us. Once again we feel helplessly frozen. We fight against the pain. When will this end? [. . .]

Field Recruit Company Training

February 1940

The first hour of work in the morning is the most difficult. Two groups line up, twenty paces apart, and form one unit along the long hall of the side wing of the barracks. From the main building, the monotonous barking of orders reaches our ears. It's always the same thing: "Lower your left shoulder!" "Lower the trigger toward the outside!" "Put your right foot forward!"—"Not so far!"—"Yes, exactly!" "At ease!" "Attention!" "Eyes right!" "Sound off!" "Right Face!" The noise is endless. Then there's a short break. Lance Corporal Stusken tells his Bavarian yet again that although he'll put up with his jokes when he's not on duty, at the moment he needs to obey orders. Then the first sergeant appears from around the corner. And soon the commands are flying even more quickly. Flat hands slap against our rifles. "Hass, of course you'd arrive a half an hour late!" The first sergeant intervenes: "Hold on tighter, you have enough strength in your arms, don't you? And when was the last time you shaved?" . . . "Of course it's Müller again. NCO Jarausch, Müller is to practice again today afterward with Lance Corporal Quade." And then that cloudburst is over. Our taskmaster has shifted his attention to the next group. A glance at my watch—another fifteen minutes to go. Still, there's land in sight.

An hour later, the group practices individual combat training. This is the famous training for "terrain north of our quarters" that appears daily on our agendas. We are now familiar with every aspect of this broad field; know where it bends and where it climbs, where one can walk on the snow with care and where it reaches above one's boots and where one sinks hopelessly into its depths. We've repeated all the possible variations of the rather few basic formations hundreds of times. Rows of riflemen spaced three or eight steps apart; chains of riflemen right and then left; changing positions; opening and then ceasing fire. We've used the oak tree and the southern ridge of the forest as compass points so many times—"A thumb's length away toward the woods!" or "To the right of the high trees." And yet we've been experiencing something here that changes every day, and that leaves its impressions not only in our views but also in our whole bodies. This is what it is—even in the midst of this frozen winter nature is all around us; we're not just walking around worn-down floors or staring at bleak, dirty walls. The snow is always new and different, depending on how frozen the surface is; its depths sometimes ball up or fall apart. The wind is constantly singing a variety of tunes in our ears; it's the living breath of this landscape that enters our own bodily rhythms and makes our impassioned struggles part of its life. Today the wind whipped out of the northeast of that particular corner of the woods and the snow lashed out around us. "Turn around, turn around, back to the street, back to our quarters"—every heartbeat repeated the thought. And then the commander opened his mouth, refusing to give in to this game: "Head to the corner of the woods, riflemen!" Then the wind was out of the south, and its icy wetness seeped into our arms and legs. And then it died down altogether. Sunshine and brilliant snow. However, we had to summon all our energies to break through enemy lines, marked by the high wall of snow along the street that led back home. "Forwards, march, march—Hurrah!" We all sunk in the drifts along the walls. But we saved ourselves by grabbing onto the crowns of the young fruit trees that are still sticking up out of the snow. We're back on the street. Our morning exercises are over. We can go home. [. . .]

Few Distractions

February 25, 1940

[. . .] Today was our first quiet Sunday in the last four weeks. We needed it. [. . .]

Yesterday we spent two and half hours in the snow. Then we got our inoculations, cleaned the parade grounds, bathed at the sawmill. I had an interesting conversation there with a worker who had been expelled from Posen. He had owned a home there and now sits here in misery; he served in the German army, took part in the world war, and has been expelled "quite innocently." Another worker [I met] was a Polish Communist. The men earn 3 to 4.50 zloty daily, and that in the face of quite awful inflation. "If the Russkis were here just eight days, then everything would fine." [. . .]

During the past few days three death sentences have been handed down [against German soldiers of the battalion]. Two of them involved drunken conduct. Awful. One is a father of three children. The major submitted an appeal for clemency. But his life is messed up anyway. The morale of the troops in Minsk is pretty low. People are complaining that our superiors have botched the question of leave and that there's no possibility for sociability or distraction. So everyone ends up drinking. But please don't say anything about this to the officers' wives. The officers know about it all anyway. [. . .]

Becoming Real Men

February 27, 1940

[. . .] Supposedly we're now to move seventy km closer to Brest-Litovsk. The companies will be distributed in the area around Łuków [close to Lublin]. [. . .] We're going to remain a company of recruits. The second wave should arrive on the 17th. Then the company commander will keep our people here for eight more days. They've already started complaining that the companionship among themselves and with us will soon be shattered. And they're already being pestered in other ways as well. We spent three hours in the snow in the fields. The major came yesterday and today. He's coming again tomorrow. Each time he stays a long while and takes great pleasure in our efforts. Today the company commander said to me, now we're all men; before the Landesschützen were all just women. That's complimentary in a number of ways, of course.

The two men were shot in Minsk today. Today one of our men is appearing before a court-martial because he stayed away four days longer than his allotted furlough and was then arrested in Magdeburg.

Spring is arriving slowly here as well. It's still 12 below at night, but we have colorful sunrises in the morning and during the day, the sun shines so brightly that the top layer of snow is starting to melt. Above all else the sky is so soft and mild, so different from the days of winter, and we are starting to see birds. [. . .] We're getting tanner every day. And since our caps sit low on our foreheads, it looks pretty funny. Every day I look at my recruits and see how their faces have changed; almost all of them are strained and a little tired, but they've also become more chiseled and harder. And at least in terms of how things work purely in terms of soldierly life, the company commander is right. [. . .]

More Disappointments

March 1, 1940

[. . .] The day before yesterday [Boehter-Schulze][9] was here and talked to the company about the court-martial. It was pretty upsetting to him that this had happened in his battalion. We're not supposed to write anything about it. But that order came a little too late. In any case, don't say a word to the officers' wives. He then took another NCO and me to Minsk and held an hour's lesson in the afternoon for those *aspiring* officer recruit candidates. Our written exams didn't please him much. He was pretty short with the both of us, and afterward, Lieutenant Herrmann (with whom we were supposed to ride back to Mienia), kept us waiting for two hours on the street without giving us any notice. The whole experience was a frustrating strain on us both. Please don't

[9] The battalion commander.

say anything to the women. It won't help, and will only make our situation worse.

Old and New Authorities

March 3, 1940

[. . .] I'm not surprised about the money. Fixed costs here have always eaten up a large portion of our salaries. But that's related to the way we spend our time. And it's so hard to save up. I have to spend a lot for beer for the group and such things, so I'm regularly short on cash. I think if I were an officer I would never be able to make it with my salary. But that is probably only likely if the war lasts a long, long time. And we'd rather not hope for that. I can't help but get upset about a certain kind of arrogance that people still possess at heart. But now it's even less justified than it was in the past, when officers, the aristocracy, and others still fulfilled certain social and political tasks that have been taken away from them. Today, distinction is justified for the sake of military authority. And it's precisely this idea of military authority that appears quite questionable to me, because it doesn't possess any support within the *Volksgemeinschaft* that now serves as our political ideal. There is a large, unsolved contradiction between political and military organizational ideals. I could go into details that would clearly show how the whole idea of the *Volksordnung* (belonging to the party and its associations) is ignored and suspended during military service. But that can hardly be maintained in the long run. Either the officers will once more assume "political" responsibility (which doesn't mean a "dictatorship of the generals"), or the army must conform. We need to address this question (and why not?) in a positive and constructive manner. But that of course is objectionable. Instead, one must conform as a matter of course to all the customs and mannerisms. This topic is as old as the destinies and tales of the past two hundred years. Practically everyone tries to resist, but then must adhere [to the norms] after all. Yesterday Lieutenant Schulze (who was slightly drunk) complimented me again. That I can adjust to so many circumstances. This week we have to make sure to put a lot of pressure on the recruits during the Sunday inspection. My health is ok. Today I have a slight cold. [. . .]

Trying to Become a Soldier

March 5, 1940

Your letters from Friday and Sunday arrived today. I'm so happy that the mail is moving quickly. We can have a much closer and livelier exchange. Today I have the chance to give my letter to Bauerhorst.[10] It will be there with you soon. I'm so happy that you can find such joy in music again, and that you didn't have to be there alone. I feel the same way that you do. I'm ever more anxious and want [to see you]. Certainly in part what makes life so difficult are the constant concerns and the high expectations. But it's not only that. Every week I feel that we are losing irreplaceable possibilities to be together, irreplaceable because we have so much to make up for. We can hardly comfort ourselves with [hopes for the] future, because it seems to me at least to be extremely uncertain.

Until now I've always tried to find the meaning of my work here (or the way to discover that meaning) by taking my duties seriously. But that is starting to look questionable to me when I see that our work here demands so much of us that it would only be justified if we really all were going into battle.

---

[10] A comrade going on leave.

I'd really like to get through these weeks and then see if I can gain more clarity when things are quieter. Blaskowitz is supposed to come Sunday evening with his staff. You can imagine what kind of pressure that puts on everyone. One really has the feeling that we're just now starting to understand what it means to be a soldier. After Sunday evening we're to take our leave. And everyone thinks to himself that nothing could be better. And then we try to pull ourselves together and try to get through it all. We've also got more snow with temperatures around zero degrees. This morning it was impossible to go outside because the snow was blowing around so much. Everyone stumbled around in the freshly fallen snow and couldn't carry out his maneuvers in the proper manner. At least that what's my pedagogical side tells me. As a soldier, one has to demand the impossible and make it possible, I guess.

We've become a real infantry regiment. But our division is still called a Landesschützen division. So the regrouping won't really have any practical consequences. [. . .]

Officer Candidates

March 7, 1940

[. . .] We have a new man in our quarters: officer candidate and lance corporal Rücklies [?], a Magdeburg SA-unit officer. [. . .] He's an old soldier from the world war, in his mid-forties, robust and experienced. But there's something strange about this kind of officer candidate. He's one of those practical and savvy men who serve the party organization. He doesn't necessarily lack knowledge in certain areas. He's also been around a lot. But he has hardly any interest in intellectual or cultural things. Over the past few days I've been thinking a lot about how we worked educating future leaders. He appears to have no inner distance to his own life

167

and work that might come from knowledge of other cultures. Personally, I'm always disappointed when I lose yet another chance to find someone with whom I can talk a bit. When they first started talking about officer candidates who were coming here, I had some hope. But it's dead and buried. We all discuss the usual: food, drinking, women, work, and a little bit of politics. [. . .]

I hope my last letters haven't troubled you, because they've been rather melancholy. It's nothing more than the extreme stress that robs me of intellectual energy. When Sunday is over, things will be quieter. And then when the new recruits arrive I'll try to arrange a bit of freedom through the lance corporals ahead of time. The best news would be if there were some truth in the rumors about peace from the outside world. But one doesn't dare hope. [. . .]

The General Visits

March 9, 1940

Now the dreaded day is over, and we have our first rest of a long time. [. . .] Everyone had cleaned and polished. Because of the snow our uniforms aren't too worn. So we made a rather good impression this morning as we were almost all assembled in our courtyard. The major had arrived early at 7:30. It was an important event for him, and he was pretty agitated, while the company commander was fairly composed. We stood there a few minutes, and then came Lieutenant General Schenkendorff,[11] the commander from Minsk. Blaskowitz of course didn't make an appearance. The major walked the formation in the usual manner, and found our line and dress impeccable. Then, according to the plan,

[11] Max von Schenckendorff (1875–1943).

the drills were supposed to start. But the general didn't stick to it. At first I walked him to my group and was introduced as a reserve officer candidate. He asked a few questions but then moved on quickly. And then we drilled, each of us with his group, in the courtyard. The major moved from group to group, examining each one carefully. My group came up for target practice and recumbent shooting. He threw himself next to them on the ground to watch them. Everything went well, and then he disappeared. The general was more unrestrained, and didn't stick with him, but stopped here and there and spoke to the men. Suddenly there was a whistle; the company was called to attention; we thought we'd have to carry out a maneuver in the fields. But instead (after an hour) we heard the general's final words: he had a lot of praise—for the company leader, the officers, and the trainers. We marched off to quarters. The general examined our rooms, talked to the men, was introduced to the "officer candidates" (but formally, without any personal words), and disappeared. Then the major had us assemble in the courtyard; he praised us and said that it was too bad that we couldn't carry out our maneuvers and said that we were now free to go. I went to wash with the men but otherwise spent my time reading and writing. [. . .]

I'm now anxious to hear if Lieutenant H[errmann] will make any changes in the trainers. If he keeps me on, I'll stay. The positive aspects of our clear tasks outweigh everything else. And my health has been good until now—I belong to the few who haven't spent any time sick—and so I'll hang on. Unfortunately it looks like our next move is now set. We're supposed to go to a village—Kosow[12]—near the Bug between Warsaw and Bialystok, but that's not settled yet. [. . .]

[12] Kosów Lacki is a small town a few kilometers away from the Bug.

169

Reserve Officer Candidate

March 10, 1940

[. . .] At 10 we started a fast march. Things went fine the first ten kilometers. But then as we turned around, we had the wind in our faces, and we could hardly fight against it. Small pieces of ice and wet snow pelted our faces. And the whole time we had to keep our pace. The men were brave. Only the lance corporal had reached his limit. But he held on. Then we had to crawl a stretch and creep under a cart. And we did it. Then we had to throw a hand grenade. But our group failed at that. So it's likely that we'll move down to last place. I feel bad for the men who gave it their all. The storm raged all afternoon. It grew colder. Now, this evening, the wind has died down. But it piled up tremendous drifts. Sometimes I think that in the future it will be hard for me to live without this basic and unadorned proximity to nature. But we'll be feeling it in our limbs over the next few days. Just now Lieutenant Sachse came to our room and said that we had done well. He didn't tell us what place we took. I'm very happy.

Even more so because I learned today that I've been named a reserve officer candidate; Lieutenant Sachse told me so on behalf of the major. There's a lot of work that went into that. And one can't say that it's only about contacts. So I'll have to give up reading books and thinking for a while longer. It's strange, how life has moved bit by bit away from the course that I had set for it; how it forces one to say yes to things and to embrace them. Now I'll have to see how I can continue to make a good impression on Herrmann. He was very pleased with our efforts—also by the fact that we had refused to split up our group and divide it among the others, as had been discussed yesterday. There's a lot more on my mind, but now's not the time for it. [. . .]

Pride in Achievements

[March 11, 1940]

We sent our recruits away today. We had a warm goodbye and then they marched away in such good form and singing so well. [. . .] We had the best marching time. Only our mistakes with the hand grenades pushed us down to second place. Lieutenant Herrmann congratulated me and I was happy that I could get recognition, especially from him. But I'm terribly tired. Last night's celebration was a bit too much for me. There were too many people and too much noise and smoke. I've just been sort of dozing yesterday and today. We haven't had too much to do. This afternoon I took a nice two-hour walk with the lance corporal. We took a lot of photos, for the first time according to my taste; and we talked a lot. It was a huge relief, even if we were walking around with loaded weapons.

We start training again tomorrow. But hopefully we'll have some time to rest. As usual, our departure has been put off. I'm including the map with the new village. Please send it back to me. We keep saying that we're getting ever closer to Germany, toward eastern Prussia. But that's a kind of gallows' humor. Because Kosow will be cut off from all culture and the connections will be really bad. [. . .] It will be a hard life there. We'll use the school there for our quarters. We're taking our beds, tables, benches, etc. with us. Our regiment will then be at the farthest reaches of the border. On Sunday, the general told the officers at their celebration that the battalion Boether-Schulze was the best of his Landesschützen battalions. [. . .]

171

Arrival in Kosow

[. . .] March 17, 1940, Palm Sunday
We've finally arrived. It was a pretty difficult trip. [. . .] Our
room is really nice, even though fourteen of us are in one
room, but all the common rooms—kitchens, latrines, etc.—
are in bad shape. [. . .] The place has 2,800 inhabitants, and
it seems to be an agricultural town with many Jewish im-
migrants from the western part of Poland. [. . .] Hopefully
things will get better than they look like now.
   Be well

> When moon and stars meet in the sky,
> Then heaven's vault glows in the night.
> And constellations dance with true delight,
> Shining their light on earth from high.
> Humbly you cast a glance, yet daring
> You feel a glow encircling your brow,
> The doors of heaven seem to open now.
> You sense that forces for your life are caring.
> Need we find words, which will this image show?
> How much I long toward you to go,
> Till we can meet each other once again!
> In peace cathedral bells are chiming,
> I feel you in my arms reclining,
> From God's grace a life grows anew. [. . .]

New Surroundings

March 18, 1940
I'd like to wish you a happy and blessed Easter. I wonder if
these greetings will reach you? We've been cut off from all

172

contact with home for days now. Nothing is arriving. And I think it must be the same with you. [. . .]

The school grounds lie somewhat on the outskirts of this small town with its one-story houses, above which rises the proud, but somewhat desolate church tower. It's a simple building with rather comfortable rooms and with large, regular windows. All around it the Prussians have set up in the small houses and farmhouses. [. . .] The Germans have been busy. They've surrounded the whole area with barbed wire. The numerous paths between the farmhouses have disappeared. A lovely new log house now serves as quarters for the officers. Other barracks brought from home have been set up and are already inhabited. Nearby is a primitive wooden structure, about which one should be silent; it's a worthy counterpart to the run-down buildings that were designed for Polish schoolchildren. Until eight days ago, East Prussians had inhabited the school. They don't appear to have had any great aspirations to domestic comfort. But they were swimming in butter, bacon, and ham. Their beds were made out of such large planks of wood that one has to assume that their good food had its results. Today, our Magdeburgers, who aren't as well fed but who are more fastidious, have given the building a different look. Our things that yesterday were still in the entryway are now stored in the cellar. A group of mostly Jewish women and young boys have scrubbed and cleaned up. Most of the rooms are therefore a little more inhabitable. Unfortunately, we won't be able to move the huge bedsteads since we can't make new ones until the recruits arrive and we've only brought a few of our own from Mienia. But things don't look as hopeless as they did yesterday evening. [. . .]

Yesterday all the rumormongers were hard at it. All kinds of stories were swirling around: air raids on England; a meeting between the Führer and il Duce [Mussolini]; possible peace negotiations in Paris—no one could name a source. Things are worse because we are so cut off from newspapers and radios. Hopefully the mail will arrive in time for the holiday. [. . .]

Making the Quarters Livable

Wednesday before Easter 1940 [March 20] We've been without mail now for about eight days. We learned today about the fall of the French government, but nothing more. We lose ourselves in speculations that reveal all too clearly our desire to return home. It's been a rather uncomfortable week. Only the holy event remains mute.

Our company commander has had his way again. He found some space for us. So we're all hard at work again. [. . .] Our rooms now have new beds, like the ones made for the barracks of the labor service at home. The Detmold recruits set out today. They'll arrive on Good Friday or Saturday. At least everything is somewhat civilized, and if we keep working at this pace until tomorrow evening, people will at least have beds, tables, and benches. I haven't had to work with the others. The company received 110 books from the Rosenberg collection,[13] and I've been cataloging and examining them. There are some good volumes among them: Keller, Freytag, Fontane, and Schaeffer; among the foreign authors there are [books by] Flaubert, Jacobsen, and Björnson. You won't need to worry about sending me anything to read.

Yesterday I spent an hour in the town toward evening. Things are similar here as elsewhere: one can bear the

---

[13] The party sent books to the army called the "Alfred Rosenberg Donation for the Army." NSDAP/Reichsleitung to the adjutant of Reichsleiter Alfred Rosenberg, March 15, 1940. Bundesarchiv Berlin, NS-8/247, Bl. 116.

country roads with their log houses and thatched roofs in all of their poverty because they reflect the surroundings in which they have developed. But the marketplace looks like a parody of old central European cities with its pitiful houses and businesses. The imposing church seems therefore even more surprising: it's a modern gothic building made of yellow brick. The walls are large and simple and there is little ornamentation, so the overall impression is a favorable one. [. . .]

New Recruits Arrive

March 22, 1940, Good Friday
[. . .] Our recruits arrived at 5:45 p.m.—from Westphalia. [. . .] Most of them are workers, locksmiths, shoemakers, etc. Perhaps they'll be a bit more energetic than the Bavarians. Of course, now they're tired and not entirely with it. Unfortunately I lost my humane and honest lance corporal. He's leading his own group now. His replacement is indifferent and opinionated. I think I'll have to go around him. I didn't have to work along with the others. But with all the noise in the quarters one couldn't get anything done. So I'm pleased that things will now be underway again.

There was supposed to be a service tonight. But it was canceled at the last minute. So we'll spend the next few days hard at work and without any kind of celebration. [. . .]

Sensing One's Limits

March 29, 1940
[. . .] It seems that the pace is going to be sped up further. To our amusement, the company leader pulled a tendon yesterday as he was trying to demonstrate some special maneuver. When one sees how hard the men are pushed and knows

175

nothing can be changed, then one loses one's temper and wishes those in charge the worst.

It's difficult for me to go into details. Today five reserve officer candidates came into our room, and some of them are real loudmouths. I have even less opportunity to think than before. [. . .]

Basically it's difficult to get through each day, both during and after duty. I hardly want another promotion. Because that would mean I'd be sent to other units, perhaps even to Döberitz.[14] The best result would be that this won't last much longer. My energy is going to be spent at some point. The new reserve officer candidates have brought along a new arrogant tone that has become foreign to us. During the last few years they've been doing these exercises regularly, and were promoted, but now they've just been called up again. They don't even have seven months time spent in Poland under their belts. That's obvious in their whole manner. [. . .]

The New Spirit of Education

March 31, 1940

Our two easy days are behind us now. Yesterday the swearing-in ceremony was short and simple. Around noon the division general, Freiherr von Wrede[15] arrived quite unexpectedly; he seems to be a very pleasant officer, not one of those bellowing types. He carefully inspected the whole camp and even checked out the latrines. In the afternoon we had a nice walk. We spent about three hours outside. I'm becoming accustomed to the landscape. It consists of far-reaching, sandy

---

[14] The army had an infantry school there.
[15] Theodor Freiherr von Wrede (1888–1973).

waves. Near the farming villages, the fields string out in small strips up to the hills. [. . .] Yesterday we were in a farming village that stood out among the neglected villages as a piece of real culture. The wooden houses, the fences, were all smartly cut and painted. There was a respect for the natural surroundings. And the people were clean and orderly.

But then right next to that image [we were faced] once again with incomprehensible misery. We passed a Jewish cemetery, the new kind now in use. The old one lay across the road, with its worn stones. Sand was being raked out to the sides. Bones were rolling around in the trench beneath. Stacked up in the new cemetery are stones with primitive images: the seven-armed lamp; lions that hold the laws between them. We can't make out any graves. Freshly chopped pine branches have been scattered between the stones. "The Polacks from the neighboring village cut down the forest during the winter." Now the poor Jewish people crouch between the stones and are gathering the pieces together. At the wayside an older woman sat with a young girl next to a bundle; she was silent and expressionless as we passed by. The recruits were affected. Not our reserve officer candidates.

There are two teachers and one director of a business school. There's also an SS-man (a draftsman in an airplane factory) and a somewhat older foreman. These are the new middle class. National Socialists down to the bone; as far as they express their beliefs, they appear to believe in God. When they tell stories it's always about their exercises and what they've accomplished; of course the bars they've visited are always highlighted. So they're a new type of reserve officer that fits perfectly into the present. They expect to be sent to Döberitz and then to the Westwall when they've completed one or two training courses here.

177

[. . .] I hope that I can finally settle down here and get used to the—according to my judgment—completely mistaken way things are taught here without becoming enraged at every encounter. In any case I'm often thinking now about pedagogical matters. One would need to know a lot more here. So, for instance, what a man like Gneisenau[16] thought about this tradition from the time of Friedrich Wilhelm I. The whole thing is based on the fact that the men are constantly pushed beyond their limits, so that they lose any sense of initiative. Then they're putty in their [superiors'] hands, and they ask them to perform on the basis of a blind sense of duty; then they allow them a limited amount of freedom when this forced behavior has become like second nature to them. One of the methods that belongs to this kind of education is that no one can ever face his superior secure in the knowledge of his own achievements. The individual is always wrong and always messes things up. The result is an astonishing rise in the average performance. But on the other hand, there is a terrible lack of discipline when the pressure from above decreases, now just as it did in 1918. I think that this education was only possible when it was based on the belief that there is something essential about being a human being that is indestructible, even in the afterlife. At least then the individuality of each man and his freedom was secured. . . . But now, when everything is focused on living for the moment, this kind of education is sinister. Older Prussian traditions—emptied of Christianity—are being transformed into the spirit of the SS. I would like to speak with Franz about these things. [. . .]

But I won't torture you with such thoughts any longer. Please don't show this letter to anyone; at least not this page.

---

[16] Prussian military reformer during the Napoleonic wars.

Perhaps I never should have written it, but sometimes one has to get things off one's chest in order to get through each day. Tomorrow morning we'll certainly hear: "We need to make up two lost days of inactivity." Too bad that we still have Sundays.

The Misery of the Jews

April 5, 1940

Dear Franz,

[. . .] Our situation is changing at the moment insofar as we are expected to perform even harder and we often have conflicts. Our leadership believes it can increase performance by always criticizing, calling everything inadequate, and extending the length of duty. I try to keep psychologically free of the inescapable anger so that the troops do not have to suffer from it. [. . .]

My days and my abilities are filled as never before. My Polish isn't improving at all, and I barely have time to read anything else. [. . .] Tomorrow we'll march and Sunday we'll have our usual walk. The truly paralyzing things here are the people, especially in the town, where the number of Jews has been doubled by expulsion from the West; they live in horrible squalor and misery.[17] [. . .]

I am very glad that I can at least *sub specie aeternitatis* believe in the meaning of these months. From a national-socialist point of view there is much criticism of the remnants of the old spirit among our superiors. "They have started again where they left off in 1918." That is the mood among the comrades. [. . .]

---

[17] Polish Jews from the annexed areas were sent to the General Government. At the beginning of 1942, approximately 3,800 Jews lived in Kosów. See Golczewski, *Polen*, 452.

179

Renewed Confidence

April 7, 1940

[. . .] People really fall under the spell of a powerful force. It's strange how this plays out in terms of generational differences. The older comrades are generally tolerant. This became clear today when we had our first field service since Christmas and the recruits weren't allowed to attend because they had to muster for a roll call. This upset those who don't even belong to a church, for objective reasons. But the younger ones felt entirely differently about it—they expressed their intolerance toward everything—the church, the Jews. The simpler men like our recent recruits haven't yet been influenced by this way of thinking. I observed this during our afternoon walk in the manner they behaved toward the Poles. I don't think there's any way to prevent such developments except prayer and attesting to something beyond this world. This isn't about "spiritual" forces in an idealistic or even an enlightened sense. This is becoming very clear to me from my experiences and is more important than any theology that we have clung to for far too long. [. . .]

My calmer view of these things is a result of today's service and a walk. The service took place for about fifty soldiers in the Catholic church. [. . .] I really began to feel better after our walk in the beautiful snow; the wind from the east was strong and raw. We bought eggs again. It's always amusing to go into the Polish farms and to look into their kitchens. Most are outfitted with very few things, but there are great disparities in how clean or orderly things are. [. . .] People were mostly friendly. Many of them shook our hands. Some didn't want to take our money. So we traded with cigarettes. I got ten eggs for 47 pfennigs and a pack of Juno [cigarettes].

Nazi Imperialism

April 9, 1940

I think that people are sitting tensely next to the radio and waiting to hear the news that will answer the question: "What will England do now?"[18] We're getting only scraps of news but we've heard enough that it's electrifying. Personally I took the news quite hard. Now the old Europe ("Europe or Christendom") is finally over. We could still have accepted the attack in the east as a part of the limited inherited idea of [the Holy Roman] Empire. Now Germany is taking on the struggle for world dominance. Here we see at once the strange historical conditioning of National Socialism, even in the area of foreign policy. Imperialism is alive and well.

Franz will interpret the events more positively than I can. Therefore I'll keep this brief and be silent about my fears (not about military events). Why should I burden or confuse you, without being able to have a real conversation? [. . .]

A Slow Sapping of Strength

April 14, 1940

[. . .] Overall, things have been pretty quiet today. I certainly need the rest. I'm pretty exhausted. And of those NCOs who started here together, two of us are sick again. As a result, the newly arrived reserve officer candidates have been working more. We'll get more NCOs in eight days, since we've learned that we're to receive 230 recruits on April 23. But between now and then we have an inspection. This time everything seems so very different. No one is looking forward to it with any kind of ambition or a desire to achieve

---

[18] German troops landed in Norway and Denmark on April 9, 1940.

anything. The failings of the new lesson plans mean that nothing works; and then all the complaints fall on the heads of the NCOs, which naturally stifles our initiative. But in the meantime we've undertaken a number of things that extend beyond basic training; the day before yesterday for instance we marched and set up tents and ate with our field kitchen. I couldn't enjoy this respite very well, because for the first time last week my feet and legs were really hurting. But it was lovely to see the landscape. Lots of heath and moors with pools of water, brown junipers, and low shrubs. Every now and then we came across an isolated village. [. . .]

Your news about the cancellation of religion lessons was very disconcerting, as was your report of your conversation with Frau Schulze. I guess we won't be able to place too much hope in the possibility of a future in Magdeburg. [. . .]

Failures

April 18, 1940

[. . .] The inspection lasted from 8:00 a.m. to 12:30. It was completely different from last time. The divisional and regimental commanders were present. Each group conducted formal basic training and field training. Then there were lessons in the platoon. The result: the parade exercises were good; the field training is still not good enough. The group leaders are now going to be reviewed. That's to happen in the next few days before the arrival of the new recruits. So our hoped-for day of rest won't come to pass. It's understandable, if one considers that the younger soldiers may have to fight in case of an emergency. But then we would need different trainers. So the war has taken on a new aspect for us, and that answers your question about whether or not I can find some meaning in life now. Life at the moment is so difficult that we can't even ask ourselves such questions. We stand before a task that we are not able to fulfill because of the manner in which it is presented to us. And we can't get out of it, because there aren't any younger NCOs, as we didn't have compulsory military service in the years after the war. [. . .]

I could do the older drills really well, and on prior days I did well in the various exercises in front of the company leaders and during the preinspection by the first lieutenant. But I don't know enough about field drills because I lack all basic knowledge and training, and that means I'm unsure. And then of course there's the fact that I'm exhausted. But I'm not giving up. Things will go on, day by day. And if I should ever feel any serious injuries, I'll report in sick. One day this torture will be over. [. . .]

Further Worries

April 26, 1940

[. . .] This week hasn't been easy. This is probably the first time in many years that I haven't read anything other than scripture verses, daily devotions, and training manuals. There's always something new. During one free hour, when the recruits have their lessons, we now have class with the company commander. Our duties last until 8 p.m. And the work on our obstacle course continues apace. I went to the doctor on Thursday because he had requested I stop by. He felt that my heart condition had improved, but that I should continue to take valerian drops. I'm writing that as an immediate answer to your question about the reserve officer candidate course. I'm not going to do anything that could increase my stress levels, because I'm thinking of the future. If I'm picked, then I'll pull myself together. We have a certain understanding now about what it means to be in the army. And I have to say we aren't really fit for this kind of life. I think that in the future we'll all be sent off when the regiment is finally filled with younger recruits, because we really can't keep up with the twenty-five-year-olds. Soon there won't be any older regiments where we could live a more quiet life as a sergeant. I think that in July we'll be sent somewhere farther west, and then I'll consider whether or not I can apply for an exemption. That assumes that the war will continue in this protracted pace. As far as that goes, there are many postings that aren't as safe. I can really only talk about most of this with you face to face. There's nothing easy about trying to become an officer here. Of all the expectations we had on the 20th of April, none have come to pass.[19] Things look really different here than for the troops in the West, especially since they live in nice, privately owned quarters. I'm not considering any posts closer to the front. I'm not sure if we shouldn't give up on thoughts of a lifestyle based on the assumptions that officer [equals] university. I hope you understand me correctly. I'm not at all tired or resigned. But we should talk about that as well. It's just the very serious question of whether or not my strength will hold out long enough to make it. Here as well as in the intellectual world of my career, much depends on external recognition. [. . .]

Hopes for Leave

April 28, 1940

[. . .] The more we worry about our future, the clearer some possibilities become. But I still can't say anything for sure. The first members of the cohort born up to 1896 started to

---

[19] April 20 was Hitler's birthday, and this was obviously linked to hopes of promotion. See Rudolf Absolon, *Wehrgesetz und Wehrdienst. Das Personalwesen in der Wehrmacht* (Boppard, 1960), 232.

leave today. We'll end our recruit training at the end of July. Between these two events I hope I'll have some leave. Then I think I'll be able to have a better sense about a number of things: my future service, a possible exemption. With my leave in the middle I'll have three more months of training to get through, if it doesn't get too hot there. [. . .]

How Many Steps?

May 1, 1940

Today is the first of May,[20] and it's cold and sunny like the past few days have been. We just swore in the new recruits; otherwise we're off duty. But we don't yet know if we can go out. May 3rd is the day the Poles celebrate their constitution, and we're on high alert. Tomorrow, Ascension Day, they'll likely have a service, just so we don't get too carefree. Luckily, I'm doing better healthwise. I can thus get more pleasure from my work. The tone in this group of recruits seems much better. The sunny days are beautiful, as are the young seedlings and the soft greens of the birches and the pastures. [. . .] The sergeant major is going on furlough during Pentecost, after he jumped down our throats when we asked him about possible leave time. Unfortunately there's a lot that's not right there. But I don't want to dwell on these stultifying trivialities. [. . .]

I'd like to write you something meaningful. But I don't know what. Over the past few days I've read a little bit in Yorck's Italian diary[21] and looked forward to all the wonderful things that lie ahead for us; one can catch a glimpse of the

---

[20] Labor Day, made a national holiday in Germany in 1919 celebrating workers and socialism.

[21] Count Paul Yorck von Warthenberg, *Italienisches Tagebuch*, ed. Sigrid von der Schulenburg (Leipzig, 1939).

beauty when it is written in such a wonderful form. When will we be able to travel to the lemon groves of Taormina? Perhaps we should start a special savings account so that such dreams (even if they are far off) can be realized. But maybe it's more practical in the meantime to learn Polish. One reserve officer candidate, who is a teacher, told me a few days ago that all the teachers who live in the district of Gelsenkirchen who took part in the Polish campaign have been ordered to be ready to be called up for service in the East. Eleven [men] volunteered. A further thirty-five were posted. I wouldn't be all that surprised if that happens to us one day in a similar manner, especially if our cohort were to be discharged in the near future. And yet I don't know if I'll be released if I'm a reserve officer candidate. That also makes it difficult to ask for an exemption. I need to figure out all of these things during my furlough; here it's impossible to get any clear answers, especially since our sergeant is so strange—he's too insecure about his superiors to give a clear answer. Yesterday Weitbrecht[22] (who had my military address) sent me the enclosed essays. I'm pleased that there is good content for an issue of the journal that is attempting to attain a certain level of quality.

And world events? Everyone seems to think that Norway is a huge success, but that's just one more step forward. How many steps do we have to take before we reach the goal? [. . .]

Exhaustion

[May 5, 1940] Exaudi[23] 1940

Thank you so much for your understanding letter from the 30th, in which I really could not detect any lack of empathy.

[22] A co-worker on the journal.
[23] Exaudi is the sixth Sunday after Easter.

I only think you fundamentally underestimate how difficult this training is. We have reserve officer candidates here who've gone through similar training. I believe them when they say that they face very different demands than the ones we do. They say to themselves that such courses were only tolerable because they were limited in time. Even a very fit and younger SS-man said to me recently that he would rather have chosen not to have become a sergeant, than adding another training course to the one he'd already completed. Of course one would be willing to take on the burden, if the goal were worthwhile. But I cannot hear an echo of any kind of independent responsibility from our lieutenants here. I don't know if you fully understand how terribly complicated modern warfare is. A great deal of intellectual energy is also a part of it.

So those are once again the reasons why I shouldn't do anything. We're all exhausted. Of the NCOs, two are in the infirmary (one with a sore throat, another with an infection); a third has just returned (groin pull). I shouldn't be ashamed if things go similarly for me. After all, I only called in sick for a half a day during the recruit training and still did work indoors. I'd like to be able to take part in the eight-week training course in June and July here, because there will be a lot of new things that I don't know yet. That will mean a difference in any case. I'm only considering an exemption in case I have to do boring prisoner guarding at home or in the rear. [. . .]

Battle in the West

May 10, 1940

Pentecost is just around the corner. But at the moment, the holiday, and everything that goes along with it, has been overshadowed by the news from the West, and everyone is

187

terribly agitated.[24] Each of us feels he knows that the real battle, and the real bloodshed, will begin. Who knows what the near future or beyond will now look like. [. . .]

A Night Exercise

The evening before Pentecost 1940 [May 11, 1940] The heather is now starting to fade. I'd like to lay my head in the dry heath and sleep with the waning day. But I'll pull myself together and keep watch. It's banal now to speak of the junipers looking like ghosts during dusk. But don't they appear again in places where once I hadn't seen them before, dark, shrouded in shadows and I can't tell how they've gotten there? I duck under the broad branches of a young pine tree. Who knows, perhaps it's better to make myself invisible. The opposing spy patrol and the darkness of nature—can wait for me. Who can decide, who can tell what is right? But I pull myself together. I can't let myself go thus. I have responsibilities. My comrades are here. Yes, but where exactly? They lie in their trenches only a few feet away, covered with earth, buried under the cut pine limbs. Why are they so silent?—I have forbidden them any conversation. But now I'd like to go over to them and check on each one of them. But why is there no sound of human activity? Why does nature seem so strange? The sounds of barking dogs are most familiar. They remind me of houses and courtyards. But the regular croaking of the frogs, as it rises and falls still again, comes from another world. What kinds of birds are those that sound so strange? To whom are they calling? Why are they out?

[24] The German attack in the west began on May 10, 1940, and ended with the occupation of France, the Netherlands, Belgium, and Luxembourg.

How low the clouds are hanging in the dark sky! Why have the stars disappeared? Over there lies the West, but even there, in the evening sky, everything is shrouded. And there is our homeland. But isn't that where the battle is raging! Suddenly everything is awake and alive: All of the pressure of the last few days while these two powers engage in a decisive struggle. But that's not all. Suddenly I remember that it's Pentecost. Tongues of fire from heaven; spirit from heaven. People hear the one voice.—How strange, how odd, how incomprehensible at this hour. What does this have to do with this night and its muffled nature?

I bury my face in the earth. Who can bear this? It seems that all the powers in this world and in the next are rising up and trying to grab me. Who can resist their calls? Suddenly there's a flash of fire, and shots resound. The spell of the night has been broken.

Planning for Leave

May 22, 1940

I've worried you unnecessarily; my attempt yesterday evening was successful. I can depart on the 25th. Because that's Saturday, I'd like to stay in Hennigsdorf during Sunday. I wrote you why. If you get the letter on time and can come to Hennigsdorf, I'd be happy about that. I'd like to speak to Frau von Tiling in Berlin. [. . .] I'd like to gain a certain sense of clarity, because we now are a lot closer to being deployed. But you shouldn't take these wishes too seriously. They're only secondary. [. . .] I have to return on the 6th (unfortunately!) [. . .]

Leave from May 25 to June 6, 1940

189

Impressions of Warsaw

June 7, 1940

The most amazing thing about these five or six hours was seeing how tenacious and animated people who live in modern
cities can be. It's somewhat alarming that they can survive
amid the ruins of their entire political and economic system as
if nothing had happened, but that also has, without a doubt,
something grand about it. Streetcars crisscross the traffic
arteries of the city; in each car all the seats are occupied—
where are these people going, since all of their workplaces are
mere rubble? Crowds press along the sidewalks; every bench
in all the parks is occupied. And yet I have no idea how these
people make a living, especially when one sees the terrible
inflation evident in the signs of the store windows.

As far as I can tell, above all else, all the official government buildings and the important structures like train
stations, factories, and gas works have been systematically
destroyed. But entire city blocks also lie in ruins. Now everything has been removed that seemed in danger of collapsing.
But the wrecking crews continue their explosions. There are
bare firewalls everywhere. Mighty mountains of roof tile debris are piled up on the ground floors [of buildings]. Often
the doorways and window openings have been covered up
with stacked-up bricks. Likely there are often still corpses
buried there. In fact, people say that mass graves lie under
the bare grass on the "Sachsenplatz"—but there is no sign of
this. Elsewhere, indications of life and destruction lie closer
together. Some apartments in the tenements have been restored somewhat, right next to those with empty windows.
Wood has replaced the broken glass. Some merchants in
the Praga district near the destroyed Eastern Train Station
have relied on such methods. The pieces of glass have been

placed between the window frames, thus allowing a view at the goods on sale—at least those things that are still available. In the city center there are still tastefully decorated windows filled with goods. But even here, if one looks inside the stores, one sees only empty shelves. The rich display of goods in many of the delicatessens is a testament to the fact that money must be on hand in some places. One can buy anything there—but at inflationary prices.

Among the historically significant buildings, the royal palace has suffered the most. The roof has been fully destroyed; the interior is burned out. It will likely be torn down. The nearby "Krakow suburb" with its many remainders from the time of Stanislaw Leszczynski[25] and the years thereafter (late baroque and classic periods) has suffered a great deal. Especially the rows of ministerial offices and other official buildings. We went up the steps of the former war ministry and observed the effect of the bombs as evidenced in the destroyed roofs and the burned-out rooms. Welders were there, trying to cut the bent iron trusses and to remove all the metal available (doors, locks, heaters)—perhaps for the Hermann-Göring Fund?[26] Pilsudski's simple classical Belvedere remains undestroyed.[27] Unfortunately the entry to the "royal baths" of Lazienki was closed off. Generally this city has never really possessed any great works of art. Even the dimensions of the public buildings are quite modest. And the two high rises in the city don't make much of an impression. In comparison, Budapest (to mention a comparable city), is much more impressive, but also has a very different nature and history. I was most impressed by the historical and architectural significance

---

[25] Stanisław I Leszczyński (1677–1766), king of Poland.

[26] Göring had called for all metal to be collected on March 14, 1940.

[27] A palace in the Łazienki Park.

of the old marketplace, the center of the city in the fifteenth and sixteenth centuries. It's a broad, almost square site surrounded by closed house facades. The small streets lead up to the corners of the square. The houses aren't too tall and are painted in muted colors. There's nothing of great artistic worth here, but the Gothic brick openings, stripped of plaster, and the forceful forms of Renaissance sculpture speak of the vitality of the past. At one corner, the street has been cut off by a new wall with glass shards on top—is this the start of the ghetto?[28] I will long remember the gesture a man made at the post office, as he pressed his eight-year-old son to his side, because he saw that I had come up behind him. I noticed then for the first time that he was wearing the yellow star.

What will Warsaw look like in ten or fifteen years?

Back in the Thick of Things

June 8, 1940

It's already been almost two days since I left you. It's often distressing to see that the things that one looks forward to are over as quickly as the things one is afraid of. Outside, the wind is sweeping through the wheat. When we arrived, the snow was still deep on the fields. And now the question is whether or not we'll see the wheat harvested? We've already made great leaps to break camp. We've now become a riflemen field replacement company, and so we'll soon be sent off (to the western stage?). If I had known that our days were so numbered, I would have limited my luggage. I'll look to see if I can send one thing or another back home. [. . .]

---

[28] In November of 1939 a section of the city center, largely inhabited by Jews, was closed off. In November of 1940 a ghetto was erected, set apart from the rest of the city by a wall. See *Enzyklopädie des Holocaust*, 1525–49.

The company gave us a warm welcome. We didn't have to do any work today. But supposedly the recruits aren't very inspired or perceptive. These are the cohorts born in 1904 and 1905. I'm curious to see how things will go. There could possibly be a lot of changes. Two of the reserve officer candidates were sent to Siedlec[29] to a school for NCO aspirants as trainers, and so a lot may change.

At least for a long while now I'll be able to cope with things more easily when I think about the memories of our wonderful vacation and in the knowledge that you can deal with our separation, both inwardly and outwardly. [. . .]

Future Worries

June 12, 1940

Now things are back in full swing. It didn't take too much of an effort to get back into things, but especially with this heat we need some strength to get through. I help myself by making the more industrious NCOs do more than is otherwise my nature. That means that especially in the afternoons I can have some time off and can lie down on my bed. The room is comfortable, much quieter [than before]; my three comrades are extremely polite and obliging. Otherwise, the sergeant major has asked me to be the acting platoon leader, for the sake of my training, as he puts it. That's good, because I have to learn how to do it. But I've strained my voice in this dry heat. I think though it will be all right. I went to the dentist and he has started to fill one of my molars.

There are only two topics of conversation among my comrades: the great military and political events and our departure. It seems to me that this is what will happen: a

---

[29] City in the Masovia district.

part of the old reserves will be brought together as a guard company. The other recruits will be taken to a training base where there will be a proper regiment. Whether we'll stay or what else might happen is still up in the air, so we actually don't know anything. Nor does anyone know when things will happen. Now we're supposed to limit our luggage to the absolute minimum. [. . .]

The weather is slowly becoming milder. The evenings are beautiful now, wonderfully clear and colorful. Starting in the morning with work we are getting used to the summer. We wake up at 5:15. We have a lunch break until three. [Added:] I've just learned that those areas in Warsaw that are cut off by walls are those in which the corpses still lie in the basements. Supposedly some 38,000 civilians are still missing in Warsaw, so the number of the dead overall can't be so high. What will become of Paris? [. . .]

More Military Ambition

No date [June 16, 1940]
[. . .] Today we took seven comrades to the train who are being sent to Warsaw to learn how to train troops. I was perhaps the only one who wasn't particularly envious of them, especially because I really appreciate how much it means when one can sit in a pleasant space and have a cup of coffee or a glass of beer without having to stink of sweat or leather. Yesterday during a visit of the first lieutenant some comrades were picked out; this happened after the new division general (the old one was sent to the western front) had decided last Friday that we had too many trainers. So tomorrow my most valuable assistant will be leaving (I had him last week through Sunday). He doesn't have a store by the way, but a workshop in the Berliner Strasse, where he used

194

to do real artisanal gold work mostly for private customers. I'll need to see how I can avoid the afternoon indoor duty, or it will be too much. As it is now, we get up at five and have a ten-minute run in the early morning. We have a three-hour break during the afternoon. But because it's so hot one can only just lie in bed, sleep, or read novels. [. . .]

Our recruits aren't any worse than the earlier ones, although eight days ago people were complaining about them; they are quite convinced that they're far too old and are being treated much too harshly. We may have tightened the reins a bit over the past week—to good effect. My group had the best results in shooting, because I'm showing more of a certain military ambition. Riding went tolerably well, but a lot of water will have to go under the bridge before I can enjoy the "greatest joy on earth." After this group of recruits both of our new sergeant majors (twenty-five years old) are going to go to the officer reserve course. Now generally it looks like our move won't happen any time soon. I'll be pleased if I can get used to things here as a sergeant major in familiar surroundings before I take on new tasks. [. . .]

It's a great opportunity for Franz that he is now right in the middle of things.[30] I'm quite disappointed that we can't get a sense here of the exciting events in the West. It's hard to do them justice when one sees the ferocity of the German attack in the face of which the France of 1789 is completely helpless. Napoleon must have felt the same way when he attacked in the East. Today's news reminds me of Alsace.[31] It's fortunate that everything has happened so quickly and

[30] Franz Petri was active in the German military administration of Belgium and northern France as the head of the university section.

[31] Alsace Lorraine was annexed by the German Empire in 1871 and returned to France in 1919, only to be reannexed in 1940 and returned in 1945.

Training recruits, spring 1940

has been therefore relatively mild (I'm using Franz's term). But the French troops must have been destroyed in streams of blood in the face of the endless attacks of the tanks and Stukas.[32] What a destiny! [. . .]

The French Surrender

June 22, 1940

[. . .] Frau von Tiling gave a lecture in Dresden yesterday, and because she was tired and unprepared she failed miserably. Incidentally, she didn't even mention my article, and now it's almost time to publish the July volume, and I suspect the situation there is just as disastrous or even worse.

[32] German dive bomber.

196

We've been waiting all day for more news of the armistice and its terms. We're concerned to hear that the English [airplanes] have now made it to Berlin. But generally we are all preoccupied with our own personal sorrows and troubles. [. . .]

Flagging Spirits

June 24, 1940

[. . .] We've really taken on too much the past couple of weeks. The result is that the recruits want nothing more than to get away: leaving Kosow is their only solution. Our chief is now suddenly so ill that he can't get out of bed and has to let others dress and undress him. They're talking about having him sent to Warsaw to the infirmary. We can't really even think about work. It's sad that in such moments one can only think: "Hopefully it's not too bad." Then we would be looking forward to a few easier weeks. The mood here is therefore very critical; I spoke about it before. As long as we could justify the fact that the recruits were going into battle (or that we were going with them), the harshness of our training could be justified. But now with the collapse of France, we're asking ourselves: What for? And why am I not home yet? Or at the very least they're thinking about what they can still experience and what kind of "booty" they can collect to take home with them. [. . .]

Lives in the Shadows

June 29, 1940

It's almost midnight. I'm the "officer on duty" and have to review the sentries between 12 and 5. So I'll just stay awake. We had a party this evening, after we had our inspection yesterday and this morning. The regimental commander was there. The whole thing didn't have any real "zip" to it, but

197

it went well enough. There's a backlash in pushing them so hard in that we have to let up ourselves. Now things are quieter. Unfortunately it was stultifyingly hot again today. Fifty more recruits are arriving on the first, and they'll sleep on straw in a newly erected barracks. Two hundred and fifty more are to get here on the 5th of July, so that each trainer will have fifteen to sixteen men. But I'd rather focus on these more innocuous days than worry about how that will work out. The party wasn't particularly enjoyable, because no one had any energy or desire to prepare something, so a funny, but loudmouthed recruit set the tone. At nine I checked as our patrols cleared the streets. Everything in front of our post disappeared, our men in steel helmets with their weapons at their sides fanned out, and the noise from the party drifted out through the half-open door. According to [each] temperament or destiny, we got cheeky or fearful looks. It's a symbol of our times, when life disappears behind the walls and then one lives in apprehension. The Jews and Poles are gossiping about an imminent Russian invasion, but we don't believe them, otherwise I wouldn't write about it. [. . .]

Summer Vacation

July 2, 1940

We're now enjoying our "summer vacation." We don't have too many hours of work. It's possible to straighten things up, read some (military) books, and take a walk in peace. Sunday I went bathing, and yesterday evening I walked with Erich Quade for a long time between the fields and the woods. The night bore down upon us, making the rye damp and heavy. Today I went out a little earlier by myself, to take some photographs. Some comrades have gone off to Warsaw, but I'd rather not give up the quiet, especially since I naturally have to expect all kinds of new challenges. On Sunday we were invited to the dedication of the officers' quarters and had to drink punch (without any seltzer water). It took a lot of effort to stay sober and clear. We've been eating with the officers since Monday; and it's boring and time consuming. And it's difficult to eat one's fill because the officers apparently look down at the food from the field kitchen as just a formality, while meanwhile they let their boys make up the difference on the side. I'm going to have to step up more in my duties even though I still don't know the exact arrangements.

[. . .] It's quite an unexpected and wonderful gift for us that Franz can write with so much inner confidence about the Belgians. It's good that he can help to make sure that things aren't ruined there. Apparently a lot of fighting is going on behind the scenes.[33] The terms of the French armistice make it likely that the result will be advantageous, but meanwhile I read a press commentary in the Warsaw newspaper today that made apparent how much "one" hopes to make sure that tensions remain high toward the French. I hope that Franz can continue to keep writing about such positive impressions, and I especially hope that the civilian administration doesn't take on a different spirit.[34] [. . .]

Departure from Poland?

July 5, 1940

[. . .] We've been in a state of uncertainty for two days because we know that changes are coming but we don't know

---

[33] For the military administration see Wolfram Weber, *Die innere Sicherheit im besetzten Belgien und Nordfrankreich, 1940–1944* (Düsseldorf, 1978).

[34] On June 25, 1940, a civilian administration was established in Brussels that clashed with the military. See Umbreit, "Kontinentalherrschaft," 67ff.

what will happen to us. The only thing that's clear is that our recruits are no longer coming here and that the men of the cohort 1901–07 will be picked out to go serve as guards in the East. Each of us makes up our own private fantasies about what will happen to us. Will we go to the West, or be sent home in the near future? In any case, it looks as if for now the worst is over. I'm a little sad to see our recruit company dissolved like this. We still have sixty men to train here. So the trainers will likely be scattered about. One shouldn't rule out the possibility that one or the other of us older men will be sent to guard duty. No one's volunteered for this.

Please don't send anything for a while—except for the tactical book. I don't have a lot to do and am trying to make up for my lack of military knowledge. We reserve officer candidates aren't often challenged to think about higher, tactical issues because we use all our strength to get through our daily duties. But perhaps that won't be necessary much longer. Today and tomorrow I'll send you five packages of books (the Polish ones). I think that Poland is now over for us. There's a sense of departure in the air. I ask myself how things will turn out, and whether I've used my time wisely. It doesn't look like I'll become a lieutenant now either. [. . .]

No Quick End to the War

July 20, 1940

[. . .] Perhaps the book by Schütz,[35] which I've been reading since my furlough, has helped me to find some inner peace. It's quite rich with pastoral encouragement. [. . .]

---

[35] Paul Schütz, *Das Evangelium. Dem Menschen unserer Zeit* (Berlin, 1939).

We heard the Reichstag speech[36] on the radio yesterday. Now I'm not counting on such a quick end to the war. We don't want to become impatient if we have to wait for each other longer, in case we get stuck here in Poland, or somewhere else. [. . .]

Leaving Kosow

July 23, 1940

It's our last day in Kosow. Tonight I'll be going with one-half of the company via Warsaw to our new destination. [. . .] This has been a valuable period for me, especially because we didn't have any artificial distractions. Now I'm regretting not having learned more Polish. But it wasn't possible with our work.

Over the past few days I've written a few letters regarding the journal. I'm including a page that I'd like you to keep so that you are informed when there are questions. I'm not daring to hope for an early release, especially since the war against England is only now beginning and will actually now spread all across Europe. [. . .]

The Role of the Church

July 30, 1940

Dear Hans-Lothar,

[. . .] If one wants to encapsulate in a formula the way in which the role of the Protestant Church is being transformed today, one will have to say that the churches are

---

[36] Hitler gave a speech in the Reichstag on July 19, 1940, in which he made strong threats against England. Domarus, *Hitler*, 1540–59.

being ultimately confined to their religious tasks by National Socialism. That does not impose anything upon the Lutheran churches against which they would need to resist. Because it belongs to Luther's insights, which he asserted emphatically and fully conscious of its implications, that the world and God's kingdom are two separate areas for our understanding (though they certainly belong together in their final basis, namely in God). [. . .] Today the state, that is, the party, takes away from the churches the quite extensive area of cultural tasks, which had belonged to them hitherto. In the past there were always numerous young people who became clergymen because—aside from a certain religious sensibility—they also were attracted by the political, social, artistic, or scholarly challenges of being a pastor. [. . .]

But all of that is now collapsing rapidly. The war is destroying an immense amount of religious *custom*. Therefore at its end the field is likely to be free for a radical limitation of the church to its religious task. Whoever wants to become a clergyman today should not look for these peripheral areas. In his office, he must be ready to renounce all of them without inner resistance. If I am allowed to speak graphically: With inner freedom—but not without pain and concern for the future of his people—he has to be able to witness how the Magdeburg Cathedral will be turned over to the party, the choir dissolved, and a small flock of the congregation assemble in a private room to hear the Gospel and pray for the church *and the world*. He must possess the inner freedom to bear without protesting that an outside misunderstanding interferes even in that area, which is the true property of the church. [. . .] That is, he must really be able to believe, pray, love, and hope. [. . .]

Reminiscing about Poland

August 2, 1940

[. . .] Much about my life here during these days has been almost ideal. I hope you won't take it the wrong way when I put it so positively; of course the bitter BUT always accompanies my thoughts—I mean the combination of orderly soldierly duty, partly in the open air, and the quiet work on the article on the New Testament during the late afternoon. [. . .]

I got through the party and the trip to Warsaw. I'm even used to all the beer drinking now. In Warsaw we each had too many people to watch over. So it was pretty impersonal and boring. We went to the movies (*A Canned Marriage*[37]) in the best movie theater in Warsaw with modern amenities; but the film was silly. The story took place in a world of luxury and unlimited possibilities, a world that still hasn't disappeared from the movies. The newsreel that preceded it was also disappointing. But I guess I just had bad luck. [. . .]

An Idyllic Life in Germany

August 9, 1940

I can imagine that you're waiting for news. But take it as a sign that I'm doing *very well* that I'm writing only now. If I were to wait to tell you everything that's happened, then I wouldn't be finished until tomorrow. And this letter needs to go off to the train. So I'll begin with the most recent events. We're here near Ibbenbüren, quite a few kilometers away from the Dutch border. The border train station, Oldenzaal, is located a good fifty kilometers away from our train station. We're spread out

---

[37] *Ehe in Dosen*, a comedy about a divorce by Johannes Meyer, Germany, 1939.

all over the place, housed in private quarters. I'm living with Arno Wildt together with the managing director of a small coal mine. At the moment we're sleeping in a small house somewhat off to the side of the manor, but if we stay any longer we're to move over there. At noon we eat down in the village at the field kitchen. But usually we pass on our victuals and eat our meals with the landlord and his wife at a table set with linens in a wonderful setting. They are a married couple without children who live here near the mine in an enchanting villa with a lovely garden. Everything is so clean it shines. The lady is pleased that she can have company to relieve her loneliness (she is almost fifty and quite harmless, a real housewife). Her husband is intelligent and competent. [. . .]

I'll just describe for you what we did yesterday. Then you'll see how wonderfully we're doing. All right: first, we slept until nine, then had breakfast at a well-laid table, with eggs, butter, and tomatoes. Then we descended from our mountaintop and went down to have lunch at the centrally located restaurant where we had roll call, drank a few glasses of beer and some schnapps. Then we took a nap and had a little trip in our landlord's automobile over to the Weser canal, and on the way we had beer, schnapps, bread and butter with two eggs. Then we conversed in the garden, ate dinner (potato salad with eggs and ham), took a short walk, and listened to the evening news. Don't laugh! It's quite amazing to be able to experience German life in its wonderful security and variety after our time in Poland. [. . .] We could spend a few good weeks of quiet here.

But what is to become of us? I'll write openly, as I always have, about what First Lieutenant Sachse told me. They're going to make guard companies for France from the rest of the division. The preparations are to be finished in a few days. But you know how such things are always changing. Today there's an officers' meeting at the regiment. Perhaps we'll learn more then. Just one more thing: it's not so bad with the English planes. Last night there was nothing. I mean there *was* an alarm, but we slept through it. We saw quite a lot of flak fire off in the distance. A few bombs have landed here and the destruction is evident. But it's nothing drastic. You needn't worry. I'm writing that quite openly because if you look at a map you'll think: "They're right in the middle of the English flight path." So it's better that I just tell you exactly how things are. [. . .]

Like a Vacation

August 11, 1940

It's Sunday morning. [. . .] We slept in again and had a good breakfast. Now our spirits are so relaxed that it takes a bit of a push to start moving again. And I have so much to thank you for—your two letters; [. . .] and especially all the work you did. I'm sorry that my article arrived just when you had so many other things to do. But I'm pleased that you're fine with it. I'm looking forward to seeing the July–August issue [of the journal]. If we stay here I'm going to have to exert myself if I want to get anywhere with the essay. It's hard to get out of vacation mode. We eat, sleep, sit in the garden with our landlords and tell stories, take short walks, and go over to the restaurant twice a day for roll call. [. . .]

A Visit in Dünne[38]

August 19, 1940

My Sunday leave is over. I had two very fulfilling days, and I'm especially pleased that things went well on a personal

---

[38] Protestant religious community in Westphalia.

level. Stork's wife is always very nice, and I could speak with him freely and openly, when we didn't talk about those theological questions that divide us. He talked a lot about the church and theology. He readily answered all of my questions. We're actually very close in our assessment of things. Proof of that is the Luther paper you received recently, which was what had moved me to go to D[ünne] in the first place. Our different assessments about what has been preserved of theology shouldn't lead to an outright break, even if the collaboration of the Dünne people will be further limited to the occasional article in our journal. [. . .] Stork asked me if I was interested in his position at Dahlem. I said no. The reason: it's just a camp counselor job. I think in the long term it would be difficult to do any theological-literary work there. But I wanted to write you that and ask your opinion. Overall I had once again the feeling that I am making my own way rather isolated from others, especially when I heard of the individual and professional relationships people at Dünne enjoy. I heard about lectures, visits, working groups, talks with famous contemporaries. That seems to be one of the prerequisites required to do intellectual work. Perhaps the fact that our journal is in decline is due really about 90 percent to a lack of that kind energy. By the way, the July–August issue is very pleasing. Have you seen it yet? [. . .]

No decisions have been made yet about our future. I would have gladly waited for news before I come over to Magdeburg on a long weekend, which is possible in theory. At the moment all of us are quite unsettled inside. But perhaps one could speak with the chief once to see if he can do without me, say, on the first of January. Politically tension is very high. Will the offensive succeed? What will the United States do? [. . .]

Furlough from September to the beginning of October 1940

Not Really Needed

October 10, 1940

I've been away from you now for twenty-four hours and have the first hurdle behind me. I knew from the start that it wouldn't be easy. That's why I was so low yesterday and so numb that I could hardly say anything. [. . .] I didn't have any problems during the trip and found a bus that got at least close to the base. Night had fallen when we arrived in Bernburg. I was sent hither and yon until I could find an empty room in which I could spend the night. [. . .] In terms of my duties, things look familiar; I actually won't be needed. I've been assigned to a platoon leader, a sergeant major who has twenty-one years of service, so I'll likely just trot along beside him. That has the advantage that I can see how things are run without having to try too hard otherwise. The young recruits are here, the sergeant and the NCOs are so young, around twenty-five to thirty, and they've had active duty and done training. I really don't understand what I'm supposed to be doing here. If there had been any sort of purpose then it could only have been that I would "learn more." But perhaps everything happens just by chance; if so, that's rather ironic. Therefore I have to keep sitting down and memorizing things by heart so that I can tell the recruits word for word what is expected of them here. We've eaten lunch and dinner twice at the officers' quarters; the base is new and is nicely situated at the edge of the city. The large, high-lying Bernburg castle can be glimpsed off to the distance over the trees. But Bernburg also has a lot of factories: Junkers and the Solvay Soda works are here; the place is overrun and supposedly there's nothing to buy. [. . .]

207

Forgotten Paperwork

October 12, 1940

A beautiful, peaceful Sunday evening has arrived, and I wanted to send you at least a short greeting, even if it doesn't get to you on a Sunday. I had hoped to get out of the building at least once this afternoon, but there was nothing for it. I was tied up until 6:45. The plan of duty for tomorrow doesn't look any different than in Kosow. Church services are in the morning here, and they're announced in the old manner: "There's no pressure; free-thinkers can stay away from service and get cold feet." Here too we have to take our group out in the afternoon. Things are starting to settle down in terms of my duties. I'm the one who is called out when someone is needed, but I don't have a clear sense of responsibility. I really have to approach the whole thing as a new training period (how many does that make?). If one dispenses with anything "personal" then things will work, and one can report with pride that one served in an "active" regiment. The recruits are to be seen and treated from the point of view that they must serve their two years. There's a lot of bawling out, often rightly so, but it seems that people spend far too much time on mere formalities. For instance, we accomplished at least as much in our old manner of cleaning for inspection. [. . .]

It's a shame that I didn't manage to send the paperwork in. They don't want it here. I'm supposed to submit it directly. The only other possibility is that you'll have to make a sacrifice and venture into the male-dominated world of the Augusta street.[39] Because I really don't want to let the

---

[39] The Augustastrasse housed the local garrison administration for Magdeburg. Thanks to the state archive Saxony-Anhalt for the information.

documents leave my hands. You would have to ask that they check proof of my Aryan descent right away by examining the paperwork, so that you can take the records with you.[40] I think they'll do everything with the proper courtesy. Please wear something nice, so that they will strike the right tone right off. I'll try to send the paperwork to you via registered mail as soon as possible. But it might be days before I can find a chance to do so. It would be best if you could go there at around 10; then it will be less busy than it might be at 9. Room 40. Division for reserve officer candidates. [. . .]

Don't take the whole thing here too seriously. I'll be able to stand it for a few months. But then I'll be ten years younger and 100 percent fitter. Then I'll feel ready to take on anything, or I may want only to have some peace and quiet. So let's wait to see what happens at Christmas. [. . .]

Bureaucracies

October 14, 1940

[. . .] It seems to me that a lot more time and energy is spent here oiling the machinery. In Kosow, all of our time was filled, up to the last second. We spend so much time here with roll call, hunting here and there, complaining, threatening. There's always somebody yelling somewhere on base. If we have duty at the compound, we spend two hours marching there and back. We actually had to drill for only three hours today. I think what will be stressful in the long run is the whole bureaucracy. Having to salute, report, stand at attention, keep one's eyes open for the major or the captain, worry about one's uniform, etc. I have picked up a few

---

[40] Proof of Aryan descent was required for officers, according to paragraph 15 of the military law. See Absolon, *Personalwesen*, 20.

threads of human contact. Luckily my servant is a bright, honest man. [. . .]

I sent the documents to you this afternoon. Unfortunately, the major saw me in the city as I was there. He asked me at noon pretty sharply, "Were you at the dentist or were you on leave?" But my answer obviously appeased him, because afterward he favored me by handing me the soup terrine directly. Earlier I would have been more upset about that than now. I think that I've been outwardly too nonchalant the last few days. I should have shown more enthusiasm and firmness. But I just don't care anymore. Today one of the platoon leaders told me I should try to get my own platoon; he would like to leave. But I don't do it; instead I listen and learn until the right moment comes. Even if that means (which is surely possible) that my promotion is being held up because of it. Do you think that you could just go to the recruiting office [. . .] and innocently ask the sergeant how things will go from here? I think that you can do it better than I. What I want to know is whether the decision lies with the troop where I'm at, or if the decision was made by my earlier regiment and can only be delayed if they want me to prove myself as a platoon leader. But I am trying not to take things too seriously, because it would be good if I became more familiar with garrison life. On the other hand, I could relax if I were released from this bureaucratic red tape. [. . .]

Endless Sacrifices

October 16, 1940

[. . .] Eight days have passed since I arrived, and I must admit, thing are going better than I thought they would at first. [. . .] The young trainers have their weaknesses—they're immature and lack experience; I'll be able to get used to garrison life. Every now and then I make a mistake. But one can learn. Yesterday and today I basically stood in for a platoon leader who wasn't here. Yesterday we even rode—over plowed-up fields and through the park along the Saale—but not for very long. We stopped for a bite to eat. Nonetheless, it was beautiful, and I didn't have any trouble keeping up with the others. So it's good that I took those lessons. If only you didn't have to suffer because of my continued absence! I often ask myself if there will come a time when things will be different, when we won't be asked to make sacrifices for one thing or another.

The other reserve officer candidates were full of the endless tasks that lie ahead as well as of their trust in the Führer, just like Korth.[41] [. . .] The [air raid] alarms every night cost so much energy because I have to still supervise [the recruits]. Everyone else is asleep on straw sacks on the floor of the cellar; no one speaks a word. I need to make sure that I can get some sleep. [. . .]

Feeling like Soldiers

[October 27, 1940]

I don't want to write you a long letter on this Sunday evening. I hope that we'll see each other in a week. Then we'll be able to talk about a lot of things. I just want to thank you for your Sunday greetings and tell you that I thought about you again today. I went with the "Christians" to a café. We were all tired, but we could say some important things with open hearts. They've taken me into their circle without

[41] Dr. Konrad Korth from Stolp, a colleague who worked on the Tiling Festschrift.

reservation. This morning we four were at church with the same pastor who had made such a horrid brew of German-Christian songs last Sunday—he is a former member of the BK (Confessing Church) who is only tolerated because of the war! We listened to a warm, serious sermon about the false servant. After we ate I set out immediately with thirty recruits; the others had visitors. We took a lovely autumn walk along the misty Saale for an hour, and I listened to some very strange life stories. Then, somewhat tired, we had beer and schnapps at the same café where last Sunday we had coffee and cake. At the very end everything got less strained, and on the way back they were really in high spirits and felt like soldiers. Then I sat quietly in my room and read. [. . .] It's depressing to see how the older ones among them struggle with the question of what this "duty" actually means for their lives, and whether one can account for it when there are so many other "important" things to do. No one is completely satisfied, neither the pious ones nor the worldly ones. [. . .]

An Accident

October 31, 1940

Unfortunately I am going to have to disappoint you once again: I can't come. I had a slight accident yesterday (Wednesday). While we were training inside I fell down an open staircase and have a slight contusion on my right knee. I'm to stay in bed with cold compresses for three days. It's not bad, and you shouldn't worry. I even went into the city yesterday to visit Pastor Kluge from the castle (we were invited to dinner). Unfortunately there's still no news about the training course. [. . .]

Waiting for a Diagnosis

November 7, 1940

I'm sitting here in the reception area of an infirmary in Wernigerode and am waiting for the X-rays they're going to take of my knee. I was examined yesterday in Ilsenburg by the troop doctor and today by an expert. Without an X-ray it's difficult to say anything definitive. The knee has felt a little bit better every day, but it still hadn't healed, and so I wanted to go see a doctor. That means that I'll miss a few days of training, but if the X-rays come back clear, I hope to be able to stick with it. It was very difficult for me to have to sacrifice the chance of becoming involved in a meaningful military activity. But it would have been worse to have a permanent injury in my knee. I've spent so much time yesterday and today waiting. This morning I experienced daybreak on the streets of Wernigerode and so enjoyed myself; on Tuesday I watched evening fall as I took a walk along the Ilse valley. [. . .]

Recuperating

November 22, 1940

The X-rays and bandages are behind me now and I can see a little bit how things work here overall. I should actually say how things work case by case, because in regard to the big picture I don't have any news. I have no idea how long I'll stay here. [. . .] It's certainly much prettier here than in Bernburg. There aren't any serious air raids, so we don't have to worry about that. The food is good. I read during the day, as before. The nights are long. Lights out at 9:30 at the latest, and no one can sleep. [. . .]

213

Recovery Is Slow

December 10, [1940]
You'll be waiting for news, but can also imagine why you haven't received any—everything is just moving forward slowly. Today all of the doctors were here. The result: they'll remove the splint. I'm to see how the knee is slowly and carefully. It's thus certainly possible that they won't need to operate and that I'll spend Christmas neither in Magdeburg nor in Wernigerode but in Bernburg. I took a bath yesterday and went down to the basement to do so, naturally without a bandage. The knee is stiff from my having been in bed so long. But that doesn't mean anything. However, there's nothing definitive to report today. [. . .] The splint is gone now, and I'm bending my knee as I lie in bed. I hope I'm on the mend. [. . .]

Infirmary Blues

[December 15, 1940]
It's Sunday. The house is quiet. Anyone who could do so has gone out on crutches. Two of my comrades have done so. The third one is lying in bed with a fever from a throat infection. Outside, what was a beautiful sunny day has now turned dreary and gray. I wrote a few letters. I can't really concentrate on my reading. I don't know if that is a Sunday afternoon feeling or if lying around inside is slowly making me tired and empty-headed. And I had received some missionary literature from Frau Privy Councilor [Schmidt] and something arrived from Holtermann as well. Please don't send me anything trivial. If I read here, I want to concentrate on what is necessary for the military and on my Greek, so that I don't feel that I'm wasting my time. That's why I'm continuing to write down excerpts and take notes. I've read almost all of Sophocles now

214

and I'm starting with Euripides; it's strange and fascinating. I read Greek again as I reviewed the Platonic dialogues that deal with the death of Socrates. Yesterday evening I read Dehn's *Speaking about Death*.[42] It's impressive to see how an entire worldview could grow out of the death of Socrates—the immortality of the soul that belongs to the same realm as spiritual values. This really emerges in the Platonic dialogues. [. . .] So this time of forced rest hasn't been entirely fruitless; but it certainly has reawakened my desire to talk with others, and with young people, about these ideas. The image of the Socratic students in the Phaidon is so tempting seen from my intellectual isolation. [. . .]

Plans for Christmas

[December 17, 1940]

[. . .] I still don't know if I'm going to be operated on or not, but I have the impression that the head doctor doesn't think it's necessary. If possible, don't tie yourself to plans to spend Christmas here. If I have to stay in bed, you would quickly find a longer stay here rather unedifying. There's supposed to be leave only in very special situations. But if I'm released here, I could get furloughed from my squad. We're celebrating Christmas here on Friday; I'm to read a small piece from Dwinger, in which Christ makes an appearance. [. . .]

Christmas Draws Near

December 19, 1940

Today the head doctor came and examined my knee carefully. The findings are almost normal; I can bend my knee

---

[42] Fritz Dehn, *Das Gespräch vom Tode* (1938).

and move it; the swelling is gone. I'm to get up and walk with my leg bent. I asked again about surgery, and he said again there is no 100 percent guarantee it would work; he knows of people who can do very heavy labor with a knee that hasn't been operated on. In this regard I trust him completely.

Today Frau Haek[43] sent someone to ask me if you were coming. I said you would arrive on the 26th. She's to prepare a room for you. Please write. If you got a Plato book from the library, then please send it.

Christmas is getting closer. How did you celebrate at the Alumnat? How are you doing? Are you coming? [. . .]

Celebration

December 20, 1940
Downstairs our Christmas celebration is coming to an end. I came up because it was too loud and smoky for me down there. The first part, as you can see from the program, was very Christian. The superintendent spoke (but for too long and he was boring). That meant I didn't do my reading. [. . .]

His wife's visit over Christmas

Imminent Release

January 3, 1941
This is your first evening back at home. I hope you didn't get stuck in the snow. It wasn't too cold though. I hope you got to Magdeburg safe and sound. It's good that you have some quiet before the boys return. [. . .] They examined me for release today. My chart notes that I still have some slight pain

---

[43] Local landlady.

that grows after I've been walking and that the knee is not completely healed. I'll get my suitcase on Monday and then depart on Tuesday. [. . .]

Sick leave January 1941

Religious Dilemmas

January 13, 1941

Dear Dr. [von Tiling]

I feel the need to thank you once again explicitly for your essay[44] after I have been resting for a fortnight at home. I have been ruminating a great deal about the task of carrying the weight of the modern distance from God for others, about which you speak in the second part, and I react like your interlocutor: I shudder from it, but I have to concede that you are right. The liberating aspect that nonetheless accompanies this is that you have succeeded in making plain the entire worrying and caring for our time as a task of faith. This view reveals our distance from both "fronts," which we have always maintained: against the [Nazi] opportunists and against those content in their Christianity. But such a path is only possible in a double radicalism: Only when the search for understanding tries to penetrate to the final end will it succeed in revealing the reality in which we live today, and only if faith is complete can it be supported by God, because that quest for knowledge is not, as your essay explains, an intellectual process. That was probably the fault of the nineteenth century, which persists in the ideological efforts of all

---

[44] Magdalene von Tiling, "Das Evangelium in unserer Zeit," *Unterweisung und Glaube* (January/February 1941): 100–109.

217

camps, even the pseudo-Christian one. But here it is rather a matter of dedicating one's life to this world. [. . .]

Are there people who will heed this call? It seems to me that you have ultimately posed the question of the purpose of our entire work. While perusing the last journal issues on pastoral theology or the young church during this leave, I have encountered a lot of activity in the area of applied theology. [. . .] Everywhere the spirit seems to be the same: that Pietism of the Confessing Church, which draws on the aftereffects of [Karl] Barth and works with great earnestness, but knows nothing of the ultimate needs of our time. You write that I ought to criticize this thoughtlessness. That I cannot do, because I don't have the personal insight into it. But if one really wanted to help in this situation, one would only be able to do it on the basis that you have indicated, in sharpest opposition against the subjectively earnest sloth. I don't think that one can wait any longer, because it seems possible that the war will drag on, continuing the suspended state in which we live for a long time. [. . .]

Back in the Swing of Things

February 3, 1941

Now I'm back in the swing of things. I've already taken over a platoon of the old recruits and had duty outside Sunday and this morning, and didn't feel anything in my knee. [. . .]

What do you think about my trip to Berlin?[45] Unfortunately, we have duty next weekend, so I can't get away next Sunday. You'll have to wait fourteen more days. But mother was so happy that I don't regret it. Yesterday as I was leaving she said, "It was a holiday, and an unexpected one." Of

[45] Apparently he had just visited his mother there.

course she went to all kinds of trouble to make me comfortable. On Saturday evening after a nice bath we both went to bed early and slept until 8:30, without being awakened by the cold. So it wasn't even all that tiring. But I did arrive with the late train and only got to the base at two in the morning. [. . .] Things are already pretty hectic. [. . .]

Failings as a Soldier

February 8, 1941

The peace of the weekend is upon us. [. . .] The training is much more intense than it was in October, because the battalion commander is now interested in it and was there for an hour yesterday. Most of the time we have to ride without stirrups, even when galloping or jumping. One can learn a lot, but it's exhausting. Today nine new recruits arrived, but I won't have anything to do with them. I'll stay in charge of the platoon with those who came in December. We still haven't received orders about their departure. Today the company commander told me that my voice isn't loud enough and my commands aren't energetic. That doesn't surprise me. But I can hardly change that. So I think it will be a while before I'm promoted. I've gotten used to the casino because I threw some dice and drank some schnapps. I don't know how I should behave in the future. There's hardly any other opportunity to break out of one's "social" isolation and one slowly dies in it. But the alcohol does make one horribly tired the next day. [. . .]

Reinjured

February 10, 1941

[. . .] My knee is slightly injured again, after all the marching, riding, running about on Saturday, and too little sleep. I'm sad, because work—caring for others and working on their behalf—makes me happy. But I'm not going to worry. If I can't do it, then I'm going to call in sick. It's been a difficult start; I have to write a lot in my free time and prepare for the next day, because I'm unfamiliar with a lot of things. In a fortnight things should be a lot easier. I hope I can hang on until then. Please keep your Sunday free, unless you have personal obligations. I need it to rest.

This evening, our company's new lieutenant—an East Prussian estate owner—called twice to tell me I should come into the city. But I can't, I need to take care of my knee and prepare for tomorrow. [. . .]

The Demands Are Great

[February 16, 1941]

Dear Franz,

It's almost your birthday again, and it's unlikely you'll get to celebrate it at home. [. . .] I remember very distinctly a few seminar discussions we had almost twenty years ago about the relationship between historians and political actions. Now you're in the middle of politics. You're surrounded by the air of great events and difficult decisions. I know you well enough to know that you'll be able to look beyond the small irritations and see the big picture. I hope that you'll be successful in bringing the "Nether Lands" back into to the empire, even if it's only in small steps at the beginning. I can imagine that this current task will provide you with the will and the strength to look in quieter times back to those decisive moments in history that have provided the foundation for past greatness and ruin as well as background for today's challenges. I would be more at peace if I knew that these tasks could be restricted to the Central European

Officer candidate, spring 1941

space. I think that everything is pointing to the moment when our destiny will carry us further out into the flood of world politics. I have a difficult time thinking on such a scale. I hope we don't overreach. In any case, it means that there will be no foreseeable end to this war. Overall we see

221

signs that we are to redouble our efforts. Our own personal destiny won't remain unaffected by these developments. I hope that you can remain in the work that is appropriate to you.

I'm writing you this letter at my own desk—I have Sunday leave. Lotte has carved out a quiet day and is taking good care of me. I'm enjoying it, because my work as a platoon leader, in which I have to go out in the wet and the cold and interact with very different kinds of people, is really taking it out of me. My promotion has been put off further, because of course for the demands of the replacement army I lack the soldierly vigor I would need for hurrying things along. I'm going my own way in peace and quiet and am trying to do justice to the demands as far as I can, without trying to achieve the impossible. [. . .]

A Decision

[Postmark: March 7, 1941]
Perhaps you'll receive this Sunday greeting, as I've just received a letter from you. We've just lost a part of our platoon, quite suddenly. Sergeant Leuchte as well. I'll have to step in today and tomorrow with the others (a night march) and I won't have any quiet at all on Sunday. My knee is all right. That's always a reason to be thankful. I have enough to eat. But I've gone through my socks. Please send me some. [. . .] I think I will go ahead and write Franz my acceptance.[46] I've been looking at the whole thing too narrowly. I'm not sure if (1) the academy will take me, (2) whether the military will

---

[46] Apparently his brother-in-law was trying to obtain a research position for him at the Academy of Sciences.

agree, and (3) whether the school authorities will let me go. One can try and see what will happen. [. . .]

Waiting for Approval

April 2, 1941

The week is almost half over; that was easier than I had thought it would be. Yesterday I handed over the second platoon to a newly promoted twenty-seven-year-old sergeant; I'm supposed to make an inventory of the armory and will start on Friday with the new recruits we're expecting. [. . .] But at least I've finished my work, written a few letters. I wrote Lohrisch and told him about how things stand, in case a request arrives.[47] If he wants to do something about my exemption for the school, then he can. I'll talk with the captain about it tomorrow. I'm just waiting to hear about being sent to the Landesschützen. Probably they would be more likely to release me there, so I would have to ask to be transferred immediately. But that can't happen without approval of the squadron leader and the battalion commander. [. . .]

A New Balkan Front

Palm Sunday [April 6], 1941

Because the previous officer selection is now finally over, everything has to be turned in [for my exemption]. Please look up Boether-Schulze's address and bring it with you. Please have the enclosed card notarized and send it off.

---

[47] Hermann Lohrisch (1882–1951), director of the Cathedral School in Magdeburg. *Vereinigtes Dom- und Klostergymnasium Magdeburg, 1675–1950. Gedenkschrift*, 165.

[. . .] Tomorrow [. . .] I'll go over to the new recruits, some of whom don't understand a word of German. We're all still reeling from the day's events. This afternoon in the casino we heard the explanations and appeals, with somewhat ambivalent feelings in regard to the legal justification, although no one can doubt the military necessity.[48] Now suddenly all the administrators have been transferred. Who knows if the wave will wash over us some day. That makes it even better that we can still be together. [. . .]

Always a Disappointment

April 21, 1941

And now you should get a note from me. You've thought of me so faithfully, and it does me good every time. Even if you write that you're going to give me a good scolding I'm not afraid. I don't intend to play the self-confident husband. At the moment I'm all too aware of how much I owe everyone—the recruits, my comrades in the casino, friends and relatives, and not least of all, you. Easter made this very clear to me, especially in terms of my private affairs, and the week thereafter made it apparent in terms of my work. But I just can't find the strength any more. There's nothing particular that I should show the doctor. Otherwise I would have already seen him. [. . .]

German Lessons

May 2 [1941]

[. . .] Things are a lot easier now thanks to the largesse of our current commander. [. . .]

---

[48] On April 6, 1941, Germany attacked Yugoslavia and Greece.

I have a request. The company commander asked me to give a lesson in which the Polish recruits and the comrades can be shown how they are ethnic Germans.[49] So [I need] something about the German migration into Upper Silesia, the Teschen area, something about the language. Could you write to your Silesian colleagues and ask for some materials? We're trying to overcome their feelings of inferiority and convince the comrades they shouldn't feel superior. Starting next week they'll get regular German and math lessons. . . . [. . .]

An End to This Kind of Work

[May 24, 1941]

I'm sitting alone on the terrace of the mountain hotel "Ziegenkopf." It's evening. The day is ending in grays and blues. The bright green leaves of the beech trees are growing dull. I spent all afternoon alone in the forest with a book. It was a welcome relief after the stress of the past few days. We now wake up at 4:30 or 4:45 a.m. We work until 6:15 p.m. After I drew the ire of the regimental commander today with my platoon on the parade grounds, I really do want to put an end to this kind of work, even though I'll miss the opportunity to teach. I'll write tonight to Lohrisch and Hermann.[50] If I can't get an exemption, I'll try to get transferred. We left on a march yesterday at 5:30 a.m., and went fifteen kilometers into the Rappbode valley; we picked up branches during the day and then after another fifteen kilometers we

---

[49] About 200,000 Poles served in the army as "ethnic Germans." See Jerzy Kochanowski, "Polen in die Wehrmacht? Zu einem wenig erforschten Aspekt der nationalsozialistischen Besatzungspolitik," *Forum für osteuropäische Ideen- und Geistesgeschichte* 6 (2002): 59–81.

[50] Hermann is probably Gertrud's brother; as an old party member he had contacts in the NSDAP.

were back at 7 p.m. That's too much for me. It doesn't make any sense to grit my teeth and get through it, because any possible solution would take weeks. I'm looking forward to being together with you, even if the hours get shorter every time. I would like to enjoy the evenings with the freedom of someone who has completed his work and can therefore be doubly grateful for his blessings. [. . .]

Leaving Blankenburg

June 3, 1941

I left Blankenburg with a heavy heart. There's no reason to keep that a secret. I knew that I would face new tasks and troubles, the meaning of which (despite all the lovely words) is difficult to discern for my life. I especially felt that I had to enter a new phase of loneliness just when new experiences could have forged ties with others. Your openness for all things living during these last days of Pentecost, and the way in which you look to the future, have meant a lot to me. I've often asked myself why my attempts to find the right path, just as in Bernburg, often lead to more difficulties. I can only guess. I suppose it is because in everything—both earthly and heavenly—our desires never end. "For I am a stranger with you, an alien, as all my fathers were" [Psalms 39:13]— that was the text of my grandfather's funeral oration, as well as my father's, and one day it will be my own.

The Blankenburg days were filled with such brilliance, such perfume and bird song. Seriousness and stress would have returned, and so I don't want to complain, but give thanks. My trip (as usual) didn't bring any human contact. I was likely too tired and withdrawn. But during the long hours of tense sitting, in which one had to maintain one's posture, I encountered some unexpected and beautiful vistas and inner joy. [. . .]

Arrival in Amiens[51]

June 5, 1941

My first evening in Amiens. [. . .] I visited the office and introduced myself to the officers. I was then shown my room and I unpacked a bit, and I slept a few hours. In the afternoon I went to the orderly room and got an overview of my tasks. When one has settled in it's a quiet enough existence; 8:30 to 12 and 2:15 to 6; paperwork. Every once in a while an hour for exercise or drill. In between, many private conversations, letter writing; people coming and going. I don't know how long it will take me to know enough so that my predecessor can leave. Only now is it becoming clear to me how easy many people have had it the whole time. But that hardly makes me happy. This has little to do with being a soldier. I'm thus constantly thinking about the exemption. If a request came soon, then they would curse and let me go. If it takes longer, they might keep me here. Besides being separated from you, it wouldn't be all that bad. [. . .] My room is quite nice. It's in a pleasant, clean home with a private bath and maids. [. . .] Madame is in Paris, but is coming back today and she speaks some German. Up until now I haven't been able to make myself understood. [. . .]

French Impressions

June 7, 1941

Outside a thunderstorm has unleashed a downpour. Our street, which descends into the old city center, is flooded with water. It's nice to be able to sit in comfort in one's room

---

[51] City in northern France in the department of the Somme.

without having to go out. Just now, after a roll call, I took a short walk through the half-destroyed streets on the lookout for a bookstore. I wanted to get you something, like I did last year in Warsaw, since I can't be there with you on your birthday. You should expect a small birthday package in the mail. [. . .] We have ample rations. [. . .]

Except for the cathedral, the city has little to offer. The city center is partially destroyed, but it likely only possessed the character of an average provincial town. [. . .] The house where I'm staying is respectable and clean. [. . .]

The one downside is my work. I don't see how I can learn all the regulations in such a short amount of time and said so today to the adjutant quite openly. It was ridiculous to send me here.[52] [. . .]

The Journal Ceases Publication

June 17, 1941

Dear Frau Doktor [von Tiling],

I received the May edition today, which makes it is clear that the journal needs to stop publication. I'm not indifferent to its fate, especially when I see how the others are flooded with illustrated magazines and the most inane novels. But perhaps we should look on the bright side. You'll be pleased that this burden will be taken from you. And overall it's good to take a short break and start anew, should it be necessary and possible after the war. Personally I'm sad that my hands are tied and that I don't have the chance to prepare anything. But perhaps I'm just impatient and unwilling to learn and do that which there is to learn and do. I'm not sure what the near future holds for me. At the moment I'm lying in the infirmary

[52] Konrad Jarausch was therefore sent back to his previous unit.

after a small but necessary operation on my feet. I hope the question of my exemption is settled soon. Otherwise I'll have to look for other work, because our training of the reserve battalions is more closely linked to active duty. That has its benefits in comparison to the other field and reserve units, but it takes a lot of strength, and I'm too tired at the moment to find the energy. My brief introduction to life in France ten days ago was extremely helpful. It's sad to see a defeated people living among the ruins of their nation. I'm actually happy to be away from that atmosphere, which was marked by a sense of dissatisfaction regarding unrealized possibilities. [. . .]

Attempts to Get an Exemption

June 18, 1941

Thank you for the efforts you've made on my behalf. I'm sure it cost a lot of energy to wait everywhere and then to carry out such difficult conversations. Thank you as well for reporting everything so faithfully. Your letter arrived today with the first card this morning, just as I was sent out of the infirmary. I was disappointed by its contents in that I was really counting on an exemption and didn't have any doubts that it would be granted. I'm not imagining things when I have to acknowledge that H.[53] doesn't want me. But now the holidays are before us, and it may be that things are running slowly in the provinces. At least it's good to have some clarity in regard to this.

Of course I'll send Hermann the address he asked for, but I won't put too much stock in his letter. There as well it needs to be acknowledged that Riedel didn't do anything because he thinks it's hopeless. If I wanted to try something, I could go to the reserves and attempt to get posted somewhere else.

---

[53] Possibly a reference to the first name of the director of his school.

That would only be possible if the war lasted long enough. It's useless to stay here without the prospect of an imminent release. I can't be promoted. And the demands are just too great. The company is going to march to the Brocken[54] tomorrow, stay there Friday and return on Saturday in the evening. That's how things go, week in and week out. I'd like to ask you to go visit Frau B[oether]-Sch[ulze]. But please don't emphasize the question of whether something can be done about the decisions regarding officers (it's also getting far too late; the cut took place almost eight weeks ago!). Perhaps you could ask her for advice about whether I could find a job more suited to me. Maybe she could give you her husband's exact address. Then I might be able to use the time productively until I'm fully healthy again. [. . .]

I've had about enough of all this talk about intellectual activity, because no one has ever really offered me a chance to do it. The journal is going to stop publication. You've probably already seen that. [. . .]

Feeling Overwhelmed

June 21, 1941

[. . .] I just wrote B[oether]-Sch[ulze] but emphasized my future deployment. Because (1) I don't think they'll cancel the cut, especially judging by what Riedel thinks, and (2) I don't want to have to start over here again with the same old song and officer training. The only thing that would help would be an immediate promotion and a transfer to the reserves. But that's impossible.

The company marched seventy-two kilometers to the Brocken and back, starting Thursday evening at 9 p.m. and

[54] Biggest mountain of the Harz range in central Germany.

returning Friday at 8:30 p.m. The NCOs here with me slept for two hours up there. And it was beastly hot. Today and tomorrow they'll likely have free. But if on top of such efforts I had to go riding, eat at the casino, etc., my life would be pure misery. In addition, rumor has it that the regiment will march to Altengrabow to be trained on the parade grounds there. There are limits to my perseverance! I know how it felt to be out in the heat last summer in Kosow, and I have no desire to experience it again unless it's absolutely necessary. I don't think things will end any differently than the talk with Hermann, who was all enthusiastic and then did nothing. [. . .]

The Invasion of the USSR

June 22, 1941

As 10 p.m. I heard a repeat broadcast of the Führer's announcement [regarding the invasion of Russia].[55] What solemn news, and how amazing it is to hear of the real state of things after so much official silence. I've been thinking quite deliberately and without any nervousness about whether or not it would be best for you to prepare for a longer absence from Magdeburg. I'm not sure it would be good for you to return at the beginning or middle of August, even if we weren't trying to be pessimistic. I'd like to ask you to do the following: (1) take the important papers, including your savings book, with you to Wernigerode; (2) can you take a suitcase with the silver (and some laundry) to Prof. Meyers or to the Schulze's? (3) ask in any case how you can access our money from afar.

I think that all my worries about my future in the military are now superfluous. One will have to do what one is ordered to do. But don't fear. Keep yourself free from all trouble. Pray and

[55] See Domarus, *Hitler*, vol. 4, 1726–32. Plans for the invasion were top secret.

read the psalms and the songs so that you can prepare yourself for your coming tasks [of having a baby]. Don't be overcome by worry or sorrow. If Bruno and mother come to Wernigerode, they'll help you in all things, if I shouldn't be here any longer. But at the moment I'm not ready to get my marching orders yet. Perhaps we'll have to train the last reserves. [. . .]

Personal Matters Are Unimportant

June 23, 1941

Dear Franz,

It's high time I wrote to you. You know all about my experiences from Lotte. You'll understand that I often don't feel like writing. My lack of outer success is stultifying, especially when it's not clear to me what I should do. I have some quiet now that I've returned from my failed attempt in Amiens. I had to have my nails removed on my two big toes and have been in bed ever since. I am on my feet now but am still off duty. Lotte has tried to intercede for me personally in Magdeburg. I don't think there's any chance for me to become an officer, and I don't want to be one, if I have to start here once more as a trainer. It's too demanding physically—one could make the effort if things were serious, but it's hard to do so at the garrison. I think that once I can move, I'll be sent from here to the reserves. [. . .]

But enough of such things. Personal matters have become unimportant again in any case. We weren't surprised by yesterday's news. It's somehow liberating when one knows the truth. But we should be allowed to be concerned about the military and political tasks that rise before us ever higher. One shouldn't blame the private if he is at first disappointed to hear that the war will last longer. One can't free oneself from such thoughts. I hope our inner strength lasts. I can't help but worry about the many loved ones I know who have moved East during the past few months. [. . .]

Another Campaign

June 23, 1941

It's sometimes frightening to see how one day is followed by the next. The campaign has already taken on an air of normality. Life goes on. The reports from the front have a new paragraph; that's all. But it's good that way. [. . .] I'm on my feet as of today. It's a whole other life. The toes are healing so well that I doubt I'll be here fourteen more days. I spoke with the first sergeant about the reserves, and I think I can stay here in the vicinity. One of the NCOs who replaced me and teaches German to the ethnic Germans told me he's been diagnosed with a heart murmur. [. . .] I don't want to have to endure such things. If B[oether]-Sch[ulze] can help me find a way to become an officer that I can actually accomplish, I will gladly exert myself. But otherwise, I'll pass. [. . .]

Uncertainty

June 25, 1941

[. . .] The regiment is to go to Altengrabow on July 21. I don't know if that includes the days spent marching there. Otherwise, the battalion would need to leave at the end of next week. I hope that by then I have an answer from B[oether]-S[chulze]. By the way, it is possible that this will take much longer. [. . .]

Perhaps our fears about the Red Air Force were exaggerated. That would be good news. But you're prepared now in any case. We're waiting for the first reports; hopefully things will go quickly there are well. [. . .]

Education and Self-Awareness

June 26, 1941

[. . .] I received the enclosed letter from B[oether]-S[chulze] today. I'm a bit uneasy as to how this attempt will end. But I don't want to go into it. [. . .] Let's wait and see. [. . .]

I think that my freedom will come to an end this week and so I'm going to concentrate on Plato. The trouble you took to pack and send the books was worth it. I see the connections more clearly now. I'm largely concerned with the question of education through continual striving for understanding. This has more do to with the way in which people need to know themselves and function in the world—that means initially the community—which is not so much a matter for the schools. The relationships are so deep and far-reaching that any criticism is forbidden, because it smacks of aesthetic individualism. The questions are: how can a self-aware education fit within the parameters of an ethnic education (for Plato this meant educating those who were capable of duties on behalf of the community, duty in service of the community that is taken up by the individual and carried out by him) and how can this be possible in the eyes of Christianity? There are similarities and differences when one looks at Goethe's work, where there is no reference to politics ("One must write as one lives, first for oneself, and then one also exists for related beings"). Goethe follows up that sentence with a fierce attack on Lavater[56] and his belief that "Everything that lives exists outside itself." Here pedagogy and biography live close together. Pieper[57] represents the Catholic compromise between the Greek-Aristotelian world

---

[56] Johann Caspar Lavater (1741–1801), pastor and philosopher.
[57] Josef Pieper (1904–1997), *Über die Hoffnung* (Leipzig, 1932).

234

and Christianity. [. . .] You can see that I've been wrestling with big issues the past few days. And yet I am lacking for all that the clear answer "to what end" regarding the possibility of pedagogical and political action. [. . .]

Expecting

July 1, 1941

I was so very pleased to get your letter yesterday. I think everything is unfolding in its natural course. That you're in Magdeburg and that mother is near. I know that doesn't help you much, but it will please her a great deal. And at least you're not alone at home. She can call someone if necessary. Perhaps I'll even be sent somewhere near you!! I was at the doctor's again today to get my bill of health and had to report to the company chief. He asked right away if I wanted to go to the Landesschützen. He said things were pretty difficult in the company during the last few weeks, and that I perhaps couldn't keep up. I agreed and pointed out that in many other instances it's hard for me to keep up, like in shooting. He denied this and said he hadn't noticed. It had more to do with my physical abilities. That was gratifying, especially since he's an old soldier, who's served more than twelve years. He closed with the sentence: "All right, we'll report you to the Landesschützen in *Magdeburg.*" I think that's the best solution, even in regard to the question of my officer candidacy. If the war lasts longer, then I can perhaps try there for the third time at least to become a reserve officer candidate. As for the rest I can be transferred from there to anywhere else, in case B[oether]-S[chulze] has something else. I don't know how long it will take for the transfer to come through. If it takes a few weeks I can certainly get through it here. I'll come for sure on Saturday. [. . .]

Transfer to the Reserves

July 24, 1941

The days go by and your hour comes ever nearer. I wish you much courage. Then everything will be twice as easy. I'll hopefully be with you by the day after tomorrow. I received news from B[oether]-S[chulze]. The commander refused, because I'm physically not capable enough, and advised me to be transferred to the Landesschützen. B[oether]-S[chulze] regrets not being able to have accomplished more and will make further inquiries there. [. . .]

Furlough from August 5 to 11, 1941

Part III

_

War of Annihilation in Russia

The German attack on Russia on June 22, 1941 radicalized World War II into an unprecedented "war of annihilation." The struggle with the Soviet Union was not just a conventional great power conflict, but an ideological crusade against communism that sought to extirpate the "red menace," as the infamous "commissar order" reveals. Hitler, Nazi leaders, and volkish intellectuals had long dreamed of conquering "living space" in the East—a racist fantasy that required the ethnic cleansing of most of its Slavic population. Moreover, the invasion of Russia also added further Baltic, White Russian, and Ukrainian territories with heavy Jewish populations to the Nazi sphere, leading to the culmination of anti-Semitic persecution in the "Holocaust by bullets" that inaugurated systematic genocide. By blurring any real distinction between combatants and civilians, this racist imperialism expanded warfare beyond the front and cost millions of innocent lives. Already during the fighting, the anti-Slavic repression and anti-Semitic genocide began, because Hitler's New Order had no place for Russians or Jews.

The invasion of Russia also clarified Konrad Jarausch's military future, since he was sent to Dulag 203 in the central front on August 11. After a transfer to Stalag 204 in France had not worked out, the need for experienced personnel to guard the hundreds of thousands of Soviet prisoners prevented his reassignment or release from service. The *Durchgangslager* were the initial reception camps that operated fairly closely behind the front in order "to hold and guard" the prisoners who had been captured in the fighting, and to sort them for shipment as laborers to Germany or killing by the SS as ideological enemies and racial inferiors. Dulag 203 was attached to security division 286, which was supposed to protect the advancing tank and infantry units by maintaining their communication lines and preventing partisan attacks. Since young soldiers were needed for the push to Leningrad or Stalingrad and the offensive toward Moscow, "securing and ordering the towns crossed during the fighting" fell to the older comrades in the reserves. Hence Jarausch was sent to Dulag 203 in Kochanowo and later on moved to Kritschew in Belarus.

Once again he was fascinated by his encounter with the unknown East and sought to make sense of his conflicting impressions of Russia. While the landscape somewhat resembled northern Germany, the culture and politics appeared fundamentally different. Daily contacts with POW helpers and translators led him to admire the Russian people's immense capacity for suffering, especially among the women, and made him gradually see them no longer as enemies. The visible remnants of Old Russia he found congenial, since the villages with wooden houses seemed inviting, and signs of deep religiosity among the peasants intrigued him. In spite of encountering newly built train stations, schools, and factories, he remained critical of "the Bolshevik system" due to drastic tales of human suffering from the Stalinist transformation into the modern Soviet Union. But the more he found out through conversation and reading, the less he believed that "the Russian could be completely defeated in the few weeks that separate us from winter." Moreover, he worried about the material and spiritual destruction of Europe that would leave a trail of bitterness, clouding the future.

His letters also reinforce the impression that the Dulags faced a near impossible task under the chaotic conditions of the fall and winter of 1941/42. The rapid initial advance produced so many prisoners that the collection camps were simply overwhelmed. When 20,000 POWs crowded into a facility designed for one-tenth as many, disorder and hunger were the result. Guarding such a large number with 150 soldiers required the repeated use of force. The basic decision to feed the prisoners with what could be collected in the occupied territory itself put them at risk, since too little was left on the scorched earth. Part of the problem was also a lack of transportation, as the retreating Red Army had destroyed roads, bridges, and railroad tracks. Another part was the inclement weather, because rain transformed the dirt roads of the *Rollbahn* into groundless mud, while early snow froze trucks in their tracks. Moving with the front, the Dulags could never stabilize their infrastructure and had to improvise constantly. Finally, due to their own food problems in October the Wehrmacht leaders reduced POW rations to below the minimum requirement, callously ignoring their likely death.

In this mess Konrad Jarausch was put in charge of one of the field kitchens of Dulag 203, covering an entire subcamp. Trying to reconcile a sense of duty with human compassion, he attempted to feed the fluctuating number of POWs in his charge as best as he could. That meant constantly having to fight with pursers about receiving adequate supplies, such as edible potatoes, flour for bread baking, and very rarely some scraps of [horse]meat. It also required finding large enough kettles for cooking a watery soup and then getting bowls for the POWs to hold their limited ration. Moreover, it necessitated scrounging up wood to heat the stoves or ovens and organizing both a handful of soldiers and a dozen prisoners to get the cooking done. Racist SS officers objected to these efforts, and cynical nationalists simply told him to forget helping Slavic subhumans. A Christian sense of charity nonetheless compelled him to intercede personally to maintain order, beating back the ravenous, even firing shots so as to be able to give the weaker prisoners their share. When there were only a few hundred in camp this task seemed

241

doable, but when thousands suddenly arrived, it became impossible.

Making reference to the passion of Christ, the letters from Dulag 203 provide chilling descriptions of the "quiet dying" of Russian POWs. Their detailed accounts of the mass death as well as their sympathetic perspective are unparalleled in Western literature. His reports indicate that many prisoners were already half-dead on arrival at the camp, since they were dejected, exhausted, and starving, having marched long distances. After they reached transit camps, many did not receive adequate shelter in the stables, factory buildings, or schools that had been converted for this purpose, but had to sleep on the wet ground. Their rations were grossly inadequate and nutritionally unbalanced, since they were only fed twice daily, generally with two helpings of soup and a chunk of bread. Finally, the breakdown of transportation and the lack of guards slowed efforts to move them on to better facilities. Crammed together with inadequate sanitation, prisoners deteriorated quickly and dozens passed away each night. In disregard of the Geneva Convention, more than two million of the about 3.3 million Russian POWs, captured during 1941, appear to have died during the marches and in the camps.

Konrad Jarausch was deeply shocked by this "boundless suffering" because it took place under his own eyes and he was helpless to alleviate it. In order to assuage his conscience, he sought out some educated prisoners who also helped him keep order, thereby seeing them as individual human beings and establishing a level of mutual trust. In order to communicate better, understand the kitchen help, and talk to other POWs, he began to take Russian lessons from an interpreter. Such efforts also led to human encounters, in which POWs would recount their suffering under the Bolsheviks and each would exchange pictures of loved ones at home. During Christmas 1941 several POWs gave him little gifts to express their gratitude and an opera singer also performed selections from the repertoire, Russian folk tunes and orthodox hymns. No doubt, some of these contacts were not entirely disinterested, since they would improve survival chances for the prisoners. But on the whole, he judged them genuine and began to sense a deep solidarity beyond enemy lines. This feeling of shared humanity made him question the conflict's legitimacy, since it had become "more murder than war."

In spite of his relatively privileged position, he ultimately paid with his life for his involvement in this atrocity. In order to improve morale, the command of the central front had issued extra rations of food and spirits for the holidays, and his working and sleeping quarters were somewhat sheltered from the cold. But the breakdown of order as a result of defeat had created an epidemic of typhoid fever in the Russian population that also spread to the POWs. Since the disease was transmitted through lice and washing facilities were limited even for the guards, there was no effective way to prevent contagion. Normally the disease resulted in a high fever that dehydrated the body, wasted the flesh, and made the sufferer sink into a coma. While most young men survived, over forty-year-olds with a heart condition were particularly at risk because the army had no effective medicine against it. On January 11, 1942, Konrad Jarausch was transported to the field hospital in Roslawl where he struggled until succumbing on January 27. While there was a bitter logic in suffering the same fate as the POWs, his death was nevertheless tragic, because he had just turned against the war.

These letters from Russia shed some light on the complexity of individual or collective involvement in wartime atrocities. As a Prussian patriot, Jarausch participated in the nationalities' struggle by selecting prisoners and helping refugees, even if he did not physically take part in ethnic cleansing. As a volkish nationalist, he knew of but did not personally assist in the killing of communists, the decimation of Slavic elites, and the genocide of Jews, for whom he felt some pity. But as a master sergeant, he was directly involved in the mass death of Russian POWs because he was unable to provide them with the necessary food in spite of his efforts to mitigate their suffering. Stemming from chaotic circumstances, racial prejudice, and political design, this killing behind the battlefield was the result of a new kind of *Vernichtungskrieg* (war of extermination) that broke the norms of modern civilized warfare. Jarausch's experience suggests that neither the apologetic "myth of the clean Wehrmacht" nor the critical accusation of the Holocaust culpability of the entire army are quite correct. Instead, his fate demonstrates how annihilationist warfare could turn doing one's duty into becoming an accomplice of crime.

Konrad Jarausch's correspondence from the Soviet front therefore raises troubling moral questions about which values should predominate in wartime—a sense of national obligation or a commitment to transnational humanity. In spite of some personal idiosyncrasies, the letters are representative of the attitudes of many decent, cultivated Germans who supported the Nazi program of national renewal, only to find themselves embroiled in another world war. Throughout them the author is torn between his support for the war effort and his distress over the suffering inflicted by conquest. The stark evidence of Nazi brutality in the mass death of Russian POWs sharpened this conflict of conscience between his wish to belong to a national and military community and his feeling of compassion for the many victims of Hitler's hegemonic dreams. In the end, Konrad Jarausch

Stationing in Russia, 1941–42

resolved this dilemma by overcoming some of his nationalist enemy stereotypes and choosing solidarity with the suffering POWs. Starting out as a cautionary tale about the evil consequences of NS complicity, the letters eventually tell a more encouraging story of the possibility of recovering a shared humanity.

Letters from Russia,
August 1941 to January 1942

Traveling and Worrying

August 12, 1941

We've arrived in Warsaw after a quiet and rather comfortable trip. There wasn't much to see. A thick fog blanketed the landscape. I've had a little breakfast and freshened up and am waiting for the command center to open for news of my next assignment. In between fits of sleep I thought about you a great deal. I wonder if [the popular remedy of] sitting in the streetcar helped [start your contractions], or if you've gone to see a doctor. [. . .] At around 10 a.m. we're to move on—via Brest-Litovsk to Minsk. I'll likely stay in that area. It's really quite far behind the front, so please don't worry.

The Lenin House in Minsk

August 14, 1941

The city lies on some small hills above the green meadows of a river. It meanders along where the hills meet the low rolling fields; it consists of gray buildings surrounded by gardens. Down by the river (where the banks are likely swampy and where it probably often floods), the ribbon of the city disappears. Instead, the built-up center stands up sharply against the slope of the hills. From here, the city appears as a unit unto itself. It's really fascinating for those of us here in the rear to be able to see how a new shape is starting to emerge, one in which urban life has moved to a new stage of development. The few church towers (in themselves not so imposing) hardly stand out from the overall panorama. Instead, signs of the changing times are what spring into view.

246

The apartment blocks and shops (not very high) are dwarfed by the massive community buildings. It would be foolish to try to downplay their influence here: they stand out from the indistinguishable masses because of their clear, geometrical lines as the epitome of architectural expression. In the face of such an example, it's easy to see that our attempt to have church towers rise above the city skylines as if they had sprung organically from the middle of a medieval city was ill advised. Doesn't Bolshevik art only express exactly what we once were and are? We are limited in terms of the artistic means at our disposal that would allow us to build in such a manner. Of course we can't rely on decorative elements or any other freewheeling fantastical designs. All we can do is put together the basic forms (which are and should be identical) so that some kind of pattern or design can emerge. The Lenin House, the Belarus parliament, is such a building. And yet it is not completely separated from history. Its plan is reminiscent of the palatial form of the eighteenth century: an open square with a courtyard in front. Beyond and above it are the receding facades of various heights. These are enlivened only by the symmetrical rectangular windows. The staircase and the balcony are reminders that the need for self-representation is something that has persisted over the centuries. The main axis is directed toward the street, and there is the statue of Lenin on a glistening, black block of granite. The monument had been decorated along the base with reliefs of workers, soldiers, and farmers. But the statue has been pulled off its podium, and it lies, broken at the knees, on the street.[1] Germans and Russians are standing around lost in thought; the Germans can't believe the style

---

[1] In occupied cities and towns, the populace or the troops toppled Bolshevik monuments.

is so primitive. Yet everyone comes up and knocks on the statue: yes, it sounds hollow—it's no great work of bronze. And it's easy to grasp the larger metaphor behind this reality. I'm reminded of the destroyed idols of the pagan gods, before which the erstwhile believers stood in ignorant awe. I'm struck by the fragility of human efforts.

Inside the building, there are grand staircases and hallways lined with marble and wood leading toward the inner rooms. Built like a western parliamentary hall, the auditorium has seats for speakers, representatives, stenographers, etc. A huge image of Stalin hangs above everything else and is flanked by other symbolic figures. The same images that grace the walls of the halls appear in the university gardens or on posters—even on stamps: the red soldier, the parachute jumper, the women athlete, the engineer, and of course the farmer and worker. The rows of seats rise in front of the lectern in the shape of a half moon. Above hang portraits of party members. On a banner above them I can already decipher the names of Lenin and Stalin next to each other.

Reliefs along the hallways depict various scenes from the revolution. A large triptych decorates one entire wall. The main panel depicts the "Red Storm" on the Petersburg palace. On one side, Lenin, among a group of co-conspirators, calls for the revolution. The bitter and determined spirit of this picture contrasts with the glow of victory on the opposite panel. Stalin speaks in terms of gleaming optimism at a huge factory while the workers hang on his every word. Our gaze is drawn toward a sunny horizon, filled with the busy industry of a happy new life.

Today the courtyard is full of parked military vehicles. Almost all the windows have been destroyed, but the building hasn't suffered any further damage. The balcony provides an unrestricted view of the ruins of the inner city—burned-out

Burning Minsk, August 1941

walls, gaping windows, missing roofs. In regular intervals one can hear the dull explosions [of the wrecking crews] and then the sound of crashing walls. Beyond the city lies an area of gardens and small wooden structures that appear to be undisturbed. What a difference between these two worlds! Here one sees the old Russian world: filthy, without any German sense of order, but yet filled with life, and right next to it these modern buildings. What links the two worlds is the lack of orderliness. One sees it in the weeds that have sprung up in the cracks on the backside of the monuments. Alas, the German troops have failed here miserably, in a most shameful manner. It was clear that we had to occupy the building thoroughly. It was also obvious that we needed to convert the large hall into a space for troops. But the manner in which we have spread dirt and disorder hardly accords with our claims to represent a higher cultural order. The latrines and the hygienic facilities are beyond belief. And that's after six weeks of occupation! The spirit that rules on the front line is in keeping with this. One is housed in makeshift quarters and then looks in vain for better lodging, until one takes one's destiny in one's own hands with a better result.

Churches in Minsk

August 14, 1941

Already on the way here I had kept my eyes open for signs of churches and crucifixes. In Poland we had become used to the fact that most villages had no church of their own. Most of the destroyed villages still had a church tower left over as a symbol. But did any kind of ceremonies take place in these buildings? We also saw occasional crosses along the fields. At times I could tell that a few of the wayside crucifixes had been robbed of their icons. And so it was that on the morning after my arrival in Minsk I noticed a church tower right next to the Lenin House in Minsk. It could have been located in one of the more modest neighborhoods in Berlin. The church was made of red brick and was Romanesque in style; it reminded me of the Kapernaum Church in the Seestrasse in Berlin-Wedding. Except that everything was more marked by poverty, and the tower was smaller. The church was likely built in the years before the world war. It wasn't damaged much on the outside. But there were no crosses or Christian iconography of any kind. Plastered on the fence posts outside were theater and cinema announcements. The main entry had been blocked off with a kind of glass wall that looked like a storefront window. A side entrance led me past a ticket counter. Inside, carpenters and others were at work. They were whitewashing the walls and refinishing the floor. A few men and women were standing around looking at what had already been accomplished. So we started a conversation (I opened with a question in Polish). I could get the basic facts despite our problems in conversing—the Bolsheviks had converted this "beautiful, wonderful Kyrka [church]" into a movie theater. It is now supposed to be turned back into a church. It was clear that people were interested in it. Were they expressing some kind of religious sentiment? Who can say?

A few hours later I was standing in front of the "cathedral" on the market square. It is a modest building of the late baroque period; we've seen a number of such churches here in the East, some with old paintings. Here, the religious character of the building had already been reestablished. A crucifix made of pieces of birch stood on the altar, flanked by flowers. In front of it stood a smaller cross that had been saved through difficult times. One of the side chapels had also been restored. An old woman knelt at a pew. Otherwise only German soldiers were milling about. There were posters announcing both Catholic and Protestant field services.

As I was leaving (tired and with heavy feet), a siren sent people running from the market square: another planned explosion, this time right next to the church. I wonder if a new Christian spirit can rise up from the rubble? Or are the reopened churches yet another part of German war propaganda?[2]

---

[2] Hitler released guidelines on August 6, 1941 that forbade any fostering or hindering of religious sentiment in the occupied Eastern areas. Rudolf Absolon, *Die Wehrmacht im Dritten Reich*, vol. 5, *1. September 1939 bis 18. Dezember 1941* (Boppard, 1988), 289.

First Impressions of the Camp

Kochanowo, August 15, 1941
(about twenty kilometers west of Orscha)[3]
When I heard how long it takes for mail to arrive I was quite
shocked. I'm so sorry you've had to be without news from
me, especially now. In general I've been struck by how difficult this transfer, with all of its accompanying circumstances,
has been. They've been waiting here for more troops (more
NCOs, etc.) since July 1. I'm the first to arrive. Obviously not
everyone is as anxious as they were in Blankenburg. There's
nothing to be done about it now. You're going to have to get
through these next few weeks alone. I hope that the good
news outweighs everything else and that the pains you had
are now forgotten. I can comfort myself with the fact that the
monotony of base life is now over; time moves more quickly
here. One can now feel something of the war again, as we
did during the first weeks in Poland, even though we're still
far from the front. The atmosphere makes people more open,
and I'm hoping to get settled here soon. Of course one has to
get used to being without the comforts of living on base. The
rooms in particular are pretty primitive. Since it's summer,
that's not too bad. In any case we are looking forward to a
change when the front moves farther eastward. I'll experience that move in the back of a truck. If the war ends in the
near future, we won't have a need for these transit camps.
But we can't look so far ahead. In any case, today as soon
as my shift is over I'll write Lohrisch[4] and say that I'm ready
to apply for a position at home. I don't want to experience

---

[3] Kochanovo, town in eastern Belarus, close to Orscha (Orsha), a larger city
and railroad hub.
[4] Director of his school in Magdeburg.

another Russian winter. The prospect of promotion is really an illusion, especially if one won't use one's connections to get it; it's better to be clear about that. I recently learned about the possibilities of promotion from a librarian who traveled with me from Warsaw to Minsk; he was experiencing the hard life of a soldier for the first time. Before, he had spent the war in elegant hotels in Brussels and Paris, where he served as a special envoy. I don't have any ill will toward him about that. But I think we need to take care of ourselves a bit. What you're going through is too much, especially because it is ultimately not necessary. I wouldn't say anything if I thought that my service was essential and extremely urgent. But I can't bear this mixture of thoughtlessness and vexation; it really is just the last straw. I only had to write that once so that you know that I'm not entirely callous about your situation, especially since on Monday I attempted to master my feelings so that our farewell wouldn't be too painful. I promise not to worry you any more with this. I'll try to busy myself quickly and integrate myself into life here. [. . .]

Arrival in the Camp

August 15, 1941

[Dearest Little Mother,]

[. . .] Here I am, far away in the East, somewhat westward from Orscha—you should be able to find it on a map; we're about a hundred kilometers away from the front. I've already seen and experienced so much. The prisoner camp is located in a rather large village on the main road. I won't have anything to do with the prisoners directly, but will rather work in an administrative position. I think I'll be able to figure things out soon. Here things are much more in keeping with the war effort, and the war is much closer than it was in Amiens.

Things aren't as orderly, and they're certainly much more primitive. Today I finally got settled. For now I'm by myself in a large room that used to be the post office. Sergeants and other NCOs are to join me here. It's a real log cabin. Around it things look pretty untidy; there aren't any gardens around here. There are a few fruit trees near the farms. Beyond lie the fields of the collective farm, and the wheat that grows there is thin and scraggly. The woods provide a looming backdrop to everything. The landscape looks like the highlands of our midsize mountains at home: large pieces of land, dark forests, fields with little on them and in between a few gray wooden houses. Our town is somewhat larger. It contains numerous official buildings, such as schools and other structures formerly occupied by the Soviets, which I still have to find out about. German troops are spread out all over the place. In the meantime, the local population is making an effort to bring in the harvest. Things are moving along in a lively fashion, and the hay is loaded on simple carts. Not as festive as with us at home. There's so much more that I could tell you. But there isn't much time, and tomorrow morning I start my duty. [. . .] I hope that I won't spend the winter in Russia, but I can certainly hold out until then. [. . .]

Settling In

August 16, 1941

I can't begin to think with any sense of confidence about how you might be doing and what you're up to. So I'll be patient and won't even mention my hopes. Instead, I'll tell you a little bit about myself, so you can get a sense of what things are like here. I would need more patience and time to describe everything here adequately. This morning when I reported to the major, he sent me straight away to the camp kitchen. I was to assist the NCO on duty there. That was somewhat unexpected, but at the moment it's not too bad. There are only six hundred prisoners here, and everything is set up and practically runs itself. As long as we don't get any new transports (which could happen any day now), I just sit around to be on hand; I also oversee how food is distributed. We've decided to take turns, so that we each are on duty for one day. But if we get new prisoners tomorrow, then the NCO who had overseen things by himself will have to be in charge. Otherwise, I survived the journey all right. I'm somewhat tired, but there isn't much time to sleep; that's always being put off until our next transfer, or until the next arrival of prisoners. One can't sleep at all during the day. The flies are terrible and really eat us up. But the night comes early. I don't have any lights in my room. So I'll be able to get some sound sleep. Our food is the same as it's been everywhere; yesterday I had some broth with noodles and today I had some peas. They cooked well both yesterday and today. Today we were allowed to buy supplies. I got 300 grams of French chocolate and cigarettes. Because of the alcohol we bought, tonight we're to have a social evening with warm food. That's a start, at least. If there were anything to buy, I could use the kitchen to make it. But there really isn't anything around, except for a few eggs, some milk, potatoes, and a few cucumbers. Because one has to be really careful with one's digestion (those flies!) it's better if one eats only what has been cooked in the field kitchens. I'm still sleeping alone in the large, lofty room that was once the post office. It's a log building, complete with beds made from freshly cut pine; they're familiar to me from Poland and are outfitted with a sack of straw. My desk is made up of a small bureau laid on its side, without a drawer. I possess one bench and a slat of wood with nails. But there aren't any lice here, and that's

Feeding POWs in Kochanowo, August 1941

certainly something. Four lance corporals and privates first
class are sleeping in the adjoining room. Behind that there
are some workrooms. So I'm well tended to. The other comrades are similarly stationed, but they have to share bunks.
I've been impressed overall with the atmosphere among the
NCOs. They've experienced a lot together, including some
tight spots. And they're better educated than most of the
territorial reserves. I don't think I need to miss the latter. I'm
looking forward to this evening [spent with new comrades].

And now just some impressions to show to you how I'm
trying to see things positively. I just ate my first serving of
Russian *kascha* [porridge]—not from the prisoners' camp, but
cooked by our Russian cooks for themselves (they're allowed
this privilege for their efforts). [I have had] my first Russian
lesson with the help of a small guidebook. My teacher was
a really young fellow from Ukraine, near Schepetovka.[5] His

[5] City of Shepetivka in the Ukraine.

name is Trohim Schewtschuk. On the table between us lay a volume from Pushkin, almost symbolically. I had a lively discussion with a really bright high school student who studied for a number of years in Berlin (his father was a merchant); we talked about Russian schools, the Komsomol, and the future of the revolution.[6] In reality, not all Russians are "swines" or "beasts." Of course we knew that before, but it's good to have that impression confirmed by firsthand experience. [. . .]

Russian Women

[August 1941]

When I walk through the camp, invariably I pass by them. They stand there with the patience peculiar to the peoples of the East that seems to us Germans to be nothing more than mere passivity. There they are: at the infirmary, where the military doctor takes care of sick Russians; in front of the command post; at the bridge; and especially across from the entrance to the camp. If there's a wind, they huddle together in groups in the sheltered entrances of nearby houses. Otherwise they just form a solid crowd across from the camp gate. Seen thus, they seem nothing more than a stupid, dumb mass intent on resisting their destinies; they cling to each other to survive. But I've looked in their eyes and seen something else. I'm thinking about one woman who a few days ago leaned against the fence, looking out toward the stream and the fields, and further into the future, where her own fate might lie. Or I think of the small group I encountered today on a village street; they were hopeful that they could

---

[6] "Revolution" means here an uprising of the population against the Stalinist regime, as was expected in the first months of the German-Soviet war.

find the one face among the hundreds of men who were being sent away today; they ignored the soldiers before them who sought to read their expressions. I was reminded of early sculptural depictions of the three Marys.[7] But then I remind myself that it's foolish to call something primitive when it's really just an expression of simple innocence.

It's obvious even in the minor details that the Russian peasantry is losing this innocence. Their clothes are made out of the cheapest materials. Their cut is the same all over the East: they wear long coats with a jacket over them; their heads are covered in scarves that are most often simply white, but are sometimes quite colorful. In general the clothes aren't very vibrant, and most of the material is washed-out and gray. Many women wear shawls, but one often sees them in coats as well. Sometimes one will see an odd piece or two: a suit, a coat adorned with cheap fake fur, or a wrinkled silk headdress. Many are clean and proper. Sundays appear to be the day to clean oneself up. But there's nothing elegant or expensive around.

The faces that peer out from beneath the headscarves are so very puzzling to us. If the women are young, then their faces can be quite remarkable in their simplicity, and in the right circumstances, they can almost pass for classical beauties. But soon enough their faces are covered with lines and wrinkles, and in their furrowed visages I see the traces of endless daily sorrows; sometimes one can note something deeply maternal as well.

As it is with the clothing, so it goes with the people themselves. Sometimes, you'll notice a pair of unsteadily

---

[7] A cult in the thirteenth and fourteenth centuries built on early depictions of Christian virtues (faith, hope, and love); the three Marys depicted the women who visited Jesus's tomb.

gleaming [eyes] glaring out at you. An agitated face. Often their tousled hair, cut in a bob, adds to the impression. One can see the beginnings of something new: ancient customs are being replaced and people believe in new goals and have a different definition of humanity altogether. But such people are really not common here in this Belarusian village. So perhaps I'll close this description of such old "primitive" ways. New prisoners have arrived. I am in charge of doling out food at Kitchen III, which lies somewhat to the side of the camp. Suddenly I see a rather disheveled, raggedy young man approach the barbed wire. Twenty meters beyond that, a young woman fitting the description I just gave you is standing in the middle of a potato field. They both freeze in their tracks at the same moment. The sentry in the observation post has seen them and is threatening that he'll shoot. So we try to shoo the woman away. She hesitates, and the young man tries to show his joy at seeing her, and to express his love for her. She then runs away. The next morning, she's there at 5. She's brought some support—a few relatives, along with the village scribe. The young man hasn't been idle either. He's wrapped a white handkerchief around his arm, just to be sure. He hopes he can thereby prove that he's an important member of the group and therefore won't be sent away on a transport. They're standing together now face to face. They kiss each other, and dry their tears. The woman pulls some bread, eggs, and sour milk from her basket—everything that she has. She smiles as she sees her husband lay into the provisions, happy that she can provide for him again.

When one sees such women waiting so patiently, or otherwise at work—either on the fields with a sickle in their hands, on a village street leading the cows out to pasture, one can imagine that the entire existence of this people rests on

Russian women waiting, fall 1941

the shoulders of these nameless women—millions of them. They have had to carry the burden through the decades, while the men, with their deliberate efforts, have missed their mark, drowning all in a pool of smoke and blood.

A few notes regarding the middle school in Kochanowo. Most of the subjects: mathematical or scientific. Russian language courses (the official language here is Russian); some German classes starting in the sixth grade. The sixteen-year-old who tells me this would have graduated in August. He wanted to be an engineer. Then he would have had further years of technical training and then an apprenticeship. He would have been supported by the state and housed in a group home. In return, he had to promise to go wherever the state would send him. His classmates were sent off to the interior when war broke out. The transport train was destroyed by German air attacks.

Dulag 203

Keep this somewhere safe and do not copy.

Camp Kochanowo [August 1941]

(Partially based on my comrades' insights)

"Dulag" is short for transit camp. Such camps serve to process prisoners once they've been removed from the battlefield and then to send them on. The camps thus follow on the heels of the fighting troops but lie beyond the battle zone. Depending on what's happening in the field, they can be filled quickly and then can become quiet again. Then one has to start building the facilities out of nothing, leaving them during further advance behind for supply convoys etc. The first time we advanced, we kept very close to the tanks, because we were part of an attack division. Now things are peaceful and lazy.

The road here in K[ochanowo] winds its way through the village and then sinks and passes over a creek. The meadows on either side of this creek seemed to offer an ideal location for a camp. Everything was fine as long as the sun was shining. But then we had quite a downpour. The creek flooded and the meadows were covered in water. At the same time, we received some 10,000 to 12,000 prisoners. They had marched thirty to forty km from the front; they were soaked; they had gone days without food and had eaten green sheaves of grain. In an instant the meadow was transformed into a muddy morass, with the prisoners sprawled all about. Their hunger drove them to the kitchens. Shots were fired to keep them in order. Some (not many) were killed. Others rolled around in the mud, howling from their hunger pains. The next morning several corpses were pulled out of the mud; only their legs or heads stuck up out of the mess.

Distributing food at Kochanowo, fall 1941

If you could see the camp now, eight days later, you wouldn't believe this had ever happened. Everything is so peaceful and orderly. There's a large, lofty building in between all the other buildings (they house two kitchens, the sentry post, storage rooms, quarters for captured officers), and thousands of men can find shelter there from the rain. We have four kitchens set up. We hand out food in the morning, at noon, and in the evening: a liter of grits and 1,000 grams of dark bread; those at hard labor receive 1,700 grams. Prisoners serve in the kitchens, as overseers, and as medics. We don't see many Mongolian types anymore. When prisoners line up to eat by the hundreds, one sees mostly Eastern European farmers and workers. Some are really young boys with impish features; they're cheeky and trusting. Probably most of them are happy to be away from [the front] and that things are not worse.

The Fate of Volga Germans

[August 16, 1941]
The night presses upon us. It feels as if the silent darkness has added to the weight of the thousands of bodies that lie around our barracks, leaning on the walls, stretched out on the cold, wet ground, or crowded together in one large mass under the roof in the middle of the courtyard. In the feeble glow of the oil lamp in the kitchen the two of us are reading the front newspaper (which is ten days old now). It's just me and our trusty assistant, the Volga German train worker. Around us the cooks and assistants are finishing up their last chores in silence. This day has been endless. Adolf asks all of a sudden: "Who was Siegfried, anyway?" He had been reading an article, comparing the Stalin Line to the Siegfried Line. I explain it to him briefly. He replies, "I've already read that story in the Bible." Even when I tell him that's not right, he sticks to his story, and informs me that the Bible *also* contains the Old Testament. "I don't know how that is with you," he explains. But then he finally recognizes that it's *Sampson* who's in the Bible. "I've read the Bible twice, all the way through. My mother had a thick one, written in

263

German script. I didn't understand a lot of it, like the An-
nunciation. But I understood the stories of people like Sampson. My brother had a lot of books, in which smart people
wrote a lot of things about the Bible. He was a churchy type;
he gave lessons and also taught his brothers and sisters two
or three times a week. He had to run away because he was
so religious. My father was a farmer. He didn't have a lot of
land, but he was considered the best farmer in the village,
and so the Bolsheviks said he was a kulak. But then he died,
and my eldest brother (the churchy one) was sent in his place
to Siberia. After a year he ran away from there, and because
he couldn't come back here, he went to the Ukraine. He
trained to be a carpenter. But because he couldn't practice
his craft, he became a guard in a factory and worked as a
carpenter at home and earned his bread that way. He has
seven children. In the terrible winter of 1931 the Bolsheviks took fifty families out of the five hundred living there
and put them on sleds and sent them to the capital. Many
of them had already frozen to death before they arrived. I
don't know what happened to them. My mother was supposed to be sent away with my younger siblings. But then
they changed the orders. Then my brother brought us to the
Ukraine. That was when I learned Ukrainian. We never
spoke any Russian at home. Our village used to be one long
street. One house stood next to the other in a long row; the
courtyards were sheltered from the street by walls. Now so
much has been destroyed. You can drive straight through
everything.

"We younger children lived together a few houses down
from where my brother lived. Then I became a soldier and
haven't spoken German in so many years that I've almost
forgotten everything."

Taking Care of People

August 18/19, [1941]

A stressful, nerve-wracking day draws to a close. I should be free this evening after our shift is up, as I spent all day yesterday (Sunday) in the camp. Actually in the morning I went on a nice walk with an older sergeant from Magdeburg (who was celebrating his forty-third birthday) to go the bakery and pick up bread for the prisoners. We saw fir and linden trees, raspberries and bellflowers. It was a beautiful summer day. When we got back we heard that the camp was to receive 5,000 prisoners. I went right over, and so ended the idyllic summer day. A thunderstorm came up from the west, and it rained hard all afternoon. The grounds were immediately slick and muddy. But things were bearable. We gave them all a bowl of soup. Tonight at least the sick and those without coats could find shelter under a roof. Their departure started today, the 19th, at 4 p.m. For every four people we handed out a 2,000-gram loaf of bread. Now at six, we're cooking soup for those who were left. I can't even begin to describe the impression that these starving, filthy figures make when they stand with their tin cans in the soup lines. You can tell what kind of people they are just by looking at the type of container they have. The real soldiers have managed to hold on to their mess kits. Most of them have just scrounged up something made out of metal—an old soup tin, a hollowed-out piece of bread, even an artillery shell. The ones who are completely broken just hold out their caps. We had proof yesterday that even these men want to get out of their own filth; on a sunny afternoon everyone bathed in the river and washed their clothes. The barbed wire was blanketed with grayish shirts.

I'm now sharing my quarters with an NCO who is a functionary in the NS Motor Corps and a sergeant (a former bank clerk from Stendal).[8] I'll arrange it so that I spend most of my time in the camp. At least there I can set the tone. I won't be able to do any reading or anything like that. And I won't have time to send any detailed descriptions. But it's also good when the days are busy. Yesterday evening we heard that the offensive on Moscow has started. Everyone here hopes that the Russian campaign will be over before bad weather sets in.

I'm curious about whether they'll keep me here in the camp. Of course it's more strenuous than sitting at a desk. But here I'm really taking care of people and don't have to deal with files and boring bureaucrats. A few days ago one of them asked me why I didn't go into the upper ranks in the army administration. If only I could be as clever and hardworking as all of them. [. . .]

Russian Landscapes and Villages

August 24, 1941

This is the second Sunday I've spent in Russia. Eight days ago the camp was filled with activity. Today I'm enjoying a little respite. In the morning I spent a few hours outside and lay under the firs near the railroad embankment. I slept a little, read a little, and watched the transport trains roll by. This afternoon I walked up to the hill some thirty to forty meters above the river valley. The wind was brisk and it blew clouds across the sun, but that just added to the beauty of the clear summer day. After lunch in our close quarters, where the flies were eating us up, I appreciated this even further. My

[8] City in the Altmark in Germany.

view extended over the forest around me toward the spread-out village, behind which an empty transport train rolled back home, having left its equipment at the front. If I hadn't just run into an abandoned Russian tank with grenades lying around it down in the forest, I might have been on holiday on the highlands of one of our mountain ranges. The forest, which lines the fields and meadows all around me, reminded me of home. And the wooden houses could have been German. At least if viewed from afar, in their misty grayness. On closer inspection, one could tell [the difference]. The lack of order and the disrepair are too obvious. Things here are like they were in Poland. The problem doesn't lie in bad planning or construction. There are some really lovely buildings in the village, if they are larger halls or two-story houses. [. . .] It's really astonishing how much these developed houses resemble the classical style; they are proof it had its origins in the North. It's too bad I can't photograph them. But I've asked some comrades to take a few shots for me. But everything takes so long because it [the film] has to be sent back home first.

What is most alienating is more their inability to maintain order. Of course the war contributes to the problem: the men are all gone. Passing troops have torn the straw from the roofs of the houses to lie on. The windowpanes are broken and the openings have been nailed shut with wooden slats. But the war can't explain everything. It must have something to do with the people themselves. By the way, an engineer in the camp told us that the Soviets were much more diligent and energetic about city planning farther east. The villages there are supposedly nice and clean, with tree-lined streets. Here, the fruit has frozen in the orchards, and no one has done anything to cut down the dead trees or to plant replacements. The collective farms have beautiful new stables—made of wood—but the old buildings are falling apart. Unfortunately I haven't found anyone who can tell me anything about the buildings around here. Our prisoner camp, for instance, was an orphanage. One of the younger boys is often playing around here. I need to ask him what happened to them.

I wonder what you're doing? If I could just get a good sense of how you are, things would be easier here. If we are to judge by yesterday's news, we'll soon be back on German soil. But the news is always veering from one extreme to the next, and my experience has shown that things often turn out differently. By the way, there is now a ban on submitting requests to return home. [. . .]

Personal Hopes

August 26, 1941

We just heard that we can send mail with a division that's heading back home—it will get there much more quickly. I need to use the chance, even though I don't have the time to go into detail. Some 5,000 to 7,000 prisoners arrived last night, and they needed to be cared for. My comrade is now on duty but when we hand out the food I need to be on hand. It is a blessing that even here every evening turns into a new day and we know that God cares for each of us. Now that I've been a soldier for over two years, I can use the comfort. Please don't worry about me anymore, but take care of yourself—and hopefully our child (I still haven't received any news)—and look forward to my return. I think that once the Russian campaign is over they'll release my cohort, or at least not stand in the way of a request for exemption. I think in any case I've already served the bulk of my time as a soldier. And it doesn't matter what the future might bring in terms of a career—we'll be together and be able to face whatever happens side by side. I hope at least that those people who are close to us—Bruno and Trude, Franz and Lene—aren't too far away. I think then we'll be able to see things straight. Today I discovered that our sergeant is a former pupil of the Magdeburg Cloister school; he went there until the eighth grade, but has fond memories of the school and the teachers there (Blondeau among them; make sure to tell him). So perhaps our work hasn't been in vain. [. . .]

At Loose Ends

August 26, 1941

[Dearest Little Mother,]

[. . .] Our days take their course. We have a lot of free time and not too much pressure at work. So much here is in a primitive state. Who would have thought that after two years of war we'd be sitting deep in the middle of Russia? And yet we're really just on the border of Greater Russia. Who knows how this will all turn out?

I'm careful to take care of my health, and I hope I'll survive Russia. We all are hoping that we'll be sent back before winter comes, when the campaign is suspended. I'm going to bathe tomorrow; I'm afraid of lice because of the close contact with the prisoners. Even our doctor had a few. But he takes care of a lot of sick people in the area. The village road is always filled with carts; the sick lie in them on bundles of straw. There hasn't been too much destruction here, and most of the harvest on the collective farms has already been brought in. I think things probably are worse farther east, near the Stalin Line and in Smolensk.[9] The sad

[9] Soviet defensive lines at the Dnieper River.

thing is that the country is already so pitiful, and it's suffered such losses in terms of people and farms. The prisoners we took in today weren't too miserable or exhausted. But mostly it's pretty sad to see how much they suffer. Hopefully we can look forward to a few decades that won't be entirely dominated by war. [. . .]

All Too Human

August 28, 1941

[. . .] The weather has turned and it's really fall now. The evening sun is shining through some grayish blue clouds. It's nice and warm in the storage room, where I'm sitting; next door the Russians are cooking for the prisoners we expect to arrive tonight. On the small stove the horseflesh the kitchen staff received today as their portion from the nag they slaughtered is bubbling away in broth. I just tried some of it. The place is filled with activity; people with special privileges come by to receive their extra rations of bread— sentries, cooks, translators, officers, carpenters, etc. Outside, the prisoners are fighting over their soup rations. Things are pretty rough and ready, but they are all too human.

I had the day off again today. That is, I was in the camp from 7:30 to 10 and then slept and read in peace. My comrades played cards. This is apparently the rage brought in by the new recruits. They play for pretty high stakes. It's going to be hard to share a room with them. Not because I wish them ill, but because we have such different needs in regard to peace and quiet. My comrades complain a lot about the living conditions, but I'm used to them from my time in Poland. We just need to be sure to "winterize" our quarters. Today we got two oil lamps, one for down in the camp and one for our

Captive Russian officers, fall 1941

quarters—of course they were from Jewish homes.[10] It looks like we might move to another camp. I hope things aren't any worse there.

We haven't seen or spoken much of higher things. Today the topic of religion came up by accident. The Russians celebrate Mary's Assumption today; it's one of the twelve high Russian holidays. The villagers worked less; how much I couldn't really tell. A young translator told me with great solemnity that there are a lot of Christians among the Russians. In Kharkov[11] (a city of 800,000), where he comes from, there is a *single* church, which he attended. One of our NCOs asked sarcastically if Stalin also celebrates the

---

[10] Army field commanders participated in the collection of possessions from homes of Jews who had fled, were murdered, or deported. See Gerlach, *Kalkulierte Morde*, 640 and 675–83.

[11] Kharkov (Kharkiv) is an important city in the Ukraine.

holiday. "I don't know about that, but what I said about the Russian people, that's true." There are some other things about people here that I should tell you. But I'd like to wait some before I do so.

A few requests. If you get any of the [cheap Reklam] classical editions, please try to get some Russian authors, as long as the books aren't too heavy. I would like to have some meaningful reading. [. . .]

The evening is turning gray. I hope that you look forward to the night in peace and gratitude. Is Tommy up to his old tricks?[12] Have you had any [air attack] alarms?

A Lack of News

August 30, 1941

Dear Werner,[13]

I wonder if this will get to you in time for your birthday? The mail we received yesterday had been in transit for seventeen days. You can see that my greetings have a long way to travel. But they aren't any less heartfelt than if we were spending the day together celebrating. [. . .]

We've seen here the misery that war brings, but we've been spared the worst of it. But the prisoners—especially those who are wounded and sick—complain a great deal. Even though the Bolsheviks tried to kill any trace of human emotion, one can see in their eyes that they feel the same things that we do. At least they're happy when they get something to eat, and as far as that goes, I have a pretty decent job. Life here is hard enough for us. Everyone is hoping that we'll be out of work come winter, and that we can at

---

[12] English air raids on Magdeburg.
[13] Werner Haß, merchant, a family friend of about the same age.

least go to Poland. I don't think lodging a complaint would make any sense. Recently someone advised me to become an administrator. But then I'd be really stuck. I was infuriated by the way they yanked me away from my furlough and took me from my wife when she needed me most. There wasn't any real need to do so. And now I haven't received any news and will probably have to wait [another] fortnight to get a letter. It's difficult to be happy about being a soldier in such circumstances.

Of course, given the mail delivery problems we're also not receiving news of any kind. We know nothing of the political events of the day. We often ask ourselves what will happen in Russia when we've achieved our operational goals and winter arrives. Bolshevism is not dead yet. It's becoming more difficult to imagine an end to the war. One often is tired, and yet one knows one shouldn't be. There's some comfort in the fact that one can get to know the land and its people. Given that there's little variety to life here, it's probably for the best that we don't get out too much. One sees the same pine forests, the same barren fields of the collective farms, and the poor villages in between. In Minsk I could explore one of the larger cities that had been destroyed. It probably looks the same everywhere in the Russian west. [. . .]

Doing the Best for the Prisoners

September 1, 1941

It's the anniversary of the beginning of the war. We all lined up because the division general wanted to give out a few medals (officers and clerks). Everything was pretty pitiful and really brought home where we rate as soldiers. But all that's over for me now anyway. Now it's just about doing what I can for the prisoners and planning for the future. We had 12,300 prisoners in our camp during the last few days. A day like today (when from morning to evening one has to take care of the supplies, the fires, and then dole out the food) is hard enough. One is constantly surrounded by the stench and the cries, beset by incessant pleading. To keep things going overall, one sometimes has to be hard-nosed toward individuals. Then there's the friction with our superiors (officers and administrators); they fight with one another and that rubs off on us; above all there is a constant pressure to economize. We can't satisfy the prisoners' hunger. Since they've already been in prison for weeks now, they're more restless. They want warmth, work, bread—and we can't give it to them. It would be good if this campaign and this camp would both come to an end. We're hearing with more certainty now that they're going to build a Stalag[14] (with fewer men), and it's to be located in the former middle school, which is the largest building in the village.

I'm doing all right. I got through the diarrhea that is a regular part of settling in; it likely won't return. I continue to eat my millet with milk. Did I already tell you that we're getting fresh butter now—a lot of it? Now and then we have an egg. Without that it would be hard to get by. I continue to sleep a lot on my days off. It would be good if I could get my own lamp for when my comrades are playing cards at the table. [. . .]

I wrote the Martin Luther Bund today and asked them for some Russian-language Bible texts and brochures. What will happen to Russia if the church doesn't revive here? I'm going to write to Cramer, too.[15] I suspect that he's serving as

---

[14] *Stammlager*, permanent POW camp.
[15] P. Cramer, colleague from Erlangen.

a special envoy somewhere. He really needs to send me some material, so that one can find some meaning in this utterly horrid situation, and before we suffocate from the work and the fatigue that goes along with it. [. . .]

Uncertainties about the Future

September 3, 1941

The wood is crackling away in the oven, as if to prove that there is no end to the Russian forests. [The dog] Floki, our newest acquisition, is whimpering impatiently. He's bored here with me. I'm alone; this room is generally full of my comrades because they don't have any stoves in their rooms. No one can stand the cold there for long. And it's just the beginning of September! Hopefully it will get a little warmer for a while. One can hear impatient cries from down in the camp. Although they are covered from the rain and have some protection from the wind on one side, [the prisoners] must be freezing to death. We're having a hard time getting them any farther behind the front. The divisions headed back usually don't have room, and if we were to use the trains to transport them we would need to post sentries, and we don't have the manpower. Hopefully we'll find a solution soon. Rumors are starting to fly again. It's hard for me to get enthusiastic about any given solution. I'm only really fully there when my job requires my attention. Now the question about whether I should sign up for the army administration is really becoming more urgent. It's tempting to think that I could return home for training starting at the beginning of November. But I'd be happier with a requisition for exemption. Perhaps I'll get some mail before the 8th and it will have some sign as to whether I can expect one.

Transporting Russian POWs, fall 1941

I hope I get some news by the end of the week. I'll be able to hold out until then, especially since my free day is almost over. Tomorrow the day will go more quickly, and I'll busy myself trying to find some protection from the cold and helping in the different kitchens with soup, horsemeat, salt, and millet. The problem here is that we have a great deal of free time that could be spent well and yet we can't [use it wisely]. I guess I'll have to deal with that as long as I'm a soldier. At least my comrades will now sometimes go into the other room to play cards to respect my privacy.

Have you heard from Franz and Lene? I wonder if his career questions can be answered now that the summer is over. I need to learn more about the East and I'd like to get to know more about Burgundy. When I look back to my days in Amiens I can almost see a hand in my fate. Things were a bit more comfortable with Madame, in the barracks, at the cinema, not to mention Notre Dame. Our entire intellectual inventory here consists of a volume of Pushkin and one of Gogol, and I can't even read the script in them.

As for the enclosed pieces [of writing], I think that they don't do justice to reality. But perhaps things are simpler than we would want to make them when we wish for an experience that helps us get through the routine.

Depressingly Comfortable

September 5, 1941

I would love to be able to respond to your news; but it's still too early [I haven't received any yet]. I've been here three weeks. Your letters should arrive any day now. Our lives are pretty comfortable. We don't even have any early duty every other morning; now I work every other day for just two hours in the morning and then on the other I work from eight to seven, with a lot of quiet time in between. They say that's the way things are until new orders arrive! We're supposed to clear the nearby highway of snow and then be divided up into smaller camps.[16] The staff is to stay here in the large, bright rooms of the middle school; they're already fixing up the stoves and making sure the windows are tight. We aren't seeing too many prisoners coming in or out of the camp. It's not clear yet who will be stationed where. It will probably be weeks until we know for sure. [. . .]

There's not much else to report. If I have the time and it's quiet, I can read a bit of Aristotle. I go to bed at nine. I sleep until five. I lie there for an hour and am the first to get up. One has to constantly brush one's belongings; things

---

[16] For preparations in September 1941 to spend the winter in Russia, see Arnold, *Besatzungspolitik*, 223.

are dusty here. Today I picked up two books at the school, [Maxim] Gorky and [Karl] Marx. The other day I drew up a schedule detailing how we could spend our evenings and passed it around; everyone said, "oh how nice," but no one wants to change their routine. Our energy is sapped by the lives we lead; each of us suffers from it. God forbid we should *do* something, or think something. Instead, we should just sleep, nap, or play cards. We're hearing the wildest contradictory rumors about the war. Only one thing seems clear—the main attack has been delegated to the flanks; even there one can't possibly participate in an intellectually engaged manner.[17] I seem to have exhausted whatever impulses were to be gained (at least superficially) from the world around me. To understand more I would need to dig deeper, and that takes patience and hard work. Because I can't see how to change things I'd like to ask you again to help me a little bit. Since everything takes so long, we need to plan months in advance (of course one can't even think about a furlough at this point. We're still all confined to quarters). [. . .]

It's a Son

September 6, 1941

Thank God the waiting is over; I'm so happy and grateful. I had a feeling all day yesterday that I would hear something, but then told myself I shouldn't be so sure. Then I kept looking for the car that brings mail from Orscha along with our provisions. Then it grew dark. My comrades were sitting down

---

[17] Hitler had, despite resistance from the Supreme Command of the Army, moved the center of operations to the south and north. See Ernst Klink, "Die Operationsführung," in *Das Deutsche Reich und der Zweite Weltkrieg*, vol. 4 (Stuttgart, 1983), 572–84.

to eat; I was sitting close to the oil lamp with my Karl Marx, trying to pick out words like "Social Democrats, Reactionary, Communism," in order to practice my Russian. I heard someone in the next room say my name, although I didn't make anything of it. And then I had the piece of paper in my hand and I was so happy and yet also sad that I didn't have anything other than a piece of paper.[18] But we need to hold our heads up so that the little fellow doesn't become a coward.

I wonder how you've been doing these past weeks? I see you had to wait a few days after my departure [for the birth]. I hope you didn't have to go through too much. It happened on the Thursday that I was in Minsk, when I walked around until I was dead on my feet; I saw so many things. Then I spent the afternoon and evening riding through the Russian countryside alone in the conductor's cab. Now the boy is more than three weeks old. I hope that you've recovered a little bit. You must be very busy all day. I'm pleased that these days will go quickly for you. I'm so looking forward to your first letters; you'll have a lot to tell me! But if you're tired or have too much to do, you can wait to tell me everything when I'm home. I'm not sure when that will be. There's a ban on travel and in any case it's such a long way away. I imagine you have a lot of visitors and you've been getting a lot of mail; I hope that gives you some comfort as there are some things we just can't change. I'm sure you've already been gathering things to send them here in the mail. [. . .]

I didn't give my comrades the usual party because there's nothing to drink here. I was actually glad of it—not because of the money, but because of my mood in general. I went to bed early and slept well. I'm a little tired today after all the tension. [. . .]

---

[18] The single telegraph sheet with the news.

The Insignificance of Life

September 9, 1941

Your first letter from the 28th arrived today; you sounded so calm and collected, it did my heart good to read your note. Our mood isn't good. This afternoon a prisoner was shot in front of our eyes, just as he was struggling through a barbed wire fence to grab a cauliflower from a nearby garden. They had fired warning shots and the guard was certainly right to shoot, but it's made us all reflect on how insignificant a single life is. [. . .]

I saw the major[19] today to give my status report. He was really kind, but too caught up in his own thoughts and troubles to worry himself about anyone else. That pretty much sums him up: he's fatherly and well meaning, but doesn't really concern himself that much with others. He didn't respond to my attempt to bring up the topic of a furlough. It would be better in any case if I could come home for a bit longer. It would be a wonderful sign of trust if the request for exemption came through for the Alumnat. But I'm not counting on that. We're no longer confident here that we can completely defeat the Russians in the few weeks that stand between now and winter. And so the army won't be sent home like last year. But that's really just speculation. Supposedly the ban on travel is going to be lifted on September 30. The authorities should know all about that.[20]

I gather that you have been having air raid alarms. The news from Berlin is making us a little uneasy. What do you do with the baby? Do you go down into the basement? My

---

[19] Major Johannes Gutschmidt (1876–1961), Hauptstaatsarchiv Hannover, NDS. 721 Acc. 90/99, no. 124/2.
[20] The ban was to end September 30, 1941, but was extended to December 31, 1941.

bunkmate comes from Berlin and has relatives there. He's with the NS Motor Corps; a pretty decent fellow. He wants to become an administrative inspector. The major told me he was happy that I haven't yet decided to take the training, but I didn't give him my reasons.

My Russian is getting a little bit better. The words are sometimes really long and the script is difficult to decipher; understanding the spoken word is even more difficult. I know it's probably foolish to start trying to learn it. But if I have to spend the winter here, it would be good. Anyway, I can barely fill my time at the moment. It's too bad that we don't get out much. The weather here has gotten nicer; it's clear and dry. The colorful sunrises are beautiful; everything is covered in fog. It smells like potato greens and mugwort. The fog rises up from the river, and the smoke from the houses lies horizontally on the villages. The nights are also clear. Today the day is ending on a cold but colorful note. The cold sometimes seeps into our souls. Why does this war have to be so hard? [. . .]

Be well, take care of the little one. Do everything you can for your health and don't worry about money. Will you be able to keep the nanny with you for a while? I feel bad that there's nothing I can send you. There's no more butter around. There's only milk and occasionally an egg or two. Our work is less strenuous than ever before, our superiors don't bother us, and our comrades are being really considerate. So I hope that I'll be healthy and fresh when you see me again. [. . .]

Worries about Exemption

September 11, 1941

Today we were just getting ready to move into the renovated school building when we got the order that we should prepare for a transfer. We're to move 200 km south of here toward

Russian POW sketching, fall 1941

Gomel (or Homel);[21] it will be interesting to travel straight through Russian territory. Still, it's hard to give up the degree of comfort we've managed to arrange here. We had brought together a lot of stuff for the camp that made our lives easier. But we'll have to leave all of that behind, and start all over again. That's war. Yesterday I spoke with the camp commander (captain) to try to win some clarity about my future. I told him about the request for exemption and showed him the letter from B[oethe]-S[chulze]. He advised me to try my luck with that and then, if that didn't work, I should try to get sent to a reserve battalion within the division so that I could be promoted. A colonel inspected the camp today. I guess everything went well. Otherwise, there's not much to report. We got our first newspaper today, from September 3. That means the mail lines aren't working. I bought a history of Russia at a bookstore in Orscha. It's not very academic. But it does give me some insight into the world around me.

---

[21] Gomel is the second largest city in Belarus on the Ukrainian border.

282

The major recently gave me a copy of the *Berlin Historical Society Journal* that had an interesting article about Berlin life by Hellpach.[22] I'll send it to you with a few other things as well as the Marx volume. Please keep everything for me. The medal comes from a museum plundered by a Russian. I traded with a prisoner here who had it with him. I have a good sketch of some typical Russians but it's too big to send. I'll send some smaller ones. I hope this "booty" arrives safely. It will certainly take long enough. [. . .]

The Specter of Revenge

September 13, 1941

Dear Bruno, dear Trudchen,

Thanks to you both for your good wishes. I hope they come to pass. How lovely it would be if this war could be followed by decades of peace for all of Europe. What we've seen here makes us wish even more fervently than before that the European peoples should have a time to heal their deep wounds and take on the tasks of peace. There is so much to do here; so much to build in order for people here to live decently! [. . .] Sometimes I'm terrified by the thought that all these people whom we had to hurt and humble deeply, might at some time band together for revenge. My comrades usually say that when the Jews are gone, other forces will be able to determine things. But history—and Russian history, which I'm learning right now—tells another story. So perhaps little Konrad will one day wear a uniform and have to fight in a war. But that's not a reason not to be happy. [. . .]

Next week we'll be moving to the area south of the Rokitno marshes. Supposedly we're going to take the prisoners

---

[22] Willy Hellpach (1877–1955), psychologist and politician.

out of a contested area and move them farther. The country-side will probably be even poorer than it is here. I hope we'll have lice-free quarters. Up until now we've only seen one or two fleas and ticks. I took a steam bath yesterday even though it's quite strenuous. It surprised everyone that the Russians have put up such a fight. If you were to see the men in the camps you wouldn't believe it. But I guess those who really fought hard are dead—up to 90 percent of them.[23] [. . .]

Prisoners as People

September 15, 1941

Today's the day for us to pack up. But this morning things are still up in the air. I'm to stay here with the rear guards and take care of our provisions. But that's not clear yet. We're getting the camp ready. Our prisoners are all gone, except for a small group that we'll take with us. The Führer has ordered the Ukrainians to go back home with the Letts, Estonians, and Lithuanians, and they left here marching and singing.[24] Our cooks also left and were quite friendly. I'm glad that the NCO with whom I share duties (from the NS Motor Corps) treated them the same way I did. We're pretty much on the same page in terms of our work. I took the opportunity to have a few conversations because the camp was so quiet. There are some interesting people here—not as individuals; we don't understand each other well enough—but as representatives of

---

[23] Due to incomplete bookkeeping in the chaos of war, the figures are somewhat inexact. Catherine Merridale, *Iwans Krieg. Die Rote Armee 1939 bis 1945* (Frankfurt, 2006), 13, indicates that by the end of 1941, 2.7 million Red Army members had been killed in action (see Richard Overy, *Russia's War* [New York, 1998]); 3.3 million landed in prison camps and 1.3 million were wounded or injured. See David M. Glantz, *When Titans Clashed: How the Red Army Stopped Hitler* (Lawrence, 1995), 292.

[24] Approximately 80,000 were released. See Arnold, *Besatzungspolitik*, 334–37.

certain destinies. Yesterday for instance I had a long talk with an Armenian who served near Tiflis with "them Germans" on a collective farm and who speaks German with a Swabian accent. Another translator of ours is a Crimean Tatar and accompanies us so we can understand his countrymen. There are a lot of Turkish people here and Mongolians too.[25] Those of us in the kitchen are taking two other cooks in addition to our Volga Germans. One comes from Moscow, the other from Samara.[26] The past few days they've been taking really good care of us, and they do their best to find eggs and cabbage in the village. Yesterday evening I had some fried potatoes with egg and a bowl of cabbage soup. So there's really no need for you to worry or to send anything. We even have some good chocolate every once in a while. Unfortunately, it seems that our mail has been disrupted by our imminent departure. I haven't heard anything for the last couple of days. The last piece I received was the envelope with the [birthday] wishes, postmarked the 2nd. I sent you a Marx volume and one by Lenin. But I guess those two packages won't arrive there before the beginning of October. I've exhausted my library in the meantime. I reread things and try to memorize them. My Russian history reading has given me a real overview of Russian customs. I wonder if we have ignored such books until now out of snobbery. I spent fifteen years trying to learn from Kliutschewskij[27] and can figure it out now in eight days. Of course I would need to add depth to my knowledge. I

---

[25] Peoples who suffered under Soviet rule and who initially collaborated with the Germans. See Joachim Hoffmann, *Die Ostlegionen, 1941–1943. Turkotartaren, Kaukasier, Wolgafinnen im deutschen Heer* (Freiburg, 1976).

[26] Samara, called Kuybyshev from 1935 to 1990, an industrial city on the Volga.

[27] Wassili Kliutschewskij (1841–1911), Russian historian who wrote a *History of Russia* in four volumes (New York, 1960).

looked at an interesting school textbook this week—*Modern History from 1789 to 1870*. It's mostly a history of [European] revolutions, followed by the nationalist movement. Economic history doesn't play a larger role than it does in our own history books. Most of the pictures are of revolutionary leaders and important street battles. It's not as if the book were denying the role of the individual in history. [. . .]

I hope my request for exemption comes through at the end of November. Or that I can at least have some leave time. I'll be able to hang on until then. Then I'd need to be outfitted for the winter: woolen underwear, a fur vest, warm pajamas, etc. But there's still time to plan for that. I hope to get some news about the both of you soon. Being apart in this manner does eat away at one's spirit and energy. That's why I'm doing less and less at my work. It's just good that I can sleep so much. I miss you so. [. . .]

Up in the Air

September 16, 1941

You often ask in your letters when you'll hear from me next. Now that our operation is in full swing we can't expect any regularity at all. We saw that on the way here: often it was just an accident if the train went through or got stuck. Overall our unit is lacking in punctuality; that's something that Herrmann always took care of. But I'll try to write more frequently so that you don't have to wait so long in between letters. It won't be every day. At least not if the Army Group Center starts to move again.[28] To me it looks as if our plans for the future are already out of date. Everything is up in

[28] Operation "Typhoon," the attack in the direction of Moscow, began on October 2, 1941.

the air. We are left with nothing to do as a result. At least the weather is warm and pleasant, so we can lose ourselves a bit. Yesterday before dinner I took a short walk through the fields and strolled along the road in the evening light. I looked into the windows of a farmhouse (it was very clean, by the way). It's disgusting how intimately our soldiers interact with the Russians; they do so despite all the rules against it and both sides benefit from it. In the end things are the same here as they were in Amiens, despite the differences. Everyone is on the lookout for "booty." It's hard to believe the things that can be found here to trade: butter by the kilo; honey, but also tarps, boot shafts that can be made into gloves; boots from dead Russians that can be traded for good riding boots, etc. It's hard to say how this will turn out in the future. In any case, no one appears to be worried about morale. We have a lot of officers and most of them could care less about their men. They just do their own thing. I haven't gotten to know anyone beyond our own quarters. I've long since given up my initial hope that I could really get to know someone here. How completely impossible that is in the long run, I wrote in a letter to Oda [Hoffmann] yesterday. It's odd but the contents of that letter have already become lost to me. If one can't interact with others or at least exchange ideas with someone else, then one's thoughts take on a strange shape and finally die altogether. Even intellectual life has to be sustained in a community. Maybe young people see things differently, since they are always looking to the future. But at our age the present weighs differently upon one's spirit. That's why the prospect of a long war is so frightening to me. I worry that the result will be a Europe that is entirely consumed with the need to restore the destroyed foundations of material existence. We've been able to survive because we've had new possibilities: first 1940

287

in Western Europe and then 1941 in the Ukraine. We are living at the expense of these people and are sucking them dry.[29] What should we expect, other than bitterness and an abiding desire to overthrow this foreign rule? This is the great moral advantage the British and the Americans possess. Our relationship to the occupied areas resembles that of the British in India or now in Persia. I don't understand how we can expect anything good to come of such circumstances. Ranke's[30] saying that every state has to live according to its founding principle has to be true for the National Socialist state as well. Such considerations should determine what one wants in the future and what one wishes for oneself and others. [. . .]

In such circumstances, my greatest pleasure lies in what you have to tell me about our child. Please tell me everything about him. Otherwise, Lohrisch is probably right that there isn't much hope that I'll get my request for exemption approved. It would be so much better for me if a request came through on behalf of the cloisters. But as I wrote to you recently, the war makes it difficult for us to know anything for sure. What kind of protection could Frau Fischer offer us? Don't you think you'd be better off with the baby and its needs with your relatives in Gnadenfrei?[31] I'm thinking about practical things, like the laundry, cooking, etc. Or are you tied in other ways there? I'm in favor of your leaving Magdeburg. The nightly alarms can't be good for you, not to mention the danger of getting a cold, etc. [. . .]

---

[29] Götz Aly, *Hitler's Beneficiaries: Plunder, Racial War, and the Nazi Welfare State* (New York, 2008), and Adam Tooze, *The Wages of Destruction: The Making and Breaking of the Nazi Economy* (New York, 2008).

[30] Leopold von Ranke (1795–1886), German historian.

[31] In Lower Silesia near Reichenbach. Now called Piława Górna in Poland.

Getting Ready to Move

September 17, 1941

The day has arrived for us to pack up and load up. I haven't really been involved in the preparations. Most of our kitchen supplies are staying here. I'm remaining as well with a few others and a captain. The trucks will be departing early tomorrow morning. They're to return on Sunday evening, and then we'll be in our new quarters. Unfortunately it's turned really icy out. I'm sitting at our warm hearth and am not cold. I hope we at least have a warm kitchen in our new camp. We spend our days in there. Over the next few days we won't have much to do. It's a good thing that I have a few books. My comrades play cards all day, and the rubles change hands frequently in large sums. In between we eat and drink. Yesterday we ate a chicken, browned in pretty good butter. We bartered for the chicken with salt. I'm going to have a few eggs this evening. Our Russian cooks love to make them for us. They're less fond of doing the washing up. That's the kind of work that others need to do for them. But we have a pretty good houseboy who polishes our boots and washes the dishes, although not always 100 percent clean.

Everything is ready. Our smaller tasks are completed. But I noticed that our small oil lamp isn't sufficient to write by. The light here at the table is so weak that I need to stop. If I move a little closer, then it'll do. Today's report talked about a large-scale operation. It looks like the decisive battle is underway. I hope it brings the success we want, so that the campaign will be over, at least in general. It would be good for everyone. Not to mention the overall situation. We need freedom in the East if we want to undertake new measures elsewhere.[32] [. . .]

---

[32] Such as finishing the war against England.

Dreams of Victory

September 20 [1941]

This will be the last letter that I'll send to you from my first Russian quarters. It's a cold, rainy day. We're waiting for our cars to pick us up. We'll need to load them Sunday evening, so that we can leave early tomorrow morning. Every half hour that goes by is aggravating. Yet we all know that things will be fine if they don't arrive today. We'll just leave later. And the unit that is replacing us will have to wait as well. Even as far back as we are we can sense a little of the action at the front, because the comrades replacing us are arriving in fantastical vehicles made for the furthest reaches of Africa.[33] So the last troops are arriving to break Russia's back.

I wonder if they will bring any mail? I received your last letter over three weeks ago. But I'm convinced that God will protect you and our child, and am not worried. It may be four or six more weeks of such extraordinary circumstances. But then things will calm down, and then one day the furlough trains will be running from Moscow or Tula to Warsaw and Berlin. I dream about such things a lot now, but that's all right. [. . .]

The evening of the 20th. Our cars arrived very late. We'll load them in the morning and then leave early Monday. Hopefully we can stay in our quarters until then. [. . .] We received a comforting report from our new post. We'll have a warm hearth there as well as a roof to shelter us from the rain. We

---

[33] German leaders planned to capture the oil fields of the Caucasus and then combine those forces with the Africa corps. It's not clear what unit is meant here. See Dietrich Eichholtz, *Krieg um Öl: Ein Erdölimperium als deutsches Kriegsziel, 1938–1943* (Leipzig, 2006).

also received the special announcement yesterday [about the end of the siege of Kiev and the capture of 600,000 prisoners]. We're going to have our hands full soon. We still haven't seen any sign of the new camp, but that will all work out.

It's Sunday morning. Everything is loaded. We have a quiet afternoon ahead of us. It's gotten a bit warmer. I wonder how you'll spend this Sunday? Nothing here is reminiscent of Sundays. At the most there are a few women with cleaner clothes standing on the street who cast glances at the soldiers. The world is so barren without God both here and at the other side of the front. I have often thought so when watching yet another one of our prisoners lie dying. No priestly words. Carried out like a corpse. Such deaths occur by the millions. This is truly the work of the devil. . . .

Coping with War

September 21, 1941

Dear Siegfried,[34]

[. . .] It was so good to hear your congratulations. At the moment I need to be cautious with my use of paper. But I could feel your joy across the miles. And I trust that God will continue to guide and protect us, even if it's often not easy. Three days before [my son] was born, I had to leave Germany. I received the news on September 5. And now almost three weeks have gone by since I've heard from my wife. So I miss home very much. I would be happy if the administration would free me to take over the Alumnat in our cloisters. I know that the work at home would be much more difficult. And I know that it will be hard for you to leave home.

[34] Pastor in Berlin.

But I'm also convinced that you'll prove yourself with the Prussians. Perhaps when you receive this, the initial difficult weeks will already be behind you. It may be important for your later work that you were "there." That's the way it is for me now. I'm in charge of a prisoners' kitchen in a transit camp. Realistically, there's very little I can do. Everything would run its course without me. But I look into the eyes of thousands [of prisoners] who are strained, tired, and filled with hunger when they pass before us for their meals, and I interact with scores of cooks and kitchen workers. One can learn about Russians in such circumstances. I've gotten to know a large portion of Belarus up to the eastern border. Tomorrow we're moving 200 kilometers farther, more to the south. We expect to be [supporting] the offensive farther in the East. Hopefully this terrible war will come to an end before winter. I'm saddened as well by the news that so many young people are dying. One wonders whether one has given them enough for life and death. And yet we know how little of that is in our hands. I've received a lot of such news from Schwedt. [. . .] And that was just in the first few weeks. One has to try really hard not to become despondent. One can't imagine the battles that lie ahead. Hopefully at least our loved ones at home will be spared. [. . .]

Travel Impressions

September 23, 1941

I have the first transport behind me. After an eleven-hour trip we arrived in Schurawitschi.[35] They're building a new camp here. In a few days we'll move farther eastward, to a place on the rail line. Here, where there are no railroads or

---

[35] Town near Gomel, close to Chernobyl.

streets, we feel as if we are in the middle of Russia. But we're still in Belarus. The next village will mark the border to Russia proper. [. . .] Perhaps I missed hearing from you yesterday so much because it was so difficult to bear the impressions I gained as we traveled through the countryside. During a trip of some 200 km we passed the ruins of Orscha as well as Mohilev,[36] which seemed to have been spared somewhat. Those were the only larger urban centers. Otherwise, we encountered merely empty villages and endless forests, swamps, wastelands, fields with stunted crops. Only a writer could capture the impressions adequately. Even just an objective description is much too difficult for me today. I'll mention only a few impressions: The morning was surprisingly beautiful; mild and sunny. A real fall day. Where the fields had already been plowed, the upturned earth contrasted with its warm tones against the blue of the woods. The kind of morning that makes your soul quicken. But even early on, this brightness seemed dulled. Along the horizon lay a long stripe of gray, dark and impenetrable. The grayness rose ever higher, until by mid-morning it had covered the whole sky. At the same time it grew colder. We traveled eastward, north of Orscha along the road that links Minsk and Moscow. Then we turned to the south. At the end we veered back once again to the northeast. To our right we could see the Dnieper River valley; we had crossed the river at Orscha on a temporary wooden bridge. We could sometimes see the course of the river from the higher west bank. We had to cross numerous valleys on our way that flowed down to the river; because the road cut through these valleys, the vehicles had a tough time of it. We broke an axle after the convoy had already lost a trailer on the way to Kochanowo

[36] Now Mogilev, a city on the Dnieper.

when the hitch came loose. North of Mohilev there were many fields, and next to the farmhouses were scattered the irregular barns and stables of the collective farms. These are long, gray wooden buildings; their roofs, if covered in straw rather than shingles, are mostly bare all the way down to the beams. In the villages we see a few more stately wooden structures, such as schools or party buildings. Overall things aren't too shabby in this area. Wooden carvings decorate the door and window frames and roofs. [. . .] Within this lovely landscape, Orscha (in ruins, almost completely burned to the ground) looks even bleaker; it must have been an important rail center and industrial city. Everything in the city center or along the rail line made of stone has been completely destroyed. Only a few streets of the wooden houses that surround most Russian cities have survived. Yet among the ruins there was a great deal of activity around the staging areas and supply posts. The next city, Mohilev, announced its presence through the appearance of some half-finished apartments near a forest. These were followed by a factory that has been seized by the Supreme Command of the Army; it too is not yet completed. The city lies up on the right side bank of the Dnieper, and is filled with white buildings, churches, and new structures. Here as well as in the valley there are extensive gardens with wooden houses. Perhaps I'll visit the city in an official capacity.

To the south of the city the countryside became ever more barren and poor. The forests were filled with pines, but mostly the landscape stretched out under the cloudless sky was moorland and swamps. The signs of war became more evident [as we made our progress]: burned-out forests, buckled trees, remnants of roads, barricades, infantry posts, blasted tanks; graves. [. . .] On the whole route we were accompanied by the old postal stations that play such a role in Russian literature. They were built in the same style: four Gothic windows, between them an entrance, also with Gothic tracings, covered with cast iron. Behind are build-ings around a square with stables, surrounded by walls. In each of the half-rounded gardens that line the entryways are now German graves. They also dot the landscape south of Mohilev. Cemeteries with twenty, thirty, and forty graves are everywhere. All of them are marked by wooden crosses, and the individual graves have crucifixes as well. There wasn't a SS cemetery to be found. We passed only about a dozen vil-lages along the eighty km long route. [. . .]

In the evening in Sch[urawitschi] we received a warm welcome from our comrades, with whom I'm now living again. We have a small living space for the five of us with a bedroom, a parlor, an entryway where I can sleep by my-self, and a kitchen, where our prisoner has his bed. We could easily spend the winter here. But we'll be able to set ourselves up similarly, after we know where we're headed. Someone prepared a chicken. Some lovely, clear broth was exactly what was needed after today's exertions. We can come to-gether after five weeks of separation by sharing these exter-nal things even though we have our differences about more important matters. But such togetherness helps a great deal.

Be well. I have never felt so strongly that I can't take care of you and our child in any practical manner. I'm so far from you now. But think about me beyond the miles, as I will of you. [. . .]

Russian Lessons

September 26, 1941

[. . .] I had my first lessons with my Russian teacher last eve-ning. He's a mathematician. One can tell he's a pedagogue.

Everything has a rhyme and reason to it, much more so than in dealing with a prisoner. He is living in temporary quarters, but despite their meagerness his rooms were clean. His wife and daughters stood at a distance, but listened carefully to our attempts. If I were to stay here, I'm sure I would make steady progress. But our prospects are not good. We're to move on. They're still just trying to decide where we'll go.

Sch[urawitschi] is a small city that has some 3,000 inhabitants in peacetime. Now only 1,300 are left. There aren't any row houses here, but just individual houses with gardens. In the middle of the city there's a square gone to seed where the Lenin monument once stood. Now it's covered with German and Russian graves. Behind it is a large brick building, a new school that now houses an infirmary. The city is the administrative seat of the *Rayon* (or county). It therefore has several official buildings. A middle school, a hospital, an orphanage; all of these are rather nice wooden structures. I ordered a lot of copies of photographs taken in Kochanowo. It will take six weeks to get them. But once you have them you can imagine what things are like. At the city's edge there's a collective farm, and we're to set up in their barns. The church has been converted and now houses troops.

Morning. We're going to leave tomorrow for Kritschew[37] near Roslawl. They're going to build a large camp there. I have some things to prepare and therefore need to close. Be well. Don't be sad if there are delays in the mail. We'll have more similar disruptions. I'm most upset about my Russian lessons. It really does seem that I will never have a single advantage from this war. There will be a lot of work in K[ritschew] before everything is up to speed. [. . .]

[37] Town in the Russian district of Mohilev with a phosphate and a cement factory. See Gerlach, *Kalkulierte Morde*, 328 and 407.

Learning Russian, fall 1941

On the Move Again

September 28, 1941

[. . .] We traveled about 100 km to the northeast and are now about 150 km behind the front; in a few days we might be even farther. The landscape that we crossed was at first just as bleak as it had been six days ago. But then we joined an advancing convoy and passed numerous bivouacs—at the end, our progress was so slow that I spent eleven hours on the road. It was bitterly cold. Thankfully after twenty-five km, our inspector came by and picked me up and I sat protected next to the driver. Contrary to our expectations we are well quartered here. The train station is located about six km from the city and has new factories, warehouses, workers' apartments, etc. We're to set up the camp so that we have more space. We're in a large apartment house with small rooms. Tomorrow they're to turn on the electricity. We'll be able to withstand the deeper cold here. I'll tell you about my impressions some other time. Today I'll limit myself to heart-felt greetings. [. . .]

Cut Off

September 30, 1941

[. . .] It's difficult not to think about events on the eastern front this year. Is the offensive on Moscow underway? That's the question. What will it look like here in Russia four weeks from now? We aren't getting any news. No mail, no newspapers, no radio. Our feelings are in flux. We still don't know where we'll be staying. We're supposed to evacuate our current quarters. The officers are constantly negotiating with the local commanders without getting anywhere. So our work has come to a standstill. We're just doing prepara-tory work: breaking up stones, getting firewood, and things like that. I personally have hardly anything to do. I prac-tice Russian and wander around a bit in the area. Yester-day we visited a huge cement factory that wasn't damaged too badly. We've also looked in at the platoons for baking and slaughtering; looked at a tank that was left behind, etc. We're pretty removed from Russian life because everything around us is filled with troops. Maybe this afternoon I can go into the city and look around among the ruins. On the way [to town] there's a small, clean building and above the door there is a sign [indicating the Orthodox faith]. It's a provisional meetinghouse of the Orthodox Church. I'd like to look around there. A rabbi must have lived across the street. Among the ruins there were printed and hand-written books in Hebrew. Those are just a few impressions I gained on the way here. Perhaps I can discover more things like that. [. . .]

Setting Up Camp

October 3, 1941

We've spent the whole week here in uncertainty. Only yesterday afternoon did we learn that we are to stay here after all and are to start building the camp under adverse conditions. Because the offensive has begun, people at the top began to exert pressure. Our quarters are pretty decent and after we spent a few days working [on them], it's starting to look more likely that we'll be able to fulfill our duties here. When the weather gets bad, things will be difficult enough. I was happy that the NCOs are taking seriously their job to build a roof for the prisoners and that they're working to be sure we can provide for their needs. Still, the officers haven't done anything at all. We're often quite offended about their frequent inability to achieve anything. But things aren't very easy at the moment, when everything is in flux and filled with troops. We've certainly learned a lot the past few days, a lot about organization and procurement.

The past few days are having a strong impression on the contents of this letter. Each day we're more occupied with these tasks, and everything else takes second place. So it goes with my Russian; I've taken it up again by following the language guide I got from Holtermann. Of course we haven't received any mail. We're hoping to get some Sunday, when the unit arrives. The automobiles will be driving back to Sch[urawitschi] early tomorrow morning. I'll give them a letter to take along. Supposedly mail leaves there via air. I'm writing at the corner of a table where my comrades are playing cards. That's why you shouldn't wonder why I'm sticking to the absolute minimum. It gets dark here at 6 p.m. The evenings are thus quite long. But I always go to bed early. Things are like they were two years ago, in Poland. A cold day or two seem to portend the beginning of winter, but then things aren't so bad after all. The women are harvesting potatoes. They are likely to be the only source of food this winter. Hunger is just around the corner here as well. We're always relieved that our loved ones at home aren't threatened with that. [. . .]

A Degree of Autonomy

October 6, 1941

[. . .] For the first time, I have some degree of autonomy here. The work is entirely different from what I did training recruits. Here the days are also not filled entirely, and one is tired at night, but not so stressed out. The past two days I've had to stand watch while they construct the second camp. Seven or eight NCOs and sergeants oversee about eighty prisoners who work to complete the kitchen, the fence, etc. The captain comes once in the morning and the afternoon and walks the entire complex with me. He finds fault and nags and carps, but then he's gone and I have the day free for myself. I move from one work site to the next, observe, discuss what is to be done, and often walk on my own through the huge factory to get a sense of the whole complex. I have an entirely different state of mind than I did at the base. In addition, when the day is over, I'm really free of obligation. We now sleep, the four of us (always the same ones), in two rooms connected to each other; our prisoner cleans for us and we look out for one another. In the morning each of us goes off, but in similar circumstances, in rooms that are attached to the storage space where we're to keep our winter supplies. We're to save up in the expectation that we'll have thousands or even tens of thousands here over the winter. That doesn't mean that eight days from now we won't just move farther east. On the one hand I should be happy to be able to see more of Russia. Everyone is saying that Tula is going to be our goal for the winter. But if we think about our furlough, then we blanch. We're so far away. And when the snows come and the trains get stuck, well, it's unimaginable. We've also hoped that we could leave before the snow. But that's no longer a possibility. [. . .]

I was really interested in the Gogol short stories. I read both of them yesterday evening and then spent a few animated hours rereading them. It's so odd that this picture of the old Russia, which resembles today's situation in countless ways (but then is so foreign because of its peacefulness) should be so full of serenity and humor. I'm looking forward to reading more. [. . .]

I think the story about the plague is just one of those sensationalist-gruesome things that Metta[38] is sometimes prone to. I'm sorry she told you that. My natural reserve protects me from almost all contact with Russians. We're being careful to make sure that the kitchen won't be placed next to the reviewing field as it was in K[ochanowo], when we had people with dysentery in the middle of the camp and yet they didn't infect us. This time all those prisoners with infectious diseases will be sent to the prisoner infirmary. I just talked to our camp doctor about that yesterday.

Apropos [of infectious diseases], I'd like to take this opportunity to inform you that I remain entirely free of lice and ticks. Fleas can't be avoided.

---

[38] Metta was a sister of Magdalene von Tiling.

Keeping Busy

October 6, 1940

Dear Little Mother,

[. . .] Many people hope that when Russia is finished, England will be ready to sue for peace. That would be the best outcome. But we can't place our hopes on that. If that were the case, how willing we'd all be to stick it out here until Christmas, or even longer! We often talk about how it will be impossible to get a furlough once the snow arrives. For now, it takes about a day on the train from here to Orscha, and then one is on the Moscow line. Here in Kritschew (somewhat south of Smolensk and north of Gomel), we have been spinning our wheels as an advanced detachment because everything was filled with troops due to the offensive. Now that wave has passed, and in the past few days we've been building busily away at a smaller and at a larger camp, one that includes a very modern cement factory. Unfortunately, the massive halls of the factory, with all of their drums, vats, and conveyer belts, are really not ideal for our purposes. We've set up a fence and built a kitchen. Tomorrow we'll start with cleaning up the sheds that are to serve as bunks. It's not clear if the tens of thousands of prisoners for whom we're making arrangements will actually arrive. We think that the front is already too far away, making our work obsolete. But it may be that the masses are so great that they can only gradually send them back to the rear, and that they'll be happy that they can hold them for a while in Russia before they are transported to Germany. At least we've finished the most important tasks. We still need to build an additional kitchen and then procure and secure supplies. So we certainly have our hands full; but that does make the time go by faster. [. . .]

302

Agitation

October 12, 1941

[. . .] I've been pretty agitated the past few days. Right after I sent you the letter about my promotion and the request to return home, the master sergeant told me that the ban on exemptions has been extended until December 31. In light of this I wonder if I should just go to the territorial reserves. I was speculating if I might be a candidate by Christmas, but I wanted to wait in any case for your next letter. Now that it's arrived, I'm going to tell the major that I don't want to be transferred. What's most important is that I can come home once, even if only temporarily. I think that the ban on travel will be lifted once the campaign is over. The extension until December 31 is likely just a security measure. But if that's not the case, then these two and a half months will also pass. And we can hope that I'll be discharged. Soon I'll learn what you've decided about whether you'll stay or go, and what to do about the Flemish maid.[39] Just do what you think is right. I won't criticize you. I won't be one of the first to get a furlough in any case. Things here now are arranged so that the young men are all sitting inside while the older ones are doing outside duty. It will be the same with the furloughs. Given these circumstances I'm rather concerned about the baptism. Can we delay it given all the uncertainties?

Work wasn't particularly pleasant last week because we were the proxies in an argument between two older officers and despite all our efforts didn't make much progress. But overall

[39] Franz Petri had arranged for a Flemish maid to assist Charlotte Jarausch. Franz Petri to Charlotte Jarausch, September 29, 1941, in the Archives of the Regional Authority Westfalen-Lippe, the Papers of Franz Petri, Portfolio 914-157, 15. Thanks to Jürgen Höötmann for his assistance.

I'm doing well: a warm, quiet room, double-glazed windows, electrical lights, and often we get extra rations. In the mornings and evenings we get millet and milk. Yesterday a comrade brought eggs and a chicken. You've already had to admit that your worries about our provisions were unfounded. Even if we don't receive packages from home to help us through the evenings, we make sure to find things ourselves. I therefore often profit from the inconsiderate comrades. If you want to send something, please just send soap, shoe polish, always something to read. I borrowed a dictionary for my Russian lessons. I can now translate the Russian grammar book that I have and don't really need anything else. I also have a primer that I'm using to learn how to write. At the moment I just don't have a lot of time because I'm on duty every day in the evenings and am exhausted by the cold air. We're now transitioning to winter. We had our first snow on the 9th, which did not melt in the shade because the air was so cold. We've had a hard frost every night since then. But I enjoy a freedom of movement and can go on my own discretion to the kitchens or the heated room. Things aren't that bad; it's much different than when one is stuck in one place during training exercises.

[. . .] I received four Russian psalms from the Martin Luther Bund in the mail today. I gave one of the pamphlets to our prisoner, who is a good, honest soul. A few days ago he showed me a handwritten prayer book that he had hidden from the commissars. They took away the Bibles from all the soldiers. It's understandable that he's not especially fond of the Bolsheviks. They all are hoping that they'll be released after the fall of Moscow. Many of them will be disappointed. This afternoon the first 2,000 men from the October battles arrived. We could give them some warm food and put them in some covered shelters. But we've already almost filled all the adequate space we have. The others are going to have to

Camp commander's quarters, fall 1941

freeze. A few hundred sacks of supplies are stacked up next to our room. They'll unload a cart full of rye flour for bread tomorrow. Tomorrow we're to start digging a clamp[40] for 72,000 hundredweight (!) of potatoes. That's going to mean a lot of work, even if we never manage to get that much.[41] Werner Haß wrote that three-fourths of the Ukrainian harvest can be salvaged and will help us over the rough patches (especially regarding our lack of feed for the animals). I also got a letter from Bruno and from the Merwarts.

It's a cold, starry night. For hours now Vassily has been sitting ramrod straight in the hallway, reading the psalms by the light of the oil lamp that I gave him this afternoon. How pathetic we are in comparison, with all of our talk and

---

[40] A long rectangular ditch in which root crops are stacked and then covered with straw or dirt for storage.

[41] Orders were being passed down to begin preparation for the winter. Three hundred thousand tons of potatoes were to be readied. See Arnold, *Besatzungspolitik*, 391–92 and 401–2.

intellectual pretensions! Vassily refuses all of the extra rations that we offer him. Sometimes he'll accept some bread and eat whatever is left over from our lunches. The simplicity of the Russian soul is not a literary invention.

I want to go to bed. The letters I received today contained almost too much for my spirit. And tomorrow things will be as simple and primitive as ever. I may need to travel a great deal over the next few days to secure some supplies. But it's pretty quiet. The SS are cleaning out [the area] in terrible fashion.[42]

Feeding the Hungry

October 15, 1941

You shouldn't have to wait long for a letter, so I'll write a few lines, even though I'm not capable of having any higher thoughts. We now have 7,000 of the prisoners who were captured during the October campaigns. Because of the poor external conditions here they are quite a lot of work. Everything is spread out and in different places. We have to scamper from one place to the next. No one is here who has a clear sense of the whole situation and who can allot forces accordingly. Everything is improvised in a makeshift fashion. I had to take the morning off because I received an immunization, but now I'm back working full time taking care of the provisions. When I passed by the dark rows [of prisoners] last night, I was reminded how I had been so occupied before the war with the idea of the "Christianity" and historical

---

[42] In November and December of 1941, 1,213 Jews were murdered by mobile killing squads in Kritschew. See Wolfgang Curilla, *Die deutsche Ordnungspolizei und der Holocaust im Baltikum und in Weißrußland* (Paderborn, 2006), 443; Gerlach, *Kalkulierte Morde*, 600.

"reality" of the miracle of the loaves. Feeding the hungry is truly a miracle that only God can perform. When one sees a man crying because a comrade who was supposed to share his portion of soup has already eaten it, one can see how redemption in the afterlife must overcome even this misery. Luke 6:21.[43] There were many wounded among the prisoners; much suffering and pain. Up until now we've only been able to give them warm food twice. If the transports continue [at this pace], that won't be possible.

The day before yesterday we learned that starting on October 25, the limit on mail packages has been increased to 1,000 grams. I'm happy to hear this, if only because it's a sign that they're planning for the campaign to end. It's about time. It was terribly cold last night, most certainly several degrees below zero. The morning brought snow, which quickly turned into rain. And then we had the most terrible autumn weather. Everything is soaked through—and now at 8:45 p.m. 2,000 more men are arriving in the dark of night, escorted by only four Germans! Things are absolutely chaotic. Luckily I don't need to leave our quarters. [. . .]

For I Was Hungred

October 23, 1941

And now almost another whole week has gone by. You'll be waiting for news. But please don't take offense when I write less frequently now. My situation is like yours. You have to take care of your child, and I have to take care of more than 11,000. Fortunately, 4,000 of them are to leave tomorrow morning. Hopefully then our numbers will stay low. It's not the work feeding the prisoners that weighs on me—although

---

[43] "Blessed are ye that hunger now: for ye shall be filled."

307

we've had some new difficulties on that front. We've not been able to get any provisions because the locomotives are broken and no trains are running.[44] We have to cook potatoes, and that means a lot of work and they take longer to cook than grits. Our superiors are now making appearances in odd ways. But the most important thing is that responsibility for the running of the camp has fallen in large part on me. There was a vacuum. So for instance the captain is fifty-five years old; his deputy (a sergeant) has been ill; the lance corporal is dumb and brutish. That's all there is here in regard to personnel. Either everything would go to pieces or brute force would decide everything. So the work has fallen on me, or rather, on the prisoners. I'm constantly reminded of Matt[hew] 25:42–43.[45] I can't stop thinking about the passage. I'm trying to do what I can. It's not much in the face of the worst suffering I've ever encountered in my life. But perhaps I can prevent further calamities. The Russians are helping me. There are a few experienced men among them. Others can at least serve to maintain order. The cooks and translators are touching in their care for me; they get me milk, eggs, a chicken every now and again, even though we've only been together for just eight days. I would like to be able to focus again solely on the provisions, as soon as I can. But at the moment the question is simply: who is your neighbor?

I'll spare you the details. On Sunday one of the Russians said to me: "This is hell." Now at least we have some semblance of order. But we achieved it with blood and tears. And next to the loud [death] is this quiet dying from exhaustion and illness. I hope Moscow will fall soon. [. . .]

---

[44] The Red Army destroyed train tracks and cars while retreating.

[45] "For I was hungred, and ye gave me no meat: I was thirsty, and ye gave me no drink."

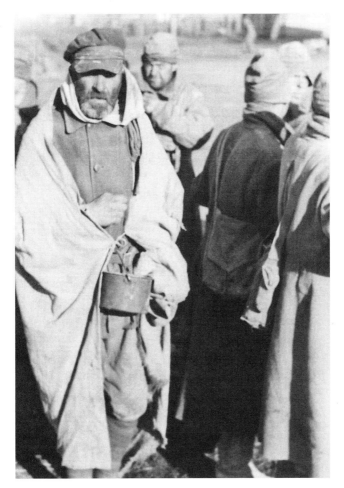

Starving Russian POWs, fall 1941

Holding On to Humanity

October 25, 1941

In the midst of all the trouble we had a quiet Sunday morning. I quit early yesterday, but not with a good conscience,

309

because as darkness fell there were still some five hundred men on the parade grounds who had not yet received their second portion of soup. But the kitchens had already given out their 12,000 portions, and we couldn't get any more than that, at least until now. There wasn't anything to be done. We left in silence and I came back and read all the congratulatory notes through again. It's really a blessing to receive such loving support. Some of the letters are really beautiful. I would love to send everything back, as well as a few things. But I'm still looking for some packing paper. The days have become somewhat less stressful since I last wrote. Friday morning we sent a few thousand prisoners off on a march. And it's a lot easier to handle 6,000 than 20,000.[46] I no longer have to play the policeman and don't need to beat anyone down with a nightstick or have them shot. Still, things are harrowing enough. Today we're finally able to have regular shifts. I'll go down to the camp in the afternoon. We've expanded our kitchen, but we'll have to give up the complex because they want to get the factory back up and running. But it's in a pretty sorry state. Every piece of wood—window frames, stairs—has been torn out and burned. Everything is covered in smoke and ash, filled with the sick and dying. We try daily to meet the demand. But we have so few means [at our disposal]. Luckily the older officers still have human qualities of the traditional sort, so that I have some support and can make things happen (like having two meals a day) against the will of the "bureaucrats"

---

[46] In a letter to Bruno on October 25, 1941, Konrad Jarausch wrote: "I have seen such images of misery that I've never encountered in my life. I don't want to go into details. It was often horrible. We (a dozen Germans) had to use the strongest measures to keep the 20,000 Russians in line. I fervently wish that such things will not be repeated. In the last few days a few thousand have been sent on. Now it's really easy, although the suffering here is still horrendous."

and many of my comrades, who don't comprehend what I'm doing. There is some room for humanity here. I listened to an opera singer from Moscow yesterday, who sang a Russian folk song for the major and then some Mozart and Wagner. I had just come back from a walk to the uppermost floor of the factory, where we had to ascertain if it was true that the Russians had stolen a corpse in order to cut the flesh off of it. We didn't find that corpse, but we did find others (fully clothed) that had been there for days.

I think you'll understand why at the moment I can't write much and that I haven't replied to your letters. That doesn't mean I'm any less happy to get them, and I beg you merely to make decisions about those things that have become necessary. [. . .] I wonder if you're in church at the moment? Here, every now and then a shot explodes through the rain. That's the sound that we fall asleep to, the sound we wake up to. But don't worry. I don't think that any of the Russians from our camp will do anything to me. "Wery gutt Komrat."

[. . .] I'm going to the camp to learn a little Russian from a teacher from the Technical University and then try to see that my people get enough to eat on a Sunday. As to what remains to us, I'm so grateful that I have our intellectual world and hope it doesn't crumble in the face of the images before me. How could one stand this otherwise, without becoming an animal?

Solidarity through Art

October 28, 1941

The days are speeding by. Soon October will be over. Will we get news about the fall of Moscow and Petersburg this month? The prisoners ask me daily as I make my rounds in the camp, "Moscow kaput?" Everyone wants this campaign to be over.

The educated Russians don't think that the Bolsheviks will ever give up. They think a hunger revolution is not out of the question (not a political revolt). I've had—now that the horrible times are over—the chance to talk with these fine, intelligent men whom the captain has called upon to assist him. I wish that, if we stayed here, we could have more to do with them. Sunday brought me a wonderful experience: the captain's translator (a teacher from the Moscow Arts and Crafts School and an old pupil of the German Peter-Paul school) invited me to a few hours of relaxation as a reward (they said this expressly as I left) in return for the excessive work I've been doing. The opera singer from Moscow sang to us (I was the only German among six Russians) whatever I requested of him: Russian folk songs, one song by wagoners on the roads and peddlers on the Volga; revolutionary songs, but also the monologue from Boris Godunov.[47] At the end, he sang at my request a few liturgical pieces that even the Russians hadn't heard in a while—"Lord, Be Gracious to Thine Servant" from Candlemas, and some Easter songs. The electricity kept going out. We sat there in the glow of the stove. We could hear intermittent shots from outside. We had two hours of real human solidarity after we had gotten to know one another in such different circumstances and knew what to expect from one another. Today one of them asked me if he could make a sketch of me. Another, whom I don't yet know, wrote down his thoughts for later publication. I wonder if we have the material for an analogue to Dwinger's "From the Hell of Totzkoje"?[48] There's enough grisly stuff to report

---

[47] Modest Mussorgsky (1839–1881), composer, wrote *Boris Godunov* between 1869 and 1874; the opera is based on a story by the same name by Pushkin.

[48] Edwin Erich Dwinger's account of time spent in a prisoner of war camp in the First World War: *In der Hölle von Totzkoje: Aus sibirischer Kriegsgefangenschaft* (Berlin, 1933).

from Kritschew. But since the start of this week the higher ups, who had previously completely abandoned us, are now starting to pay attention. We've been getting constant visitors in the kitchens. Hopefully we'll now also get more provisions.

I'm so grateful for the Reklam books [the Russian novels and short stories], which complement so well the impressions I'm gaining here. Nevertheless, the fate under which these people stand (and have even in the older stories) is pretty grim. "The Russians have always suffered; that is nothing new," one of the men said to me during our time together on Sunday. Because I have these wonderful opportunities to converse with the Russians, [my reading] will have to take a back seat. Every once in a while I read a bit in the lighter articles.

At the end [of the evening] with the Russians I showed them my photos of the [Magdeburg] cloisters and of you. Most of them also have wives and children at home and are eager to receive news of them. We're now starting to get to know the communist Russia about which we once theorized. These people are people just like us. Being with them is good and awakens thoughts and feelings that in the end lead me back to you and our child. [. . .]

Christian Analogies

November 1, 1941

It's Sunday evening. Every day we have to end work a little earlier. The world sinks into the foggy gray dusk of autumn at 5 p.m. I'm so exhausted every night that I can't use the free time very well, and I don't have the energy to write letters. I'm in the camp at 6:45 in the morning. We are faced with the same misery during the hours that lie between. One becomes rather numb to things. Because I now have to oversee the provision of 17,000 to 18,000 warm meals and 9,000 servings of bread, the sheer effort is so overwhelming that I can hardly concern myself with details. Every time I leave the vicinity of the kitchens I'm surrounded by such cries— "*pan, pan!*"[49]—I can barely tend to any one person's needs: food, bread, shoes, illness, work, release, theft—I'm supposed to help with all of that. Since most of the silent dying occurs in the barracks, where the sick are assembled, it remains out of sight. We see only the horribly emaciated corpses lying before us. I am constantly reminded of Grünewald's Christ[50] and console myself with the belief that this dying, although it is incomprehensible to us, is somehow related to Christ's death. My Russian teacher's spirit has been broken; he has stomach troubles and we aren't making any progress in our lessons due to the many interruptions. In the middle of all this—the rags, the stench, and disease—we have to keep our heads up and act like we're superior [to them] and then every now and then play a more human and empathetic role. The colonel was here today.[51] Supposedly we won't receive any more [prisoners], but instead everything is to be slowly dismantled. But there doesn't seem to be any doubt about the fact that we're going to spend our winter in Russia. His whole visit didn't really have any other practical or proximate results. [. . .]

Today I saw a brass pitcher hanging from a Russian's belt. As examined it, I could see that Christ's Baptism was etched into it. I traded a piece of bread for it. It wasn't a work of art. But as I held it in my hand, I thought about our child and was strangely moved. May God bring us together soon.

[49] "Sir, Sir!"
[50] Matthias Grünewald (1475/80–1528); Renaissance painter; the reference is to his Isenheim Altarpiece.
[51] Colonel Marschall.

Trying to Reconnect Intellectually

November 1/2, 1941

Dear Mr. Korth,

Many days have gone by since I received your letter of June 8. Even if I can't answer it at the moment as I would like to, please still accept my most heartfelt thanks. Your letter touched something in me that has been otherwise completely buried. A year ago I would have had quite a different reaction to it. Then I would have tried to respond to your thoughts and plans matter-of-factly, with the sort of distance one might have while one is temporarily on vacation. Then too I was trying to play a more active role with the journal and to stay on top of the most important correspondence. But now all of that is almost all gone. And it's hard to explain why. Perhaps it's that with this war it takes a while before one realizes how much it has changed our lives. Only a year ago, after the quick victory over Poland and France, we thought that [the war] would be a kind of 1870/71 for National Socialism;[52] a new empire would be founded as the crowning achievement, and after its end, life would be rich and full (including the struggle with the church) and it would develop along the lines imagined by the prewar generation. But now we recognize that we stand before new, breathtaking, and monumental tasks. One thus learns to keep silent in order to be able to hear again.

I don't know if I'm exaggerating, and I would be grateful to you for your honest answer. I'd like to give you a few random impressions from the last few days to try to convey what I mean. To distract myself over the weekend, yesterday

---

[52] In 1870/71 Prussia defeated France and unified Germany.

I picked up the September issue of *Deutsches Volkstum*[53] that my wife had sent me. You know what the journal once meant to me. But looking beyond the intellectual qualities of the articles, the topics were so narrowly focused: Humboldt, List, Gilly; Southeastern Europe and Russia were mentioned, but only in a historical context, without taking into consideration the present. A conversation I had today with a young Russian, carried out in halting German; he's an engineer, in his mid-twenties; he has no political ties to Bolshevism; he's completely cosmopolitan and enlightened and now is suffering in this war. Especially in comparison to the older prisoners, who are still grounded in a Christian humanism, one can see what terrible destruction this war has wrought.

You shouldn't think that I have somehow given up on what we once thought or believed. I'm experiencing unspeakable miseries as the head of a kitchen in a prisoner camp that "houses" up to 20,000 Russians. One of the strongest experiences I've had in this war is that in the face of so much hunger, destitution, disease, and death, I have not had to renounce anything that I've done as a German or a Christian. But what about the future? We need an education of European breadth in all intellectual matters—languages, history, geography. But what will provide us with the human foundation? You are absolutely right that in a situation in which we take over responsibility for the Orthodox churches, the differences between the Confessional Church and German Christians appear petty. Furthermore, the question arises— how will we deal energetically now with the question of education?

Questions about German education will now become European issues and conflict between the confessions in

---

[53] *Deutsches Volkstum*, monthly journal for German intellectual life.

Germany will become a battle for the Christian world. I would very much like to keep this larger picture in mind for our own more modest work in the future, because I fear that otherwise everything will be wrong. But I don't see any practical starting points. Perhaps you'll think this is all exaggerated. But I think if we can't work in a larger context, we have to get down to brass tacks so that we can get to the root [of the problem]. Then we'll get results. [. . .]

Please see this letter in the spirit in which it is written, out of my intellectual isolation to start a conversation about things that are also near and dear to your heart, as I know and can see from your letter. If it seems that I'm carrying things too far, please excuse me as a person who in intellectual things has only been able to make plans for the past two years. [. . .]

Making Do

November 5, 1941

[. . .] Now that things have quieted down we talk a great deal about the future. But we know nothing. Everything is equally possible: serving in a Stalag in Russia, being sent back home, furlough, an exemption. Only one thing is clear: any decision is being delayed by the stubborn resistance of the Russians.

Up until now the days have gone by quickly nonetheless because they've been filled with work. Presently the camp will have a longer break. But it's not possible to really take a break in the army. Now all of our superiors are jumping on our backs and everything needs to be built up, improved; new recipes tried out, etc. I'm interested to see if my Russian "friends" will be sent away, or whether we'll have some time to talk. Overall I haven't had as many enriching experiences during the war as I've had during the past few weeks. Really meaningful work and real live people. I'm just really tired. But I'll have a lot of stories to tell about this place.

Our kitchen is now a little kingdom unto itself. We have three stoves, upon which we can prepare about 6,000 portions at once. Everyone who stands out above the masses gets together in my room. When someone speaks slowly, I can understand a little bit. I'd like to sleep a little bit so that I can be fresher for my lessons. If I stay here until Christmas I'll have a pretty good foundation.

[. . .] Since you can't send any more packages, I'll need to prepare for the winter here as best I can. Today in the camp I got a really nice scarf from the head cook. I don't want to collect any treasures. But I don't feel bad about trading our provisions for necessary items or things that will supplement our very poor provisions. There aren't any more eggs to be had in any case now that the frost has set in. But we have wonderful full-cream milk and some meat. [. . .]

Ruthlessness against Bolsheviks and Jews

November 6, 1941

Esteemed Doctor [von Tiling],

For the first time in several weeks I've had a quieter day. I'd like to thank you most sincerely for your letter of October 20 and send you the piece you requested. You wrote in such detail about your life and work that it was a pleasure for me. We must be thankful that there are some limited possibilities for work. If only we could relieve ourselves of the personal and administrative burdens before us! But that will likely not come to pass.

I would gladly send you a similarly extensive report. But I would not want to have you read the writing copied on the bad paper [we have]. I have three very taxing weeks behind me. In the kitchen that I head up we were handing out up to

318

20,000 portions daily, and at the beginning we did not have enough stoves and lacked the necessary provisions. And so we were unable, despite all of our efforts, to do anything to ease the misery around us. Many died of weakness, sickness, and destitution. But still, the best [aspect] has been that we have been able to work together with a few mature and intelligent Russians. I have thus been able to hear and see a great deal out of the huge domain of the Soviets. But the people that we have to do with are those who are not political. Bolshevism is being ruthlessly stamped out, wherever we encounter it. The same thing goes for the Jewish element. Today in particular I'm under the impressions of such actions. Thus the brevity [of this letter]. [. . .]

Going One's Own Way

November 7, 1941

[. . .] Deepest winter has arrived, with frost and snow, icy streets, sleds, furs. It feels as if the Russians experience life more freely now. But our troops and the prisoners have to put up with so much—Jews barefoot in the snow. At least everything is out of our factory, transported by train to Mohilev. Every last piece of wood that would have offered some protection has already been pulled out and burned. Now just a few hundred men are lying around the more bearable barracks, and the kitchen has less work, and since yesterday morning I could also do something different: wash myself thoroughly, make a "visit" to my Russians, sit for my artist, etc. I haven't actually had any rest yet. But that's my fault; at least in part. It's somewhat embarrassing when one stops one's regular duties. I'm to go to another camp; go somewhere different; I'm outwardly more connected, but internally much less free. In the cement factory I could set the tone and that's the main thing. The results were good as long as there were enough provisions and people. But in the end, especially with the Russians, who are so receptive for such things, a friendly word is more important than a perfect result. So I sought out a few people yesterday and today to say goodbye. In part I learned a great deal about Russian life, so for instance that people absolutely had to support the war; [our conversations] were stammered out in bits of Russian and German. I have a few small things in my suitcase, some are presents; they come with both good and bad memories attached to them. Some of the hardness that I couldn't avoid has left bitter impressions behind. I'll tell you about that some time in person.

So I think I'll have some more lonely days ahead. There'll be work enough. I have it pretty good in comparison to my comrades, who are now moaning about the endlessly long evenings. Yesterday and today I didn't get to practice Russian. That however had to do with the sudden and painful end to my lessons: my teacher was discovered to be a half-Jew.[54]

It will, despite all my intellectual efforts, take a great deal to get through this winter, regardless of where I may end up. No one even mentions anymore the plans I once made for our group entertainment in the evenings. Everyone has to go his own way, and so I'll do the same. [. . .]

Relative Comfort

November 7, 1941

Dear Bruno,

[. . .] Because we have only a few hundred prisoners in the camp I have some peace and quiet at the moment that is

---

[54] For the SS screening and execution of Jewish POWs, see Hartmann, *Wehrmacht im Ostkrieg*, 690ff.

Lotte and little Konrad, fall 1941

quite good for me. Overall I've put on some weight from the millet and milk. Today I ate four eggs. They are of course becoming quite rare these days. I trade cigarettes to the prisoners for them, especially the head cook, the chief of police, the translator, etc. Today a painter from Moscow finished a pretty good portrait of me with charcoal and colored pencils. He really wanted to sketch Lotte with the baby from a photograph. But I was a little skeptical. He's now on leave, as well as our musician, in order to paint the refurbished church in Kritschew. [. . .]

Yesterday evening I sat for a long time with one of the Russians who speaks German and he told me about how difficult life was under Bolshevik rule. Now they are all worried about their families in Moscow and Petersburg and hope as much as we do that the Germans will soon occupy those cities. I can't imagine how many civilian casualties there must be!

321

My health is better again. But I'm really dreading the winter. Not so much because of the cold. We won't freeze. But the prospect of having to be shut up here for months on end is bleak. My comrades cling to the hope that we may still be sent back to Germany. I have to think back to the situation two years ago, when everyone was saying the same thing. Luckily the men I share a room with don't gossip in that way. That makes life a lot easier. [. . .]

Scraps of Learning

November 9, 1941

Another Sunday at war nears its end. My comrades are making a ruckus next door. They're celebrating some promotions announced today. Perhaps I need to make an appearance. Yet the mood is so confused and really insincere. But it's the first time during the past three months that there's been such noise, so I should have some patience. Otherwise the day's been really quiet, a good day for resting. In the morning we mustered and then had an inspection of the kitchens. I had a few Russian lessons in the afternoon. But my new teacher is much stricter about having a proper "Moscow" accent, so that I've almost given up hope of progressing. He's a teacher in an arts and crafts school in Moscow and is well educated, from a good family, and pious. He recited some Pushkin verses for me and I enjoyed that. He has reason to be concerned about his family in Moscow. In comparison, we're quite fortunate. You can at least tell me about the baby in your letters, and I'm always so happy and pleased to hear your news. I also just received mail sent from the middle of October, including Lene's letter, and I'm so very happy to hear that she found you so well. The packages with the books have also arrived. All of the halves [which were separated to be sent in the mail] match up. I'm very pleased to have Turgenev's works. I read a lovely story in Russian by him today, and as my teacher read it aloud to me, I felt touched by the soul of this land. [. . .]

New Prisoners Arrive

November 11, 1941

My Russian cook is truly resourceful. He has everything and can get anything; he got me a fountain pen today. I accepted it so I you don't have to try to decipher letters written in pencil. Of course I had to use it right away and send you heartfelt greetings. I can't believe that it's already almost the middle of November. The days go by so quickly and I never have the chance to complete my program. I canceled my Russian lessons today because I wasn't able to prepare beforehand. We still have about 10,000 prisoners in our camp. And since we had a break, it takes a while for everything to get rolling again. The weather doesn't help much. One would rather spend half of the day dozing in bed instead of trudging around in the snow driving things along. It's not easy to keep one's nerves with the stress. Every day we see the same thing: the same sallow, haggard faces, the same rags, especially for those hundreds of prisoners we find in the woods without papers and among whom the partisans try to hide themselves (most of them don't look like they're physically capable of any independent action). It's pleasing to see our policemen, their stomachs almost filled, march off singing a lovely Russian marching song. They sing much better and with more feeling [than we do]. Their songs aren't like the brutal rhythmic yelling of our new marching songs. And their singing creates a sense of freedom. One can forget the barbed wire for a while. Otherwise, it seems that every new group [of prisoners] is more miserable and haggard than the previous one. The first Russian prisoners I saw were still glowing with the tension of battle as well as with the raven-ousness of days of hunger. Now exhaustion and weakness show on every face. It's understandable that the mortality rates are on the rise in the camps in the West.[55]

My spirits are pretty low in regard to a furlough or a re-quest for exemptions. The promotions of the last few days and the way they've been handing out medals really under-scores how unprofessional the prevailing spirit here is; I don't expect to have furlough until it's been approved. [. . .]

More Murder than War

November 14, 1941

[. . .] Unfortunately I couldn't protect myself and I'm really pretty sick. I've been doing my duties as usual, but I really noticed [how sick I was] during my Russian lessons. It cost too much effort to concentrate, so I've skipped several times. The psychological strain is likely also to blame. The dull dying around us is just so terrible. I often ask myself what would have happened to me if I had been sent to the front. Our days are somewhat quieter now. The cement factory is housing a little more than 2,000 prisoners. This camp is to be closed completely on Sunday. But twenty-five prisoners die there daily. In the larger camps farther west, in which tens of thousands are being held, the numbers of the dead are cor-respondingly in the hundreds. One tries to help. When they come to get their food and are frozen stiff from the cold (it's

---

[55] Because the prisoners had to travel so far and because the provisions were so inadequate, mortality rates rose dramatically in the camps in Ukraine and Belarus. See Streit, *Keine Kameraden*, 130–37.

twelve below today and yesterday it was fifteen below during the day) they stagger, fall over, and expire right at our feet. We discovered another case of cannibalism today. Yet the corpses, when they are carried without clothes to the graves, are scrawny like late gothic figures of Christ, frozen stiff. The soldiers look somewhat better because they have their uniforms. There are civilians among the prisoners, many who are just in shirtsleeves—especially the Jews. It would really be the most merciful thing if they would be taken out into the forest and bumped off, as the experts put it. But the whole thing is already more murder than war. If we didn't constantly hear from the Russians about how they suffered under Bolshevism, then we could really despair of the meaning of the whole thing. We've just been thrown into this situation, incapable of doing anything other than our limited duty. It is extremely difficult to keep feeding the prisoners within these narrow limits. Our wood is wet; the potatoes we get out of the clamps stink; our waterlines keep freezing. [In the face of all of this] it would feel like snobbery if one would pick up a book.

I stayed in my room a lot today. I lay down and slept a lot. It was only three degrees Celsius in my room in the camp, which is otherwise quite bearable. [Because it's so cold] no one can expect someone to spend all day outside in the camp. I try to combat my cough with warm compresses on my throat. Our unit has no winter clothing for us. It's always the same old story. My Russian cook got me a cap. Now the only thing I'm missing is some woolen underwear, and that's not to be had.

The major came by today and said somewhat ironically (I had recently given him a piece of my mind) that I must have some *really* good friends up at the unit command, because somebody wrote again to see if I couldn't be used as a

Food storage site, converted into a mass grave, fall 1941

translator. That's out of the question. I see that I'm no use at all. I still have the hope that I'll be exempted. But won't Magdeburg already have gotten someone else? Well, it's God's will. It's useless to make any plans. [. . .]

Infinite Suffering

November 20, 1941

Dear Lene,

[. . .] Lotte has often sent me your letters. So I've been able to accompany you on your journeys. It's good when one can do so much to help. But I do hope that you both can find a firm place and be together there. One wonders at times if the new European order and the accompanying continuous state of war won't mean that countless Germans will be permanently homeless. That makes me even more grateful for the hours spent together that I can hold in my memory.

The past few weeks at the end of last month and the beginning of this one belong to the most difficult ones of my life. There is infinite suffering here among the prisoners, and it wears one down and makes one weak. Now there's quiet at least outside. Most [everyone] has been sent farther west. And we're too far back for the battles that are now raging. We'll probably remain here with a few thousand prisoners who will keep the streets and rail lines free of snow. And so one gets settled. We're in the depths of winter. The temperatures are around [minus] ten to fifteen [degrees Celsius]. But we're used to that by now. If there isn't a wind out of the east or the north, the cold hardly bothers us. Given the smaller number of prisoners it's also possible to have somewhat more humane conditions. The only good thing to come out of the difficult weeks is that I've come together with a number of intelligent and responsible Russians in an almost comradely manner. From the contact with them I'm gaining some insights into Russian life. The sacrifice will be worth it if the Bolshevist system comes to an end, and if we can create a bearable new order. [. . .]

Camp Monotony

November 21, 1941

A few more monotonous gray days have gone by. The weather has gotten somewhat milder; it must have been minus five [degrees Celsius] today. But there's no sun and absolutely no color. We now have 360 men in our camp. There isn't much work. But our superiors are giving us a hard time. The mortality rate is really alarmingly high in the two other camps. If they don't change what they're feeding them, we won't have many prisoners around come Christmas. We're handing out soup three times a day now, along with potatoes and bread. But there's no fat. We had horsemeat at times, but that's become harder to get now. I take care of my kitchen but go home every day now at noon to sleep. At around 6:45 or 7 I get together with my Russian. We often interrupt our lessons to chat. He's now sharing a room with someone who doesn't understand German. So we can speak more freely about the things that are important to us. I practice my grammar while the food is cooking. All my superiors know that I'll be reading a book whenever they stop by. Until now no one had said anything. Of course I'm constantly being bothered. But when I'm memorizing vocabulary or translating, it's not as bad as it would be, say, if I were reading Aristotle. There I have a lot of trouble making any progress, even if I try to follow the argument. In the evening we sit very quietly at our table. I read or write, and my bunkmate does that same. But it's hard to write letters. I'm starting to write Christmas greetings. But we're not experiencing any of those things that people at home like to read about. It's either all monotonous and tiresome or very, very serious. [. . .] I don't have anything to send. I sent the baptism pitcher via a secure channel to the Kritschew church. As far as I can help it I don't want it to be part of some collection of rarities. Have you actually received the two packages I sent you from Kochanowo? There were some sketches in there that I would be sad to lose. Everything here is just so unspeakably poor. The prisoners are going to great lengths to gather the material for my vest. Should I do as my comrades do and exploit this poverty, by exchanging with the women a piece of bread for their last new towels? I would rather give instead. It's too bad that I didn't think to ask you for a few small items, such as some paints (watercolors) for my teacher. But it's too late now. Some things could be found if only the mail would run regularly. [. . .]

Trying to Understand Russians

November 24, 1941

Now the last Sunday before Advent is over. [. . .] The weeks are so empty now without Sundays and holidays. There was a service here some eight days ago. But because we all live off to ourselves and because I spend all day in the camp, I didn't hear about it. You asked about the baptism [of our child]. The first Sunday of Advent will already be long gone when you get this letter. So this too I need to leave entirely up to you.

You don't need to worry about me. Apparently we're going to stay here and have all the advantages of our quarters, about which I've written over and over again. My vest is finished, next is a pair of warm slippers. The stove in my room in the camp is finished, and it heats well. We're also making sure to close up all the chinks [in the walls]. Our camp is limited to a small portion of the factory grounds. They're ruthlessly tearing things down outside the barbed wire, which is to our advantage. The mood among the few who remain is more relaxed. We often laugh with the Russians when they come for their food. This evening all the policemen had gleaming faces because they all got shaves this afternoon. That was a sight. Then they all look like children. And when they smile as they beg they can make the most winning faces. One can just imagine how they once stood in front of their lords, able to hit any note, either crying or laughing if necessary, and each time doing so with complete sincerity. I'm now alone in the kitchen with them. There's only one who speaks German, an eighteen-year-old young man from the area near Odessa, who is always in good spirits and lively. During the past few days I showed him where the Wartburg[56] is, using one of your maps.

---

[56] Castle in Thuringia where Martin Luther translated the Bible into German.

He had never heard the name Luther before, even though he's been baptized. The last in his family; his younger sisters weren't. I should be able to speak Russian better, but my teacher has hurt my confidence somewhat with his high expectations. But at least now I understand the basics needed in daily life. The day before yesterday one of our janitors told me about his religious development. He belonged to the Protestant movement. Unfortunately I wasn't able to understand too much. In any case he reads daily in the Testament that came from Wernigerode. His book of prayers, which he used to enclose in a red satin purse, is now encased in silver paper that he got from a cigarette package. And that's all of Russia for you, as it still remains in thousands of different places. If I could have understood everything, I would have written a beautiful letter to the people in Wernigerode. As it was, this Russian experience is as limited and piecemeal as everything else. How much would we all rather be somewhere at the Black Sea or in the Crimea! When I sit with my Russian, on the wall there are two charcoal drawings—to the left the "Red Square" and to the right a classical museum. I wonder what will be left of them when the city falls into our hands. My cook's wife and child live in Rostov,[57] which has now fallen to the Germans. I think most Russians are really childish in that they never stop hoping. When they get news like that they think that everyone is going to be set free immediately and that everyone can be put on a train and in a few days everything will be forgotten. One notices daily that this is a people for whom the words "bearing" and "personality" have no real meaning. But enough of these generalities. [. . .]

[57] Large Russian city on the Don River.

Hating Stalin

November 25, 1941

Dear Werner,

I thank you for your letter of September 28, which is now almost two months old. But the mail generally takes three weeks to get here, and then your letter arrived at a very difficult time for us. Some of the prisoners from Bryansk[58] were processed through the three camps that our unit oversees. I had to feed 16,000 to 18,000 men during many days, at least as far as that was possible. We had five Germans in the administration and the kitchens and eight guards. You can imagine that we had to beat and shoot. During such times the kitchen administration doesn't resemble anything in civilian life. One beats and shoots to create some kind of order around the kitchens. One takes care of the sick so that they don't starve, plays judge when provisions are stolen, etc. Now things are much quieter. The prisoners have been transported farther west, at least those who withstood the strain and the hunger—they were dying by the thousands. The real communist elements have already been eliminated before they get to us. The people who are here with us are themselves mostly unlucky victims of the Bolshevik system. So for example we have many civilians in our camp who were released from prison or work camps in order to build defenses or tank traps. They were thrown into prison because they missed three days of work. Others are sons of former kulaks, whose fathers were driven off the farms, banished, or shot. Or they come from the older bourgeoisie and have sunken into the proletarian class. They all just want Stalin to disappear so that they can quietly go home. And they

---

[58] City in southwest Russia.

lived under such trying circumstances: my Russian teacher for instance was a first lieutenant, forty-seven years old, a teacher at an arts and crafts school in Moscow, lived with his family in one room that he also shared with his father. Being able to gain such insights into this amazingly diverse Russian world is the most valuable thing that I can bring back home. There's nothing else to get here. Life is monotonous. We don't have any kind of variety. If I weren't used to finding things to keep me busy, it would be difficult to stand it here.

I have neither signed up for the administrative training, nor have I asked to start training to become a reserve officer, because my office wanted to submit a request for exemption. There's a ban for the eastern front until December 31. But those few weeks will pass by quickly. Maybe something will happen in March. Otherwise, I'm not doing too poorly. I got through the Polish winter in 1939/40 and I hope to live through the Russian one. At the moment it's ten to fifteen degrees below zero [Celsius]. But I can protect myself better now than I could then, because I have much more autonomy now. I think it's best that I not make any concrete plans for the moment and look ahead to the request. Thus please accept my thanks for your friendly offer, but I think I won't take you up on it this time. In any case I have a warm recommender in the Hannover personnel office who will do whatever is possible. [. . .]

No Enemies

November 25, 1941

Dear Siegfried,

You wrote your letter over four weeks ago, and four weeks from now it will be Christmas! Because our mail always takes three weeks to arrive, I'd like to wish you and your dear wife now my most sincere best wishes for a blessed and happy holiday. [. . .] I love the eastern landscape in the fall. But it isn't good for relaxation or recuperation. We are now stuck in the middle of winter and it's about [minus] ten degrees [Celsius] during the day. The countryside is covered with a thin layer of snow. The ground is already quite frozen through. Let's hope that the fighting in the north will soon be over. In the Caucasus there isn't any winter, at least not on the hills. So there the war will probably continue.

We've had some difficult weeks in which I have seen so very much suffering and death as never before. I used all my energies to make sure that the people had enough to eat. So many men are dying in the camps. When winter really sets in, this dying will cover all of Russia. If we are to believe the reports about the mass exoduses from the cities, we should be prepared to hear descriptions of the misery in those still unoccupied areas. But after all that I've seen, I cannot spot a single enemy amid the millions of Russians. Mostly these people are the unhappy victims of a crazed political system whose roots lie far back in Russian history. I have been a witness to this experience, which is an important, grand historical moment. I would like to understand more about the circumstances that shape these things. But unfortunately I quickly reach the limits of my abilities. Because of my lack of language skills I can't get to the heart of things. And then there's a religiosity that infuses all things. Here in our village the church has been restored. Prisoners who are singers, musicians, and artists have been granted leave in order to renew its interior and to restore the choir. I won't be able to forget a Sunday evening during our darkest hours, when the Russians invited me to visit them for a few hours of relaxation. A baritone from the Moscow opera sang Russian folk songs, pieces from Boris Godunov, and at the end liturgical pieces that the Russians hadn't heard for years. [. . .]

Learning about Russia

November 28, 1941

[. . .] Otherwise there's not much to report. It was a beautiful sunny day today, and not too cold. Nonetheless, if one has to stand and hand out food for fifteen minutes, one is frozen through. I hope that we will still have some more time like this when things are slow. I have put aside all my ambitions and am happy when people leave me alone. Of the three hundred men here, at least every day five to seven are brought to the infirmary. The reason is almost always starvation. On paper we have enough provisions, but what we get is mostly buckwheat, potatoes, and bread. A few prisoners have already been sent home. The others are restive when they see this. Still, we often wonder that they accept everything so passively. Most of them seem to exist at a stage of existence described by Turgenev some eighty years ago, despite the revolutionary and anarchist movements. There's plenty of material here to ponder and think about. During my Russian lessons today I recited for the first time a short fable. That should give you some idea about how slow my progress has been. But my teacher is really quite unhappy with my accent. He speaks in a very fine manner that is well above the kind of Russian that I hear every day. He is a very educated middle-class Russian whose vocabulary still includes the word humanity. I hope that our relationship doesn't end too suddenly. I would like to ask him so much, but when we've worked for a few hours under a dim lamplight and in front of a warm stove, we're both rather tired. I've ordered some things from Holtermann to help with my further studies. I hope they arrive by Christmas. [. . .]

Holiday Wishes

November 28, 1941

Dear Mr. Günther,

I would like to wish you, your lovely wife, and your children a most wonderful Christmas filled with festivity and the blessings of the Lord. [. . .] I worry about my wife, who must be suffering in isolation in Thuringia during these days. But the child must be a source of diversion and provide new grounds for gratitude.

The days run their course here quietly and regularly. People talk about the possibility that we'll be sent up closer to the front near Moscow. But you know how much the Prussians like to gossip. It is certainly possible that we could receive our marching orders any day now. It would be hard for us to leave the camp and quarters that we've spent the past two months setting up. But there's something tempting about the possibility of being able to see a little bit more of Russia. We can still gain something by getting more insights into this land, which is so difficult to comprehend. We are getting to know the Russians well through our daily exchanges with them. Certainly they're dirtier, lazier, and more slatternly than we are. But they do have their good sides, and these will come fully to light again once the tyranny of Bolshevism, under which they have all suffered, is finally over. Naturally I am particularly careful to pay attention to anything that has to do with the re-emergence of faith. I received some Russian language gospels and psalms from Wernigerode (*Licht im Osten*) and from the Martin Luther Bund, and I've been cautiously handing these out. Because of my position in the camp, I need to make sure that someone doesn't convert to Christianity in the hopes of getting an extra piece of bread. The temptation to do so is

335

just too great. These half-children will do anything—laugh, cry, collapse in weakness at my feet, compliment my boots, and when I reply, then they'll beg for bread. Whoever gives it to them has them eating out of their hands. It's like an object lesson in the temptation of Christ. [. . .]

Russian Resistance

December 2, 1941

I'm sorry that the mail gets to you so irregularly, as I can see from the card you sent on November 11 (which arrived surprisingly quickly, together with two packages—the Raabe and the Schinkel book).[59] I'm so thankful to you for all that and would have been able to transport myself completely into another world if I hadn't accidentally come across the enclosed announcement I found in the *Mitteldeutsche*.[60] I was truly shaken up by it. I remember the many silent walks we took in Kosow last year in the spring and summer, and the way in which Quade spoke about the boy. What I could observe during my visits was that the boy was *the* focus of his parents' lives. [. . .] They must be so terribly lonely now. [. . .]

Tomorrow my new nice translator is going away to Odessa; he's happy in part because he'll be heading home, but he's worried because the partisans like to shoot at the prisoners the Germans release because they think they are German allies. That is another Russia, one that is fighting for its life in Petersburg and Moscow and that hopefully won't be able to survive the battles.[61] Last night I was

[59] Wilhelm Raabe (1831–1910), German novelist; Karl Friedrich Schinkel (1781–1841) was a Prussian architect and painter.

[60] Announcing the death of Quade's son.

[61] The Soviet counteroffensive from Moscow began on December 5, 1941; it brought the Wehrmacht close to a catastrophic defeat. See Klaus Reinhardt, *Die*

awakened again by shots—four dead in an attempted escape. Franz wrote in much more somber tones about the situation in Belgium. They are starting to experience things there that have been customary in the East here for some time: mass shootings.[62] Yesterday I had a long discussion with the new inspector in order to secure at least the minimum required to feed the prisoners, with some success. He said to me among other things, "We need people in such positions who have robust natures who aren't shaken when a few hundred prisoners die." He's more interested in whether or not his skis are finished (which he hopes to use soon) than in his duties.

In the face of everything my Russian "studies" have suffered somewhat. But I'm forcing myself to continue with them as much as it's possible. Perhaps I can use my knowledge for practical purposes in the future; that is if I have to get through the winter here. I think that up until now I've learned enough so that I can get along in the kitchen without the help of a translator. But it would be hard for me to be surrounded solely by Russians. [. . .]

Second Sunday of Advent

December 7, 1941

It's the evening before the second Sunday in Advent. I just walked home through the stillness of the night. The cold, which had gotten down to [minus] twenty degrees during the past few days, has lessened somewhat. The wind has also died down. One can use the short fifteen-minute walk to and

Wende vor Moskau. Das Scheitern der Strategie Hitlers im Winter 1941/42 (Stuttgart, 1972).

[62] Since the first reprisals in Belgium began only in November 1942, the allusion is to the shooting of French hostages. See Wolfram Weber, *Die innere Sicherheit im besetzten Belgien und Nordfrankreich, 1940–1944* (Düsseldorf, 1968), 186.

from the camp to reflect without being hounded by the cold. Overall today was a really quiet day. I wake up at around 7 a.m. I rarely sleep through the night. If it's mild outside, the room is too warm to sleep in; when the frost returns, we have to wrap ourselves up in our blankets. Thus one can get through the night in one's bed. When I arrive in the camp, the sun is usually rising in the southeast. Breakfast has already been doled out (buckwheat soup and potatoes). I check out the kitchen and make sure everything is in order and then settle down with my Russian. I report to the captain, or a superior stops by; at lunch the inspector is regularly at hand. We talk about what we need, and chat about things. Bread, potatoes, and grits are needed. I watch them unload to make sure that nothing disappears. My cook brings breakfast—today a special treat—sour milk (like cream) with Russian bread. In between I return to my books and then inspect the kettles and the workers who chop our wood. Noon arrives, and I oversee the distribution of the rations. Today I went home thereafter, ate my Sunday roast, and took a nap. Then I went back to the camp and studied for about two hours with my Russian. We were left undisturbed so we could keep at it longer than usual. Then my Russian cook brought me the underwear that he had boiled for me and then ironed. But I saw so many dead lice in the seams that I really wasn't eager to wear it. I'll wait to do that until we move back, or until we go through another delousing here. As I was standing there our translator came by—he's a small, twenty-one-year-old half-Jew, and we talked a little bit about Russian literature. Tomorrow he's going to bring me some books. By that time it was already 6 p.m., and I left the camp and now have the evening hours ahead to write and read.

As you see, our life here is very peaceful, and you don't need to worry. Did I actually thank you for your last letters?

Military church service in the field, fall 1941

[. . .] I'm pleased that you went to services. We should wait with the baptism unless some special circumstances warrant it (Franz's visit or something like that). Our Christmas celebrations are going to be very "German." Now that the division is gone, we won't have any more church services.[63] But perhaps there won't be many people here at Christmas. Our guard company has left all of a sudden. We also have to leave our quarters and move into the main block. That's likely a friendly gesture from our master sergeant. [. . .]

The Extension of the War

December 10, 1941

We Russians do as has always been customary; we count our weeks ahead of yours so that we can take part in your lives. And so Christmas is already behind us. Our wedding day, New Year's Eve, the New Year. As I was walking from the camp back home through a howling storm, I thought about

---

[63] Chaplains were only assigned to divisions.

so many things that I wanted to write you. But now that I have the pencil in my hand I find it hard to find the right words. May God have mercy on everything that has happened in the past and that will happen in the future. Everyone's initial reactions to the expansion of the war[64] were that now there certainly won't be an end to it all. Initial successes of the Japanese will have the effect of showing the Americans how seriously they are threatened and thereby only make the situation worse. In light of this new aspect of the war I'm very pessimistic about the exemption request, assuming it's ever even submitted.

So I'll try to concentrate on the things close to my heart. A letter from you arrived today with your enclosures; it was dated November 13. Keep writing such happy things about the baby. That's the best. It's not surprising that my mother has also had to be without news for so long. The relatives of all my comrades here are experiencing the same thing. We can only take comfort in the fact that there haven't been more air attacks like those on the 7th of November.[65] The losses were apparently too high. We are all looking forward to our Christmas mail, because we remain very skeptical about the preparations that are to be made for our feast. Hopefully everything will reach us reasonably on time. The rooms we're living in now are to be turned into common rooms. Tomorrow I guess our new major is going to visit us in the camp for the first time.[66]

---

[64] On December 7, 1941, Japanese forces attacked Pearl Harbor; on December 11, 1941, Hitler declared war on the United States.

[65] British bombers attacked Berlin, Cologne, and Mannheim on the 7th and 8th of November 1941, losing thirty-seven airplanes. *Kriegstagebuch des Oberkommandos der Wehrmacht. Im Auftrag des Arbeitskreises für Wehrforschung*, ed. Percy Ernst Schramm, vols. 1–2 (Munich, 1982), 1235.

[66] Major Hartwig von Stietencron (1884–1952), Hauptstaatsarchiv Hannover, NDS. 721 Acc. 90/99, no. 124/2.

The weather is a clear reminder that we are no longer at home. The wind has been whipping around like crazy these past few weeks and the thermometer has been rising and falling accordingly: from twenty below to five above [degrees Celsius], then back to five below. Today snow blew through the area, and now the west wind is blowing so that the tarps in front of the windows are billowing out and the panes are sprayed with rain. My health is still good. I got through the cholera vaccination just fine. Thinking about having to spend time outdoors away from the warmth of the room is daunting. Perhaps if one were a news officer, things would be even worse. A year ago we were upset about my accident. Perhaps we were saved worse things because of it. [. . .]

Glimpses of Humanity

December 14, 1941

[. . .] Now it's starting to feel more like Christmas. On my birthday I was in the camp as usual and only returned home in the evening. The comrades whom I bunk with had pre-pared a birthday party for me—[they had put together] a brass lamp they had found somewhere in the dirt with a candle, six eggs, and a wooden spoon carved by a prisoner. I realized that it was nice, even if I would rather have ignored the whole thing altogether. It was the same with today's mail. Along with your letter there was one from Hans Diet-rich from the 22nd of September (!) and also a nice Christ-mas package from a pupil somewhere in the Warthegau; our Dulag was located in his village during the summer and so he got my address. My Russian was so very pleased with the collection of fairy tales sent by the *Winterhilfswerk*.[67] He

---

[67] Nazi Winter Aid Service.

sketches fairy tales for his little daughter, and it was encouraging for him to see them once again for real. The smallest among my Russian friends will get the bonbons tomorrow. When I go to the camp there are often a few three and four year olds standing along the path. When I approach they line up and call out "*pan, pan*" and they salute me to make sure I notice them. Today for the first time they received a few bonbons and I'm sure that they'll be waiting for me when I go by tomorrow. Unfortunately my little Russian girlfriend has been unfaithful to me the past few days. My little cat, who was so good at keeping away all the mice, is missing. I hope a hungry prisoner didn't catch her. I didn't know that such an animal could be so eloquent in its movements and expressions. I knew her very well as she did me. She knew when she could expect some milk and when not. I would be sorry if she had disappeared.

So there's always some humanity to be found. But then there are aggravations. The Eastern army has now really been granted leave time, but in a very limited scope, and the sergeant major announced today that there's no chance of furlough for those who've recently joined the unit. Of course we complained about that. But in reality there's not a lot we can do, because the quota is so low. So don't get your hopes up about the winter. I guess you haven't heard anything else from Magdeburg about the [exemption] request. I haven't heard anything about a possible lifting of the ban or about whether it will be extended.

Today's Sunday was of course disrupted by the news about leave. I spent a lot of time with my Russian, and we talked a lot, mostly unfortunately in German, because our conversation kept going in directions for which my Russian just isn't good enough. We both can't spend enough time with our lessons. As I was heading home at 6 p.m., the world was gleaming—we had a thaw—and everything was so quiet that I really felt the spirit of Advent. Our celebration will therefore not just be about the usual alcohol-induced troubles. My soul needs a little rest tonight, taking a break from Aristotle and Russian lessons. I've been pretty tired because of all the events of late. My ability to *speak* Russian is still really not good. I don't have enough élan or the ability to imitate [speech patterns]. And like I said, [our lessons] aren't basic enough. We should just be talking about simple things, like the weather and food, etc. Well, perhaps I'll still have a lot of time to practice. [. . .]

Preparing for Christmas

December 20, 1941

The last Advent Sunday is around the corner. At least outside it looks like Christmas. After a few really quite unusually mild days, during which it thawed during the day, the frost has returned. Snow is on the ground again and the stars twinkle in the night sky like icicles during the day. Everyone in the unit is doing his part. Three pigs have been slaughtered. There's alcohol, they've decorated a large hall, and they've even set up a stage upon which we'll have some theater on Christmas Eve. I should be able to survive it. Everyone will feel better when the first day of the year is over. At least I think that most of the men feel the same as I do, even though a lot of them are trying to distract themselves with partying and alcohol.

We still have quite a lot to do before the festivities begin. Tomorrow we'll be moving over to the other building where the other comrades are bunking, in honor of the "Volksgemeinschaft." And then our camp will be dissolved, and we'll have to set up a new kitchen. Our three camps lie very close

343

to each other. We're moving into a barrackslike building in which all the stoves, windows, floors, etc, are in really bad shape. And there isn't any glass, wood, nor a nail to be had. But now I face the whole thing with the same cool indifference as all the others here. I don't even know if I'll be in charge of the kitchen there. The rumor is that I'll take over the kitchen in the Russian infirmary. But you shouldn't worry about that. The kitchen is completely separate from the hospital. At least it would hardly be pleasant to serve "under" the young, arrogant assistant doctor. But nothing is certain at the moment, and I'll just wait to see what happens, whether it's one thing or another.

I now have a forty-year-old scientist from the Moscow Academy among my foster prisoners. He looks pretty bad. I got him some better quarters and he's getting a little bit more to eat. Now he's somewhat attached to me. He would like to learn German, and wants me to use him as a translator. But he needs to learn the basics first. He's an Armenian, by the way. If one were to hear that, one might think that everything here is so very interesting when there are so many objects of study walking around. But there isn't much time to start any real studies. It takes quite an effort as well as the resolve to find the free time to learn Russian. Perhaps in our new building the evenings will be even more disruptive.

I received an application today from Lohrisch about the [exemption] request; it was very formal by the way, as if it was just a routine, general query ordered from above. I'll answer immediately of course, after I talk to the sergeant major tomorrow about the ban. [. . .]

The Fourth Sunday of Advent

I can add a few lines to what I just wrote. The sergeant major, with whom I spoke in the presence of the adjutant,

Farewell to Major Gutschmidt, winter 1941

explained that there's no possibility of being exempted until the end of operations. But he didn't actually have any paperwork about that. So everything remains up in the air. That's just the way in which we all take part in the general course of history. My Russian teacher spoke very movingly today about his concerns about his wife and child in Moscow, whose situation is much worse. The day went by much too quickly by the way. By the dawn's light I walked through a wonderful landscape (there just aren't enough trees) into the camp. Then I came back to move. Cleaning up, settling in. A quick roll call to greet the new major. A conversation with the NCOs about our plans. Some more unpacking, then back to the camp. There I had a lovely chat with the Russian over some tea from the Caucasus and pumpernickel spread with a syrupy mixture. He never wants me to leave. As I came home toward evening the best joy: mail from you. Your letter from the 2nd and your card from the 4th. I'm so happy you sent some warm things, because the

345

cold still awaits us, and it's not clear whether our new duties will allow us to warm ourselves. The fact that they're saying we should collect warm clothes is already a sign of what to expect. [. . .]

Christmas Eve

[December 24, 1941]
On Christmas Eve I send greetings to you and with you our child with the following words (John 1:14).[68] Those are the deepest and also the most unfathomable words ever written by man. One thinks one can understand what is meant, and yet life continuously leads one to confess: until now I have not known how infinite God's love is and how never ending man's suffering is. I have experienced both in this past year. I am happy that your own experiences have led you to the former. So on this Christmas Eve we should join each other in thanking God for what he's given us with this child. That surpasses everything else. But we shouldn't forget that we can really only accept our child as the grace of God because God himself became man. How could we otherwise have celebrated the birth of our child in the face of this war? I don't know if I could agree with the atheist belief that "not to be born [at all] is the best." But the light of Christmas should outshine our own guilt, our own mortality—how much you've been reminded of that this year, and we are reminded of this daily, our hopes and desires. [. . .]

---

[68] "And the Word was made flesh, and dwelt among us (and we beheld his glory, the glory as of the only begotten of the Father), full of grace and truth."

A Russian Christmas

December 25, 1941

It's the first day of Christmas. Outside the wind from the east is driving the snow through the cold air. I sit in my warm, clean room in the camp and check in every now and then on the factory (long since plundered) that we will be leaving tomorrow; we have so many memories attached to it. The kitchen workers are singing today while they work; beautiful melodies, some of them in harmony. It's too bad that I don't understand the words and can't give you a better sense of how singular this music is. It's a holiday. And I'm happy that I can make things more festive at least within my own narrow sphere. Yesterday morning I removed two scrawny trees left over from our holiday decorations and sent them to the camp. When I went back to the camp after lunch I saw that the cooks had decorated the trees—all by themselves, one of them as a gift for me, the other as one for themselves. Mine in particular looks so wonderfully colorful; it would offend any aesthete. Lots of colorful paper flowers: red, blue, yellow, white. I don't know where they found the paper. Long streamers of colorful paper. Doves woven from straw— the translator calls them doves of peace. The whole thing would be the centerpiece of a folklore collection. Perhaps I can bring some of this back home. Then it can hang next Christmas on our tree, so that we won't forget this wartime Christmas. Underneath the tree is a "Father Frost," a kind of Santa Claus, made of cotton.

This strengthened my resolve to have a small celebration for the twelve men who work in the kitchen. As the dark began to settle in at around 4 p.m., they all arrived in my room, freshly washed, their hair combed. The drawing teacher from Moscow translated my little speech. I told them that I didn't dare wish them a Merry Christmas when they were in a prison camp, if God's son hadn't himself lived in absolute poverty and was himself a prisoner just as they were. Then the Russian read the Christmas story aloud. I told them that we Germans didn't harbor any hatred toward the Russian people and ended with the wish that we would all return to our homes in the coming year. Then I wished everyone a Merry Christmas and gave each of them a few cigarettes. At the end I arranged a small table of presents for the teacher: a few things to eat, some toiletries, and the beautiful folder of Schinkel engravings. He was quite overcome by emotion and said that he would never forget the joy of this Christmas.

It had in the meantime grown dark, and then we went home through the night, my chief cook with the Christmas tree at my side. At around seven our own party started, and in outward form everything was done with the kind of care and diligence that only a unit can do when they are stuck in the middle of winter as we are. The room was decorated completely with greenery, there was a beautiful tree, the table was overflowing with wine, schnapps, gingerbread, cigarettes, paper; candles were burning everywhere. We started off more solemnly and sang "O Christmas Tree," "Silent Night," "O Sanctissima," and then the new major gave an appropriate speech that ended in the request that each of us say a silent "Our Father" together. There followed a series of shows that at times were much better than the usual fare offered by the K.d.F.[69] troops here. There was a delightful parody of the previous major done as a shadow show. At around eleven the major left, and shortly thereafter we all did the same. It was at least a rather respectable attempt to help us get through

[69] Joy through Work, Nazi leisure organization.

the evening. I'm not sure there was any other way to do it. We have so much food that we would really like to send something home, if only the mail was faster.

Now the afternoon of the first day of Christmas is almost over. I just had a long interruption: two of our captains and a first lieutenant paid me a visit. We first talked about superficial matters, but then they began to speak about the war and then their own personal destinies. For this generation this is now their ninth winter spent at war.[70] Our camp leader is now fifty-five [years old], he has his own business, he's an interior designer. He said that when he returns home he'll have to rebuild his life over again for the fourth time. It was a very interesting hour for me. In spite of all composure [this was] a devastating eruption of feeling of the vanity of human existence: what is the meaning of life? [. . .]

But I need to go and take care of the provisions. We have carrots, potatoes, and horsemeat today. I hope this can fill them up. They know themselves, by the way, that our food is much more carefully prepared than that in the other kitchens. That's why they don't want to lose me as head of the kitchens when we move to the new building on Sunday. Temporarily I'm to take over as head of a larger kitchen in another camp. At first I protested against the fact that they were sending me as the oldest NCO over to the (small) infirmary. But on the other hand my comrades are now making more demands of us. The sergeant major even suggested [that I give] a lecture at the start of one of the officers' dinners.

After I came back home, having handed out enough food to satisfy everyone, I saw my bed was covered with mail. Included were your sweet letters from the second Sunday of Advent as well as the one from December 10, and a package with

---

[70] He must mean the seventh.

medicine. But I'm doing really fine. And we have a "doctor in the house." Hopefully the child got over his diarrhea quickly. I haven't yet received the photo (which Franz also mentioned). I did get three carefully selected and packed packages filled with clean wash from Frau Schulze. These were like a gift from heaven, because the east wind is blowing, and the thermometer is falling dramatically. Our room faces to the west, and we're warm. Please thank Frau Schulze. She was quite thorough in her choices. I'll do the same. And then there were two very sweet packages from Lene and Miss Caspar. I slept this afternoon and read a little bit. The comrades want to come, therefore I don't want to leave. Tomorrow I'll visit my Russian and talk about art and books. There's so much more to say, but that's enough for today. [. . .]

Strains in Comradeship

December 29, 1941

The days go by. The year is almost at an end. During these days one feels like taking stock. And then we should be very thankful when you both are healthy again. I received a pastel drawing of you and the child today that was drawn from a photograph. The likeness isn't very good, but it's a nice picture and it is a reminder of home. That's even more necessary now that the mail is coming so irregularly. I still haven't received all the mail from my birthday and Christmas. We keep hearing about all the "actions" they're taking to make the Eastern Army's stay in Russia easier. Shouldn't they start with the mail delivery? That would make a lot of other things superfluous.

Now it's really wintry outside; everything is white. But the snowstorm has died down, and everyone feels warm, even though it's [minus] ten or fifteen degrees. Let's hope it stays that way. We'd be able to stand it then. Tomorrow I'm going to take over the larger kitchen. There will be 2,500 men to provide for. There won't be much free time to learn Russian during the day. I'll need to keep the evenings completely free for that and will write [you] even less. Because I think that in about another three months I'll have a pretty firm foundation [in Russian]. Maybe I'll need it in order to earn my keep. If only everything weren't so difficult. Yesterday afternoon I had tea and cookies with three Russians in the camp, but I only got pieces of their conversation. Perhaps you would understand it better if you could have experienced the evening we had on the first day of Christmas. You would understand how one's energies are entirely spent just to get through every day and how little is left for other people or for intellectual things. We were invited by the sergeant major, but he was tired from the afternoon, when he had celebrated with our sentries. The others were also somewhat drunk. One of them talked about his adventures with Russian women. There was an argument; and then suddenly all our differences came to light: the old and the new, those who fought in the world war and the younger "national socialist" generation. People argued about the major and his demand that we recite the "Our Father." In short, it was hard to hold things together in some way and to maintain appearances until the bottles were empty. On the second day of Christmas, everyone was hung over and quiet. All the liquor was gone. There was a terrible snowstorm, and everyone sat in his own room and went to bed early. Now we have New Year's Eve to look forward to yet another evening of comradely companionship. We want to spend the hours before midnight in smaller groups. Then we'll have a temporary break in the celebrations. It's quieter on regular evenings than I would have suspected. Everyone sits off by himself. Gerres is usually reading. I write or read

Russian until it's time for bed. I would have quickly gone through all my books if I didn't have some Russian grammar textbooks from the local school [library]. With those I have at least three months' work ahead. [. . .]

It's not at all clear what the new year will bring. I don't think I'll be called back from the front. If it happens, that's good. But if not, there will be other adventures ahead. The main thing is that I can have a little bit of energy left for life and work after the war. That is my main concern, beside my worries about how you both are doing. Everything else—where and what kind of work I'll have, where we'll live—that's all the same to me. [. . .]

A New Year of War

January 1, 1942

It's a new year, and its beginning brings with it a tremendous feeling of pressure. I think that each of us in this year has come to terms with the fact that the future is completely uncertain. Now that war has broken out in the Far East, and there is a tense situation on the eastern front and in Africa, it seems impossible for each of us, as well as for the whole nation, to predict anything with certainty. And yet we have no other desire than to be at home next year; the Russians feel the same as we do. The adjutant also expressed his wish that I could be home as soon as possible. I take this in any case as a sign that I won't encounter any difficulties if a requisition were to arrive. So I do have some hope, but I do have to say that it's not very great. I know that you are courageous enough to keep your head up even in the face of this uncertain hope that one can't fully believe oneself. As far as I can see, the situation is really so that every last man is needed.

But now I must thank you for the great joy that you brought me. Yesterday a large collection of our Christmas mail arrived. It was almost too much to take in all at once. Thank you so much for the beautiful watch; it's a wonderful piece that hardly fits in the world [we live in]. My Russian, whom I showed it today, said that it also didn't fit into Russia at all. Someone would steal it straightaway. Well, I hope that I can bring it back home in one piece, and that it can accompany us on many journeys. It keeps very good time. The other contents of the package also arrived in one piece. The foot warmers are wonderful; I hope I can fit them in my boots. I've received letters and cards from you up to the 20th of December. Apparently the mail is moving faster now. I also got the cigarettes. Thank you for them. I handed out some to my bunkmates as a belated Christmas present; some went to the cooks, who now have to work so hard again.

How good it is that you are both so safe in peace and can receive and give some love. Absorb everything that you can that both the landscape and individuals have to offer. I hope you don't have too much to do. Everyone was pleased with the photos and was impressed with [our son's] growth. You shouldn't worry about food. I received the portrait that a Russian drew from a photograph of you both in the cloisters. It's not a very good likeness, but lovely in its own way. I also have a picture behind glass and in a frame on my wall—a present from my Russian teacher. It's a scene from a happy, traditional Russian landscape: a sled drives through a winter landscape; it's not a great work of art, but it has a special allure that is particular to this region. The dedication includes a memory of happy times—and this is not a commissioned piece like the one I have of you. I'll have a frame made for that one as well.

January 2, 1941

The day started off fine but then my comrades got a hold of me and there was no chance of escape. First I had to make hash browns and sunny-side up eggs for Gerres and me. He had brought eggs and bacon and told me that it was my duty as the head of the kitchen to take care of us—of course [he was] a bit drunk, but in the best of moods. And then a happy group who had been celebrating all day joined us for the evening. It was loud, but pretty harmless, until one of those tragicomic scenes happened that I'm quite famil-iar with. One [of them]—in his early thirties, and NCO, an SS-man with some education told me suddenly—with a great vehemence in which he lectured me for about one and a half hours—that I had completely failed. I should have, with my abilities, taken the whole company in hand and squelched the others or pushed them out of the way. And precisely be-cause of religious reasons. The whole miserable story came out: the grandfather a dean; his SS membership; how he was close to the church but not baptized in his youth. His very young wife, who didn't go to church but who read the Bible daily. I should have just ordered them what to believe in. [He claimed] many more people would have listened to me than I had thought. And then suddenly he said: "I can't listen any-more; I don't feel so great." I'm curious to see how this will develop when he's sober again. I'll tell him that I'm willing to be involved in any reasonable activity, but that I don't care to waste my evenings grousing and drinking. I don't have the energy or the desire to do so.

Overall I got through the festivities fairly decently. On New Year's Eve we had an evening with some performances, a bit of a dull rehash. And it was also terribly cold in the room. Afterward I sat for a while with my Volga Germans and Russians and let them sing Russian dance songs on demand; they were vivacious and in high spirits. Then I sent the cook to the camp with a bottle of wine and a half [bottle] of vodka. But most of [the prisoners] were sleeping. As I came back to our quarters everything was quiet. All the new year's celebrations were over. Most of them sat in their rooms and drank until deep in the night. I, however, slept undisturbed.

There's a lot to do again, even though almost everything is done in the new kitchen and is functioning. But I still have to go and check everything. And doling out the food is still such a difficult process for everyone. Yesterday it was 17 degrees [Celsius]. Today it's much colder, 25 degrees below. For the first time the Russians sent me inside today, because the tip of my nose was all white. But you shouldn't worry about a fur vest. I still don't need to put on the warm vest during the day, because I keep warm with mother's shawl, the kidney belts, and woolen underwear. In the evenings I put on the vest when the wind comes in through the windows and it's just not warm enough. [. . .]

We're starting with the evening feeding just now. With these short days, there's a lot of pressure [to finish]. But I have been able to insist that we give out food three times a day (including a portion of bread today). You can imagine what it's like for these starving, poorly clad people to stand in the cold. One often has to be tough so that things go smoothly. [. . .]

Increasing Worries

January 4, 1942

Dear Werner,

Thank you so much for your letter on my birthday. Until today it's almost the only one that's reached me at all. [. . .]

One can feel pretty abandoned when one hardly has any friendly greetings in hand on such days. But we have to share at least a little in the privations brought on by the Russian campaign. In comparison to our comrades who have to endure 25 or 30 degrees [below Celsius] at the front of the offensive, things are marvelously pleasant here. We can sit in warm rooms with electric lights and can spend our evenings undisturbed. We can forget somewhat all the screaming and misery. I hope my health holds up. I've been able to withstand the cold pretty well. One protects oneself as much as one can. When I'm overseeing the distribution of food, I have to stand outside for at least three hours every day. At 25 degrees below, that's rather a mixed bag. We now have typhoid fever in the camp (but I beg you *most urgently* not to tell that to [my mother and brother] in Hennigsdorf. They, along with my wife, should know nothing about this). Of course one can't protect oneself from the fact that one occasionally gets lice. It's become a daily habit, although not particularly one of our favorites, that we search our clothes for them. Those are our worries. [. . .]

We're also noticing some of the effects of food shortages. Our own provisions have been quite lacking at times. But everyone took pains for Christmas. We should have sent more things home, so that there, people could put away the last bit of butter for some pastries. As to our prisoners, we really don't have a handle on things. The lack of food and the resultant deaths are so overwhelming. There's just nothing else to extract from the land.

You inquire again if you can do anything for me. Our days are busy enough. We do get newspapers and magazines, although they arrive months late. But they make the rounds from room to room. I wonder if there still are more sophisticated journals like the *Leipziger* or the *Atlantis*? And then we have a lack of paper (just simple writing paper) and especially envelopes. Those would be my requests.

It's very reassuring to learn that the British won't be in Berlin at least for a long time. I hope that things are still quiet for you. [. . .]

Every Man Is Needed

January 4, 1942

Dear Miss Caspar,

Thank you very much for the wonderful Christmas joy with the package that you sent me. We enjoyed the treats with a group that would certainly have interested you. Eight days ago a Russian invited me to have tea in the camp. There we were, three Muscovites and one Magdeburger, all together. [. . .] I'm not bored. I now have to prepare food for 3,000 prisoners. Unfortunately I can't report that I can let them eat their fill. The undernourishment and diseases are just terrible. But the land doesn't have anything else to offer up. My comrades are also relying on me more, since we've gotten to know one another better. Yesterday I drank mulled wine with two of them, one of them from the SS, until 10 p.m., and we talked about the religious situation and what being a Christian actually means. And so the days fly by. The landscape is often beautiful, covered in hoarfrost and the wintry sun shines down on the snow. The winter has been relatively mild up until now. The last few days were between 20 and 25 degrees [below Celsius]. That's bearable, if one has enough to eat, has warm clothes, and a warm, well-lit place. The Russians don't have any of those things. Their suffering is terrible.

I'm so pleased to hear that you're still meeting [with religion teachers in Magdeburg]. I no longer think that I'll be exempted, although the school asked again in December. If it weren't for my wife, I would hardly wish for it. Things are so bad here now that every man is needed. [. . .] One has to spend a lot of time on things that are otherwise unnecessary; we have to search our clothing for lice daily (because of typhoid fever). [. . .]

Belief in Forgiveness

January 5, 1942

Dear esteemed Miss Schneider,
[. . .] The holidays went by quickly and well. [. . .] But now to good old Goethe! You're absolutely right to turn against the deprecation of that worldview. It's clear that the old man knew more about life than the little speechmakers who puff themselves up with his greatness. And I also agree with you that the motto "always striving to the utmost" is not the key to the whole. One has to go to the trouble of making the whole come alive with its inexhaustible number of differences in order to comprehend it without the help of such a slogan. But don't you agree that despite all tensions it remains deeply a-Christian in its balancing relationship among God, Devil, and Man? What Goethe opposed so vehemently was the Christ who is outside of us, from whom we live—that's the most important secret of our belief. [. . .]

As to everything else, I'm in complete agreement with you. We need a positive message for our youth with songs and prayers of thanks. And for the adults that should also always be the first word. [. . .] We are truly surrounded with enough misery here. During many weeks we've had hundreds of dead in our camps. But here in particular I've had to learn again that what forms the core of our belief is neither a contrived confession nor a true and honest penitence in moral seriousness, but rather alone the infinite forgiveness that outshines all suffering and all guilt. That is what we must teach. [. . .]

Facing Winter

January 8, 1942

The last few days have brought me so much mail that I just can't get through it all. And I'm also a lot busier than I was in December. So you'll have to wait to receive this letter. I also want to thank you for a whole slew of cards and letters. I'm most happy with the one from the morning of the first day of Christmas. You wrote with such joy and happiness that I could feel the spirit of Christmas again. I thank you so much for the photos. It's a wonderful thing to see them. Otherwise, I don't know where to start and how to respond to the contents point by point. Perhaps it's better if I'm just really practical. I think you all imagine winter here much more horrible than it is in reality. Sure, we have had a lot of days both last year and this year when the temperature was 25 [degrees below Celsius]. But that's just the average. We've had some days in January when there was a slight thaw. At the moment the temperatures are around [minus] 10 degrees. We put log after log onto our fire, every hour, every day, so that the room is warm in the evenings. If the wind is at our windows, then it does get cold at night. We put our coats over us. We've boarded up the windows and hang our winter blankets over them. We won't use them for our beds because they don't seem all that clean. I rarely even put on my vest. In the evenings I usually make do with my knit jacket, especially now that I have the good woolen underwear. [. . .] So I can dress warmly enough if I need to. I only have to stand outside in the camp when we hand out the food, and then I

Suffering Mother Russia, winter 1941

don't need to stay in one place and so can warm up occasionally. A fire is always burning in my room. [. . .]

Now we're preoccupied and moved by the heavy losses.
I'm including a list from the Cathedral School. It's shocking
that from Kluge's small group three men have already been
killed. Hopefully Marzahn will make it through. I also wrote
to Bernburg once before Christmas.

The dying continues all around us now that new prisoners are here, and it is occurring on a horrifying scale.

Hundreds move about in the camp around us, and they are walking skeletons. Every time we hand out food it's a tragedy. People are becoming ever more ravenous, until they are completely exhausted and then they are impervious to everything. Over the next few days we may be able to increase the rations, but that isn't going to help anymore. And I have to continue to maintain the most primitive sense of order around the kitchen. My right hand is swollen from all the blows I dispense. But when you hit one man, his neighbor jumps right up to take his place. Perhaps things will be better when we can regularly hand out bread. I now have a new translator; he's a geography teacher at a school in Moscow, but he doesn't help much when help is needed. The Bolsheviks shot his father in prison; he doesn't know when. [. . .]

Comfort in Contrast with Misery

January 10, 1942

Dearest Little Mother,

[. . .] The temperatures have been quite variable. On New Year's minus 25, then a thaw, then temperatures down to about 10 below. It's really only bad when the wind comes out of the north or the east. Then the snow comes blowing in as fine as sand, and one can hardly do anything against the wind. Overall I don't need to stand outside very much. We've gotten faster at handing out the food. Six men fill bowls without a break. Others are constantly carrying large vats out of the kitchen. In this manner, 2,600 men can be fed pretty quickly. But getting them to stand in line always results in a fight to get at the head of the line. When that happens we have to thrash them ruthlessly. Many of them collapse if you just touch them. Hundreds of them just slowly stagger around, are carried around on other's backs, or walk with crutches.

The ground is frozen stiff. There's always someone lying at our feet. At the moment in our camp alone twenty people die each day.[71] And then we have infirmaries with five hundred sick men. We are constantly fighting about what we should receive with the inspectors and the pursers who are responsible for getting the provisions—with great difficulty. Yesterday for instance a crew was sent out with eighty sleds filled with potatoes (about six hundredweights each) from Tsch[erikow][72] about thirty kilometers away. They arrived in our camp between six in the evening and two in the morning. A northerly wind was blowing the snow across the streets. Today the last sled arrived with a fourteen-year-old driver. Or when they go to get wood, about thirty men out of a group of 210 escape from the train cars. Yesterday a Russian, a father of four children, said to me: "Hitler promised us bread and fair treatment, and now we're all dying, after we've surrendered."

Bruno also wrote about the doctor. He lives right near us; there is an assistant and novice physician. They belong to our unit and are in charge of the Russian doctors and medical assistants who work in the infirmaries and the parade grounds. I've only had a little bit of frostbite on occasion. Otherwise I haven't had anything to do with them, except for immunizations. I couldn't be more comfortable. [. . .]

Depending upon the Lord

January 11, 1942

Dear Miss Caspar,
My most heartfelt thanks for the two packages that just arrived here in the past few days. The one you sent on

---

[71] A daily mortality rate of 0.8 percent; see Gerlach, *Kalkulierte Morde*, 820ff.
[72] Neighboring city in Belarus.

October 26 has also just arrived. Please don't be angry that you didn't receive an answer from your letter sent the same day. I've received various pieces of mail, which have been underway now for two to three months. It's very touching that you still take great lengths to find the good things to send. We often say that such things aren't necessary or desired when we think about how much you have to give up. And then we enjoy them anyway. But it was more important to me to hear once more about your work and about how you're doing, because it will probably be a long while before we can have a conversation face to face, given the ferocity of the present war and the difficulties in transportation. Just today an inspector who had been sent back home returned, absolutely exhausted from his attempt to reach the main road. After the train had made it the thirty-three km through snowdrifts, he had to turn back. One would rather remain here in the relative comfort that we now enjoy.

You know well that the psychological situation in which we do our work is very difficult. I won't describe the misery again. I have already taken a bit of a day off of work today in order to rest. It was necessary, since I really had to exert myself today. But I'd like to get back to your letter. It isn't true that the big tasks are here and the smaller ones at home, because actually everyone here lives by depending on home. I can't say anything about the front. But we're not soldiers who've cast everything aside in order to give themselves over completely to life, their destinies, or God. We live from that which we have brought from home, and nurture ourselves with what we hear from home. Most of us can only stand it here, because they see their time here as merely a temporary thing. But we don't dare to make any plans about the future any more after one and a half years. No one knows when this war will finally come to a provisional end or will know what Europe will then look like. The insights that you wrote about regarding your lecture about the prophets are so essential because they do not depend on where the German advance will finally stop.

I think it's a serious mistake to make infant baptism dependent upon a guarantee of a Christian education later on. That would make the miracle of the resurrection dependent on our efforts and their scope. Have you come to any conclusions in your search for a biblical foundation for infant baptism? [. . .]

Overall what remains for us is nothing more than to ask God to assume our daily sorrows. May He be with each of us. [. . .]

Sensing the End

January 13, 1942
I only have time for a short note today. I thank you so much for your many letters from the last days of last year and then those from the new one. I am touched and thankful for all the heartfelt love that speaks from each of them. May God bless our wishes for the future. Everything is now in His hands. Here it's horribly cold. But I'm well covered. Thank you so for the wonderful presents. When will you go to M[agdeburg]? I'm so pleased to hear that the little one is so full of life and high spirits.

Now goodbye and be well together with our child. [. . .][73]

---

[73] This is the last letter from Konrad Jarausch to his wife; he was already ill as he wrote it.

Grave of Konrad Jarausch in Roslawl, January 1942

Death Notice

January 28, 1942

Esteemed Mrs. Jarausch,

I am deeply sorry to fulfill the difficult duty of having to inform you that your dear husband, Staff Sergeant Konrad Jarausch, born on December 12, 1900, has died quietly and without consciousness at 6 p.m. on January 27, 1942 from stoppage of the heart in the field hospital of Roslawl (southeast of Smolensk) after a sixteen-day illness of severe typhoid fever.

Already when he was brought in on January 17, he was in a typical typhoid fever daze, which lets the patient not be conscious of the severity of his disease. The increasing general weakness of the heart kept him in a condition of intellectual stupor that was at times interrupted by deep sleep. This ushered in a stage of gradually slipping into a painless release.

I want to express my cordial sympathy to you. I know that you have to bear a boundless pain, but this fate of war joins you to all those who know to thank their heroes. These are above all his comrades.

We shall lay our comrade to rest with all honors in the heroes' cemetery, Roslawl. [. . .]

⌣ ACKNOWLEDGMENTS ⌣

In this endeavor I have been aided by two coeditors, some colleagues, and graduate students as well as several funding agencies and publishing editors whose competence and generosity rendered this edition possible. My special thanks go to Klaus Jochen Arnold, a historian of the Russian front, for providing the transcription as well as the information for the military introductions and commentary. I am equally grateful to Eve Duffy, a German cultural historian and director of the University of North Carolina Program in the Humanities and Human Values, for selecting and translating the letters. I also owe a debt of gratitude to Richard Kohn, a leading historian of the American military, for providing a broader perspective in the foreword. And I want to thank Norman Naimark and Omer Bartov for critical comments that improved the manuscript. Moreover, the archivists at the Bundesarchiv-Militärarchiv, and of the Protestant Church Archive in Hanover as well as the colleagues at the Militärgeschichtliches Forschungsamt proved quite helpful. The University of North Carolina graduate students Andrew Haeberlin and Waitman Beorn also provided several further documents. The Ertomis Stiftung supported the initial exploration, while the Gerda Henkel Stiftung financed the transcription and research in the military archives. At the same time the University of North Carolina College of

Arts and Sciences subsidized the translation and the Lurcy Fund helped with transatlantic research expenses. Conor W. McNally did the legwork on the index. Finally, Michael Werner of the Schöningh-Verlag and Brigitta van Rheinberg of Princeton University Press need to be commended for understanding the special nature of this book.

NOTES TO "IN SEARCH OF A FATHER"

~

1. Detlef Mittag, *Kriegskinder '45. Zehn Überlebensgeschichten* (Berlin, 1995); Sabine Bode, *Die vergessene Generation. Die Kriegskinder brechen ihr Schweigen* (Stuttgart, 2004); and Hermann Schulz, Hartmut Radebold, and Jürgen Reulecke, *Söhne ohne Väter. Erfahrungen einer Kriegsgeneration* (Berlin, 2004), 7–13.

2. Niklas Frank, a journalist, wrote *In the Shadow of the Reich* (New York, 1991) in the form of a scathing letter to his father, while Bernward Vesper, a 1968 radical, wrote a psychedelic fragment, titled *Die Reise* (Jossa, 1977), which was a journey into his own tortured psyche.

3. Harald Welzer, *"Opa war kein Nazi." Nationalsozialismus und Holocaust im Familiengedächtnis* (Frankfurt, 2002); Peter Longerich, *"Davon haben wir nichts gewußt!" Die Deutschen und die Judenverfolgung, 1933–1945* (Munich, 2006).

4. Wibke Bruhns, *My Father's Country: The Story of a German Family* (New York, 2008).

5. Bruno Jarausch, "Erinnerungen in einer schlesisch-märkischen Familie" (MS Berlin, written during the 1960s). For further material see the papers of Magdalene von Tiling in the Landeskirchenarchiv Hannover and Jarausch's personnel file in the Landeshauptarchiv Sachsen-Anhalt, MD, Rep. C 23 Dom and Klostergymnasium Magdeburg, no. 93.

6. The following account is based on the "Familiennachricht," 9–13, 38–44, on the short CV in his dissertation as well as on his personnel file.

7. "Familiennachricht," 46–50. Tuition was 70 Marks per semester.

8. Ibid., 50–54.

9. Friedrich-Werdersches Gymnasium zu Berlin, "Zeugnis der Reife," October 20, 1917; "Familiennachricht," 60–66 and "Lebenslauf" in his dissertation. Another friend was the future author Bogislaw von Selchow, who wrote the well-known book *Der Glaube in der deutschen Ichzeit* (Leipzig, 1933).

10. Enthused by Felix Dahn, he "decided to obtain as student as vivid a picture as possible of the Germanic era and then did especially study German prehistory and the Nordic languages, in order to be able to read the ancient Icelandic literature in the original." Konrad Jarausch to Hans-Lothar Dietze, March 13, 1940. Cf. "Entwurf Abgangszeugnis" of June 24, 1924, archive of the Humboldt-Universität.

11. Konrad Jarausch, "Der Volksglaube der Isländersagas. Inaugural-dissertation zur Erlangung der Doktorwürde genehmigt von der philosophischen Fakultät der Friedrich-Wilhelms-Universität zu Berlin," MS (Berlin, 1925), 1ff., 414ff.; Wissenschaftliches Prüfungsamt, "Prüfungs-Zeugnis," November 3, 1925 and "Zeugnis über eine Erweiterungsprüfung für das Lehramt an höheren Schulen," January 17, 1927; and "Familien-nachricht," 68–70.

12. "Familiennachricht," 68–70. According to an article on the theologian Karl Heim, the DCSV was an association "aiming at a personal decision for Christ, a willingness to follow in Jesus's footsteps, and an active engagement for spreading the kingdom of God," Tagesspiegel, January 20, 1974.

13. Letter of March 1, 1940, in the second set of excerpts by Oskar Ziegner, already mimeographed during the war. Cf. Peter Loewenberg, "The Psychohistorical Origins of the Nazi Youth Cohort," American Historical Review 76 (1971): 1457–502.

14. Staatliches Pädagogisches Prüfungsamt, "Zeugnis über die pädagogische Prüfung für das Lehramt an höheren Schulen," March 14, 1928; "Urkunde über die Ernennung zum Studienassessor," April 1, 1928; and "Familiennachricht," 70–71, 79–80; Konrad Jarausch to Lotte Petri, January 16, 1929, and May 13, 1931.

15. Known for his existential theology, Karl Barth became the mentor of the Confessing Church that opposed many aspects of National Socialism. Rudolf Bultmann instead focused his work on biblical criticism, seeking to demythologize the scriptures. The neo-Lutheran Friedrich Gogarten was initially attracted to the German Christians before distancing himself from the Third Reich.

16. Konrad Jarausch, "Die Behandlung des Markusevangeliums in der Untertertia," Schule und Evangelium 4 (1929/30): 80–85, 99–106, 123–31, 152–59, 180–86, 210–15, 231–36; idem, "Was versteht man heute unter evangelischer Pädagogik?" undated lecture manuscript in Nachlass of Magdalene von Tiling, Landeskirchenarchiv Hannover (LKAH), no. 17. He was drawn to Gogarten because of his criticism of modernity, rejection of the Weimar parties, frustration with nominal Protestantism, and faith in a theology of creation. Cf. Friedrich Wilhelm Graf, "Friedrich

Gogartens Deutung der Moderne. Ein theologiegeschichtlicher Rückblick," *Zeitschrift für Kirchengeschichte* 100 (1989): 169–230.

17. Konrad Jarausch to Lotte Petri, July 14, 1929 ("I am, as you know, working on Gogarten and trying to draw out the implications for the school"), September 5, 1930, and undated [from late 1930]. Cf. Gury Schneider-Ludorff, *Magdalene von Tiling. Odnungstheologie und Geschlechterbeziehungen* (Göttingen, 2001), and Claudia Koonz, *The Nazi Conscience* (Cambridge, MA, 2003).

18. Konrad Jarausch to Franz Petri, October 12, 1930; idem, "Schuld und Aufgabe der evangelischen Christenheit," *Schule und Evangelium* 4 (1929/30): 133–38; idem, "Volksnot," ibid. 5 (1930/31): 244; idem, "Literatur zur Schulgestaltung," ibid. 6 (1931/32): 51–53; idem, "Staat und Mensch. Ein Bericht," ibid. 7 (1932/33): 140–50ff.; and idem, "Moderne Pädagogik und Disziplin," *Philologenblatt* 39 (1931): 356–58.

19. Konrad Jarausch, "Was versteht man heute unter evangelischer Pädagogik?" and "Thesen für die Arbeitsgemeinschaft christlicher Philologen in Berlin am 1. Februar 1931," LKAH, Nachlass Tiling, no. 11; and idem to Lotte Petri, July 14, 1929 as well as late 1930. ("You well know, that in my identity I am rather more a Prussian than a German.")

20. Curriculum vitae of Elisabeth Charlotte Jarausch in "Familiennachricht," 81–82; as well as idem, "Über den Einfluss des Pietismus auf das Sozialleben in Deutschland" (MS Marburg, 1929). Konrad Jarausch to Lotte Petri, December 23, 1928; undated [May 1930], May 24 ("How nice it would be, if you were to succeed in carrying some French fire into our barbaric East"), June 6, and September 18, 1930.

21. Konrad Jarausch to Lotte Petri, March 19, 1931, and Lotte's answer of March 20, 1931. Initially they did not make their engagement public.

22. Konrad Jarausch to Lotte Petri, August 4, 1931; Dr. Sergel, "Heiratsschein," December 30, 1933. See also "Familiennachricht," 82.

23. Konrad Jarausch to Lotte Petri, December 3, 1930; May 30, and June 5, 1931. He claimed that he was "morally expelled" from the School Association because he "belonged to the enemy camp." Idem, "Die Tagung der Evangelischen Schulvereinigung und der ihr angeschlossenen Verbände in Bethel am 2. und 3. Oktober," *Schule und Evangelium* 5 (1930/31): 210–14.

24. Konrad Jarausch to Lotte Petri, August 10, 25, 28; September 11, 15, 1931; November 3, 1932; and idem to Franz Petri, October 12, 1930. Cf. Konrad H. Jarausch, "Die Not der geistigen Arbeiter. Akademiker in der Berufskrise, 1918–1933," in *Die Weimarer Republik als Wohlfahrtsstaat*, ed. Werner Abelshauser (Wiesbaden, 1987), 280–99.

25. Gerda Mielke, "Tagung der Ortsgruppenleiterinnen des Verbandes für evangelischen Religionsunterricht und Pädagogik in Potsdam am 7. und 8. 10. 1933," *Schule und Evangelium* 8 (1933/34): 204–5; Konrad Jarausch to Magdalene von Tiling, September 6, 1933, LKAH, Nachlass von Tiling, no. 17. Although he was a member of the Teachers League, the NS Welfare Organization, and the Reich Air-Defense League, he did not join the Nazi Party. "Politische Betätigung," addendum to his personnel file, August 25, 1937, LHASA, MD, Rep. 23, no. 93.

26. Konrad Jarausch in idem and Magdalene von Tiling, eds., *Grundfragen pädagogischen Handelns. Beiträge zur neuen Erziehung* (Stuttgart, 1934), 1–21, 149–75, 198–227. Cf. idem, "Volk und Volksschule," *Schule und Evangelium* 8 (1933/34): 33–37; idem, "Die Umgestaltung des Oberprimajahres," ibid., 161–65; and the message of the editorial board, "Am Ende des achten Jahrgangs. An unsere Leser," ibid., 281–82.

27. For the situation of teachers at the beginning of the Third Reich see Konrad H. Jarausch, *The Unfree Professions: German Lawyers, Teachers, and Engineers, 1900–1950* (New York, 1990), 115ff. As a result of misogyny, the Nazis reacted to academic overcrowding by firing married women teachers if their husbands were already publicly employed.

28. Alfred Laeger, *Vereinigtes Dom- und Klostergymnasium Magdeburg, 1675–1950. Gedenkschrift* (Frankfurt, 1967). For the activities of the Home for Protestant Teacher Trainees at the Monastery of our Dear Lady during 1932–36, cf. the Landeshauptarchiv Sachsen-Anhalt, Rep. A 4f., Anhang nos. 6 und 9.

29. Konrad Jarausch to Lotte Petri, undated postcard and letter, stamped on May 14, 1935, as well as letter of June 26, 1935; idem, "Bericht über das Referendarheim am K.U.L.F. in Magdeburg," LHASA, MD, Rep. A 4f., Anhang, no. 10. Cf. "Gutachten über den Studienassessor Dr. Jarausch," September 14, 1936, LHASA, MD, Rep. C 23, no. 93: "Jarausch endorses the National Socialist state just as resolutely as he is convinced of the eternal truth of the Gospel." And "Ernennungsurkunde zum Studienrat," January 26, 1937.

30. Gury Schneider-Ludorff, "Arbeitsbund für wissenschaftliche Pädagogik auf reformatorischer Grundlage," in *Metzlers Lexikon christlicher Denker*, ed. Markus Vinzent (Stuttgart, 2000), col. 52–53, and "Verband für evangelischen Religionsunterricht und Pädagogik," ibid., col. 2166.

31. Konrad Jarausch to Magdalene von Tiling, January 19, 1937, undated (end of 1938), undated (early 1939), and July 6, 1939, KLAH, Nachlass von Tiling, no. 17 und 11.

32. Konrad Jarausch, "Die germanische Religion als Gegenstand des Religionsunterrichts," *Schule und Evangelium* 9 (1934/35): 25–37; idem,

"Die Kirche im Volk," ibid., 186–89; idem, "Richtlinien für die Behandlung der germanischen Religion," ibid. 10 (1935/36): 109–11.

33. "Familiennachricht," 83; K. Cramer, I. Feußner, K. Jarausch, and M. Walther, eds., *Evangelischer Religionsunterricht in der Gegenwart* (Stuttgart, 1937). After subtracting the depression cuts, he had 485,98 Marks left as pay. Oberpräsidium der Provinz Sachsen to Studienrat Konrad Jarausch, February 6, 1937, LHASA, MD, Rep. C 33, no. 93.

34. Konrad Jarausch, "Luthers Weg zur Reformation in der Kirche im kirchengeschichtlichen Unterricht," *Schule und Evangelium* 11 (1936/37): 181–90; the editors, "Ein Wort an unsere Leser," ibid. 12 (1937/38): 1–2; and Konrad Jarausch, "Vorwort," *Evangelischer Religionsunterricht* 7–8. Cf. idem, "Entwurf eines Planes für die theoretische Arbeit und das Gemeinschaftsleben im Konvikt unser Lieben Frauen," LHASA, MD, Rep. A 4f., Anhang, no. 10.

35. Konrad Jarausch, "Wie ist Christus heute zu verkündigen?" manuscript of a lecture in Dünne on October 12, 1938, LKAH, Nachlass von Tiling, no. 11. Cf. idem, "'Ich glaube, daß Christus' sei 'wahrhaftiger Gott,'" *Schule und Evangelium* 13 (1938/39): 64–76, 88–98.

36. Konrad Jarausch, notes for a lecture to Protestant religion teachers, dated August 8/9, 1939 with a marginal comment of Magdalene von Tiling, and idem, "Evangelischer Religionsunterricht heute," undated page proof, LKAH, Nachlass von Tiling, no. 11. Cf. idem, "Die Kirche im neutestamentlichen Unterricht," *Evangelischer Religionsunterricht*, 127–57; idem, "Der Epheserbrief im Unterricht," *Schule und Evangelium* 12 (1937/38): 73–85; idem, "Nerthus und Balder, ein Lehrbeispiel." ibid., 198–202.

37. Letter of condolence by I. H. and further characterizations in the second group of excerpts by Oskar Ziegner. Konrad Jarausch, "Wie steht es heute mit der Methode in unserm Unterricht?" *Schule und Evangelium* 13 (1938/39): 48–55. Statements in a letter and phone call from two former students several years ago.

38. Franz Petri to Konrad Jarausch, March 21, 1938; Konrad to Lotte Jarausch, April 3, 11 ("Have you listened to the Führer's speech on Saturday? It was hardly edifying"), and further letters until May 2, 1938 (a fellow patient who was a teacher from Baden "has been done in by the party").

39. Konrad's vacation letters to Lotte Jarausch, July 14 until August 1, 1939, partly in original form, partly in the "Familiennachricht," 87–95.

40. Konrad to Lotte Jarausch, October 4, 1939, alluding to *Die Kriegserlebnisse des Grenadiers Rudolf Koch* (Leipzig, 1934). Most of the subsequent quotations are from letters included in this edition. But in some cases, there are also references to letters or fragments not printed.

41. Martin Humburg, "Feldpostbriefe aus dem Zweiten Weltkrieg—Werkstattbericht zu einer Inhaltsanalyse," at http://hsozkult.geschichte. hu-berlin.de/beitrag/essays/feld.htm, and Jörg Echterkamp, Hg., *Kriegsschauplatz Deutschland 1945. Leben in Angst—Hoffnung auf Frieden. Feldpost aus der Heimat und von der Front* (Paderborn, 2006), 111ff.

42. Konrad to Lotte Jarausch, September 9, 1939; idem to Magdalene Caspar, January 11, 1942. He explicitly wished for some letters to be sent on to his brother and mother, but when he was describing controversial things like the POW camp in Kochanowo, he asked that they not be seen by anyone else.

43. Konrad Jarausch to Konrad Korth, November 1/2, 1941; idem to Joachim Müller, November 12, 1939; idem to Lotte Jarausch, January 8, 1940. Cf. Thomas Kühne, "Zwischen Männerbund und Volksgemeinschaft. Hitlers Soldaten und der Mythos der Kameradschaft," *Archiv für Sozialgeschichte* 38 (1998): 165–89.

44. Konrad to Lotte Jarausch, September 22, 1939; October 14, 1940.

45. Konrad to Lotte Jarausch, January 9, 1940, February 11, March 10, 1940, etc.

46. Konrad to Lotte Jarausch, February 8, April 26, July 5, 1940; June 18, July 1, October 7, 1941.

47. Konrad to Lotte Jarausch, October 7, 1939; April 18, June 24, 1940; November 14, 1941; January 11, 1942.

48. Konrad to Lotte Jarausch, July 20, 1939; April 19 and 26, and August 4, 1940.

49. Konrad to Lotte Jarausch, September 5, 1941.

50. Konrad to Lotte Jarausch, October 10 and 27, November 3, December 3, 1939. Cf. Thomas Pegelow, *The Language of Nazi Genocide: Linguistic Violence and the Struggle of Germans of Jewish Ancestry* (New York, 2009).

51. Konrad to Lotte Jarausch, December 15, 1940; June 26, September 5, November 21, December 10, 1941. Cf. the manuscript fragment on "Humanistische Bildung heute," which pleaded for maintaining classical secondary schools, so "that the leaders of the people retain an understanding of the human condition." KLAH, Nachlass von Tiling, no. 17.

52. Konrad to Lotte Jarausch, October 21, November 15, 1939; June 25 and 16, 1941; and idem to Ruth Schneider, January 5, 1942.

53. Konrad to Lotte Jarausch, September 17, October 2, November 8/9, 1939; March 29, April 2, 1940.

54. Konrad Jarausch to Franz Petri, January 14, 1940; idem to Lotte Jarausch, April 14, May 13, 1940 and September 15, 1941. Cf. Władisław Stanisław Reymont, *Die polnischen Bauern* (Jena, 1912).

55. Undated letter, probably from the fall of 1939, in the fragments mimeographed by Oskar Ziegner; Konrad to Lotte Jarausch, June 29, 1940; and idem to Magdalene Caspar, January 11, 1942.

56. Konrad to Lotte Jarausch, July 31, August 2, October 23, 1940; Magdalene von Tiling to Konrad Jarausch, October 6, and idem to Magdalene von Tiling, October 8, 1940, LKAH, Nachlass von Tiling, no. 17. Cf. idem, "Johannes der Täufer," *Unterweisung und Glaube* 15 (1940/41): 60–66, 72–77, 83–88. But he could no longer realize his plan to write a book on "Religious Pedagogy."

57. Konrad to Lotte Jarausch, October 4, November 15, 1939; May 1, July 23 and 27, August 19, 1940; idem to Karl Korth, November 1/2, 1941; idem to Magdalene von Tiling, June 16, 1941, LKAH, Nachlass von Tiling, no. 17; and "Mitteilung des Verlags und der Herausgeber," *Unterweisung und Glaube* 16 (1941/42): 26.

58. Konrad to Lotte Jarausch, November 5 and 26/27, December 26, 1939; April 7, October 15, 1940. In Russia he was no longer able to get to any religious services.

59. Konrad to Lotte Jarausch, November 22, 1939; February 4, July 20, 1940.

60. Konrad to Lotte Jarausch, July 20, 1940; August 26, 1941; idem to Hans-Lothar Dietze, July 30, 1940; and idem to Siegfried, September 21, 1941.

61. Konrad Jarausch, "Aufgaben des Friedens," *Unterweisung und Glaube* 15 (1940/41): 36–40; idem to Lotte Jarausch, April 14, 1940; December 29, 1941.

62. Konrad Jarausch to Hans-Lothar Dietze, July 30, 1940; idem to Magdalene Caspar, January 5, 1942. For his position between the fronts of the Confessing Church and the German Christians, see his letter to Magdalene von Tiling, January 13, 1941, LKAH, Nachlass von Tiling, no. 127. Cf. Doris Bergen, *Twisted Cross: The German Christian Movement in the Third Reich* (Chapel Hill, 1996).

63. Konrad to Lotte Jarausch, September 5, October 22, 1939; and January 17, 1940; and idem to Franz Petri, January 14, 1940.

64. Konrad to Lotte Jarausch, November 8/9, 1939; and April 28, 1940. Cf. idem to Franz Petri, February 16, 1941: "I would be more at peace if this task could be limited to the area of Central Europe." Yet he was fascinated by the fact "that today a single man risks the entire force of his people to clear the path either to world dominion or to perdition." Letter of March 1, 1940 in the second set of excerpts by Oskar Ziegner.

65. Konrad to Lotte Jarausch, September 14 and 16, December 24, 1939.

66. Konrad to Lotte Jarausch, September 30, October 22, December 22, 1939; and idem to Johannes Müller, November 22, 1939.

67. Konrad to Lotte Jarausch, August 15, 1941; essays on "Russian Women," "Churches in Minsk," and "The Kochanowo Camp" of August 1941.

68. See the letters in the previous three notes.

69. Konrad to Lotte Jarausch, October 22, November 12, 1939. At the same time he emphasized German responsibility for Poland and for the subsequent peace. Letters of January 23 and February 11, 1940, in the second set of excerpts by Oskar Ziegner.

70. Konrad to Lotte Jarausch, June 22 and 27, 1940; June 22 and December 10, 1941. Cf. Karl Fuchs, *Your Loyal and Loving Son: The Letters of Tank Gunner Karl Fuchs, 1937–1941*, ed. and trans. Horst Fuchs Richardson (Washington, DC, 2003), 47ff., 110ff.

71. Konrad to Lotte Jarausch, September 14, and essay on "Voyage to the East," after September 22, 1939.

72. Konrad to Lotte Jarausch, October 22 and November 10, 1939. In contrast to other descriptions, the sporadic references to Jews in the letters seem somewhat opaque, which may be the result of a bad conscience.

73. Konrad to Lotte Jarausch, September 16, 1941.

74. Konrad Jarausch to Konrad Korth, November 1/2, 1941; idem to Lotte Jarausch, November 14, 1941 and numerous other descriptions. Cf. Christian Hartmann, "Massensterben oder Massenvernichtung? Sowjetische Kriegsgefangene im Unternehmen 'Barbarossa.' Aus dem Tagebuch eines deutschen Lagerkommandanten," *Vierteljahrshefte für Zeitgeschichte* 48 (2001): 98ff.

75. Konrad to Lotte Jarausch, October 25 and November 1, 1941; idem to Siegfried, November 25, 1941.

76. Konrad to Lotte Jarausch, October 23, 1941; January 8, 1942; idem to Werner Haß, November 25, 1941 ("They expire by the thousands"); and idem to little mother, January 10, 1942. This dedication aroused the respect of comrades who sought moral orientation from him.

77. Konrad to Lotte Jarausch, October 28 and November 9, 1941; idem to Magdalene von Tiling, November 6, 1941; idem to Bruno Jarausch, November 7, 1941; idem to Lene Petri, November 20, 1941. Konrad Jarausch was aware of the attempts of POWs to get into his good graces in order to obtain a piece of bread. But he considered these encounters as genuine. Cf. the undated scrap of paper by "Alexander," who regrets the illness of "Konrad Hugovitsch."

78. Konrad to Lotte Jarausch, October 23, December 25, 1941; idem to Werner Haß, January 4, 1942.

79. Konrad to Lotte Jarausch, January 13, 1942; staff doctor Starck to Lotte Jarausch, January 28, 1942. Without penicillin typhoid fever was generally deadly for people over forty years of age, especially if they had a weak heart. The body was buried under a simple birch cross in a small German military cemetery at Roslawl.

80. Major von Stietencron to Charlotte Jarausch, January 28, 1942; Hermann Lohrisch, "Gedenkworte an Konrad Jarausch," Magdeburg without a date; quotes from sixteen letters of condolence in the second set of excerpts by Oskar Ziegner, 7–10; Lotte Jarausch to Bruno Jarausch, February 24 and March 6, 1942, as well as "Familiennachricht," 134–37.

81. Brother Bruno did have Konrad's name added to the grave of his own father and later also mother in the Plötzensee cemetery in Berlin, but that somehow did not seem as "real" as a normal burial plot. Cf. Klaus Naumann, ed., *Nachkrieg in Deutschland* (Hamburg, 2001); and James Franklin Williamson, "Whom to Mourn and How? The Protestant Church and the Recasting of Memory, 1945–1962," master's thesis, University of North Carolina, 2008.

82. "Familiennachricht," 153ff. Cf. Elisabeth Heineman, *What Difference Does a Husband Make? Women and Marital Status in Nazi and Postwar Germany* (Berkeley, 1999), and Lilly Kemmler, Julia Ermecke, and Oliver Wältermann, "Kriegerwitwen," *report psychologie* 29 (2004): 234–44.

83. Karl Ditt, "Die Kulturraumforschung zwischen Wissenschaft und Politik. Das Beispiel Franz Petri (1903–1993)," *Westfälische Forschungen* 46 (1996): S. 73–176, and Peter Schöttler, "Die historische Westforschung zwischen 'Abwehrkampf' und territorialer Offensive," in idem, ed., *Geschichtswissenschaft als Legitimationswissenschaft, 1918–1945* (Frankfurt, 1999), 204–63.

84. Pastor Nast to Lotte Jarausch, January 8, 1954; editorial marks of my mother on first half of the letters, and typewritten transcript of about half of the correspondence in the author's possession.

85. "Familiennachricht," 156ff. and surviving fragments of my mother's correspondence. Another method to retain memory was occasional travel to Magdeburg where there were still some acquaintances, but the bombing of the city had obliterated our previous apartment.

86. Madgalene von Tiling, *Der Mensch vor Gott* (Berlin, 1950), 5: "Konrad Jarausch zum 14. 8. 1950 in dankbarer Erinnerung an seinen Vater von der Verfasserin." Cf. Gerhard Ritter, *The German Resistance: Carl Goerdeler's Struggle against Tyranny* (New York, 1959).

87. Dr. Teipel, Städtisches Arndt-Gymnasium, "Zeugnis der OIa," 30. 11. 1959; Konrad H. Jarausch, "Der Wilde Westen ist zivilisiert" and

"Krefelder erlebt USA Wahlfieber," *Rheinische Post*, July 26 and November 8, 1960; idem to Franz Petri, February 22, 1962 and 1963. Cf. Konrad H. Jarausch, "Some Thoughts on Becoming a U.S. Citizen: Countries Cannot be Made to Order," *Rundschau: An American-German Review* 4 (May 1974): 17.

88. Helmut Schelsky, *Die skeptische Generation. Eine Soziologie der deutschen Jugend* (Düsseldorf, 1963). Cf. Ulrich Herbert, ed., *Wandlungsprozesse in Westdeutschland. Belastung, Integration, Liberalisierung, 1945–1980* (Göttingen, 2002); and Konrad H. Jarausch, *After Hitler: Recivilizing Germans, 1945–1995* (New York, 2006).

89. For a similar mellowing from a Jewish émigré perspective see Fritz Stern, *Five Germanys I Have Known* (New York, 2006). Cf. also Philipp Gassert and Alan Steinweis, eds., *Coping with the Nazi Past: West German Debates on Nazism and Generational Conflict, 1955–1975* (New York, 2006).

90. Franz Petri to Anna Jarausch, May 4, 1942; Konrad Jarausch to Konrad Korth, November 1/2, 1941; and idem to Lene Petri, November 20, 1941. For a long time he sought to quiet his conscience: "The future break-up of the Bolshevik system justifies the sacrifices, at least if a tolerable new order succeeds."

91. Konrad Jarausch, "Aufgaben des Friedens," 39. Cf. the reflections of his student Arnold Nüßle on the alienation of soldiers from the church, "Der Soldat und das Christentum," *Unterweisung und Glaube* 15 (1940/41): 109–13.

92. Longerich, *"Davon haben wir nichts gewußt,"* versus Omer Bartov, *The Eastern Front, 1941–1945: German Troops and the Barbarization of Warfare* (New York, 2001). Cf. Christian Gerlach, *Kalkulierte Morde. Die deutsche Wirtschafts- und Vernichtungspolitik in Weißrußland, 1941–1944* (Hamburg, 1999) versus Christian Hartmann, *Wehrmacht im Ostkrieg: Front und militärisches Hinterland 1941/42* (Munich, 2009), 789–806.

93. Konrad to Lotte Jarausch, October 12 and November 2, 1941; idem to Magdalene von Tiling, November 6, 1941. Cf. Fuchs, *Your Loyal and Loving Son*, 110ff.

94. Letters of October 1939 and March 1, 1940 in the second set of excerpts by Oskar Ziegner and additional fragments. He also found the "SS spirit" repulsive, which forbade a humane treatment of prisoners, citing a typical prejudice: "That someone in a German uniform stands up for a Pole, I do not tolerate." Konrad to Lotte Jarausch, December 24, 1939; March 31, 1940.

95. Konrad to Lotte Jarausch, October 9, November 23, 1939; April 7, 1940; and idem to Ruth Schneider, January 5, 1942. Cf. Theodore S.

Hamerow, *On the Road to the Wolf's Lair: German Resistance to Hitler* (Cambridge, MA, 1997).

96. Konrad to Bruno Jarausch, September 13, 1941; idem to Lotte Jarausch, October 28, 1941; and idem to an unidentified privy councilor, November 9, 1941. For a similar soul searching about his war experience see the composer Gerhard Krapf's "Recollections" (MS, written in the 1990s in Calgary, Canada), 7 vols.

97. Konrad to Lotte Jarausch, December 24, 1941.

98. Jürgen Reulecke, "Vaterlose Söhne in einer 'vaterlosen Gesell-schaft,'" *Söhne ohne Väter*, 144–59.

SELECTED SUGGESTIONS
FOR FURTHER READING

∾

WAR DIARIES AND LETTERS

Anonymous. *A Woman in Berlin: Eight Weeks in the Conquered City: A Diary.* Trans. Philip Boehm. New York, 2005.

Browning, Christopher R., Richard S. Hollander, and Nechama Tec, eds. *Every Day Lasts a Year: A Jewish Family's Correspondence from Poland.* Cambridge, 2007.

Bruhns, Wibke. *My Father's Country: The Story of a German Family.* New York, 2008.

Echternkamp, Jörg. *Kriegsschauplatz Deutschland 1945. Leben in Angst, Hoffnung auf Frieden. Feldpost aus der Heimat und von der Front.* Paderborn, 2006.

Fuchs, Karl. *Your Loyal and Loving Son: The Letters of Tank Gunner Karl Fuchs, 1937–1941.* Edited and translated by Horst Fuchs Richardson. Washington, DC, 2003.

Gollwitzer, Helmut, and Eva Bildt. *"Ich will Dir schnell sagen, dass ich lebe, Liebster". Briefe aus dem Krieg, 1940–1945.* Edited by Friedrich Künzel and Ruth Pabst. Munich, 2008.

Hosenfeld, Wilm. *"Ich versuche jeden zu retten". Das Leben eines deutschen Offiziers in Briefen und Tagebüchern.* Edited by Thomas Vogel. Munich, 2004.

Irrgang, Astrid. *Leutnant der Wehrmacht Peter Stölten in seinen Feldpostbriefen. Vom richtigen Leben im falschen.* Freiburg, 2007.

Klemperer, Victor. *"I Will Bear Witness": A Diary of the Nazi Years, 1942–1945.* New York, 2001.

Last Letters from Stalingrad. Introduced by S.L.A. Marshall. New York, 1965.

Reese, Willy Peter. *"A Stranger to Myself": The Inhumanity of War: Russia, 1941–1944.* New York, 2005.

Sajer, Guy. *The Forgotten Soldier.* New York, 1987.

381

Scholarly Works

Arnold, Klaus Jochen. *Die Wehrmacht und die Besatzungspolitik in den besetzten Gebieten der Sowjetunion. Kriegführung und Radikalisierung im "Unternehmen Barbarossa."* Berlin, 2005.

Bartov, Omer. *The Eastern Front, 1941–1945: German Troops and the Barbarization of Warfare.* New York, 2001.

Boog, Horst, et al. *The Attack on the Soviet Union.* Vol. 4, *Germany and the Second World War.* Oxford, 1998.

Chickering, Roger, Stig Förster, and Bernd Greiner, eds. *A World at Total War: Global Conflict and the Politics of Destruction, 1937–1945.* Cambridge, 2005.

Edele, Mark, and Michael Geyer. "States of Exception: The Nazi-Soviet War as a System of Violence, 1939–1945." In *Beyond Totalitarianism: Stalinism and Nazism Compared*, edited by Michael Geyer and Sheila Fitzpatrick, 345–95. Cambridge, 2009.

Gerlach, Christian. *Kalkulierte Morde. Die deutsche Wirtschafts- und Vernichtungspolitik in Weißrußland, 1941–1944.* Hamburg, 1999.

Hartmann, Christian. *Wehrmacht im Ostkrieg. Front und militärisches Hinterland 1941/42.* Munich, 2009.

Heer, Hannes, and Klaus Naumann, eds. *Vernichtungskrieg. Verbrechen der Wehrmacht, 1941–1944.* Hamburg, 1995, rev. ed. 2002.

Jarausch, Konrad H., and Michael Geyer. *Shattered Past: Reconstructing German Histories.* Princeton, 2003.

Liulevicius, Vejas Gabriel. *War Land on the Eastern Front: Culture, National Identity, and German Occupation in World War I.* Cambridge, 2000.

Streit, Christian. *Keine Kameraden. Die Wehrmacht und die sowjetischen Kriegsgefangenen, 1941–1945*, rev. ed. Bonn, 1997.

Weinberg, Gerhard. *A World at Arms: A Global History of World War Two.* Cambridge 2005.

∿ INDEX ∿

Page numbers in italics refer to maps and photographs.

Adelsblatt, 112
Aeschylus, xvi
Altengrabow, 231, 233
Amiens, 232, 253, 276, 287, *227–28*
Army Group Center, 286. *See also* Wehrmacht
Asmussen, Hans, 27, 120
Atlantis (journal), 356

Barth, Karl, 12, 218
Bartov, Omer, vii
Bäumer, Gertrud, 100
Bavarians, 36, 151, 155, 160, 175
BdM (League of German Girls), 116–17
Below, Georg von, 9
Berlin Historical Society Journal, 283
Berlin: air raids on, 30, 197, 280, 340; districts of, *1,* 4–7, 11, 206, 250; Jarausch family in, 4–16; thoughts about, 280–81, 283, 290; wartime visits to, 55,109, 117–89, 218
Bernburg, 142, 207, 213, 214, 226, 360
Beuthen (Bytom), 14
Bialystok (Białystok), 169
Birkenfelde, 70
Björnson, Martinius, 174

Blaskowitz, General Johannes Albrecht, 96, 96n., 167, 168
Boether-Schulze, battalion commander, 164, 230, 233, 235, 236
Bolshevism, 7, 248, 272, 321, 327; architecture of, 247–48, 251; future of, 312, 327; attitude toward, 251, 272, 273, 304, 321, 327, 335; Nazis' eradication of, 41, 273, 316, 319; and religion, 251, 304; modernization of, 29, 240, 242, 249, 251, 259, 260, 264, 267, 272; suffering under, 29, 32, 240, 242, 264, 321, 325, 331, 333, 335, 361. *See also* USSR
Bonhoeffer, Dietrich, 26
Brackmann, Albert, 112, 123, 125, 133
Braem, Dr., 123
Brandenburg, 11, 48, 49, 64n
Brauchitsch, Field-Marshall Walther von, 126
Breslau (Wrocław), 20, *51,* 53n, 55, 58
Brest-Litovsk, 113n, 130, 163, 246
Brieg (Brzeg), 4
Briesen (Wąbrzeźno), 64
Britain. *See* Royal Air Force
Brocken, 230
Bromberg (Bydgoszcz), 63

383

INDEX

Bruhns, Wibke, 3
Bryansk, 331
Brzeziny, 103
Bug River, 114, 134, 169
Bultmann, Rudolf, 12

Camus, Albert, 39
Canned Marriage (film), 203
Caspar, Magdalene, 20, 38, 350, 357–58, 362–63
Cathedral Gymnasium (Magdeburg), 18, 34, 65n, 144, 150n, 223n, 360,
Catholicism, 29, 49, 57, 61, 89, 101, 180, 234, 251
children, 1–2, 11, 15, 60, 61, 75, 78, 126, 127, 130, 159, 163, 173, 204, 264, 313, 329, 330, 335, 345, 362
Christliche Pfadfinderschaft, 38
Cloister School, Magdeburg, 269, 291
Cologne (Köln), 19, 103, 118, 120, 124, 340n
Communism. See Bolshevism
Confessing Church, 120n, 212, 218, 316
Corinth, Lovis, 7
Cramer, Karl, 19
Cramer, P.,. 274
Crimea, 285, 330
Cysarz, Herbert, 135, 135n
Czortkow (Chortkiv), 85

Dahn, Felix, 7
Daladier, Édouard, 66
DCSV (German Christian Students' Association), 9
Dehn, Fritz, 15
democracy, 13, 16, 37
Detmold, 174
Deutsches Volkstum (journal), 316
Dietrich, Johannes, 7, 38, 341
Dietze, Hans-Lothar, 150, 201–2
Dnieper River, 269n, 293, 294

Döberitz, 176, 177
Domanin, 70, 88
Dorn, Theodor, 7
Dresden, 57, 196
Dulag 203: administration of, 253–55, 266, 274–75, 318–19, 356–57; bartering with POWs in, 283, 287, 314, 321, 328; and cold of winter, 301, 322, 325, 327, 332–23, 341, 345–46, 351, 355, 356, 357, 359, 361; control of POWs in, 241, 261–63, 280, 308, 310, 320, 331, 355, 361; daily life in, 300, 313, 319, 337–38, 345; disorder of 263, 306, 307, 342, 356, 362; ethnic selection at, 49, 239, 244, 284, 319, 320, 325, 338; food distribution at, 265, 270, 274, 300–301, 310, 313–14, 319, 328, 331, 355, 361; food procurement and preparation at, 241, 263, 270, 276, 285, 305, 306–7, 318, 328, 336, 349, 362; function of, 203, 239, 261; humanity in, 263, 311, 312, 313, 319, 342; overcrowding in, 240, 261, 265, 268, 270, 304, 307, 310; POWs dying at, 242, 261, 291, 308, 311, 319, 324, 327, 331, 333, 337, 356, 358, 360–61; 362; reading, art, and music at, 311, 312, 321, 323, 333, 347, 350, 353–54; relationships with prisoners in, 242–43, 263–64, 292, 301, 308, 312, 313, 316, 321, 327, 328, 336, 342, 344, 345, 347, 348, 351, 353, 357; relocation of, 241, 261, 282, 289, 292, 297; starvation in, 240–41, 300, 307, 311, 314, 334, 361; sympathy for POWs in, 261, 275, 292, 308, 309n, 314, 323, 327, 357, 361–62; transportation of POWs, 275, 276, 283–84, 331. See also Jarausch, Konrad, Sr., war experiences of; USSR

384